Kisti's Royal Garden

by

Walther H. Lysne

and Robin H. Lysne

Publishers Page

Copyright 2023
Robin H. Lysne, M.A., M.F.A., Ph.D.

Blue Bone Books
P.O. Box 2250
Santa Cruz, CA 95063
United States of America

Blue Bone Books is a cooperative poetry and literary press. All rights reserved under the U.S.Copyright Act of 1976. No part of the publication may be reproduced, distributed, or transmitted in any form or by any means of stored in a database or retireval system without the prior written permission of the publisher or the copyright holder.

This book is Book Three of the Legendary Woman Ancestor Series.

ISBN#: 978-1-948675-11-6

Library of Congress#: 2023909560

Ebook: 978-1-948675-12-3

I so enjoyed reading your new book, Kisti's Royal Garden. The stories, names and locations, felt so familiar to me. Having grown up in the Midwest, my Lutheran Norwegian ancestors were pioneers in similar communities. You brought life to what seemed like my own family history.

Joy Cook
Daughters of Norway Grand Lodge VP

Dedicated to Kisti Moe Lysne,
Hendrick Olesson Lysne,
and Walther Herman Lysne,
without whom we would not know
the true story of
Kisti and Hendrick Lysne,
and to my sister, Kisti Heerens Beckwith, Kisti
Lysne's namesake,
who helped me so much when she was alive,
and who I am still very close to,
even now.

CONTENTS

Table of Contents vi and vii
Robin Lysne's Prologue and Acknowledgements 1

Part One - Discovering a New Land 5
Chapter One – Leaving the City 6
Chapter Two - Crossroads Crisis 11
Chapter Three – Baptism, Berry Picking, and Glory of the Morning 18
Chapter Four – Oshkosh By Gosh 26
Chapter Five – Red Moon and Twigg 29
Chapter Six – Preparing for Settlement 36
Chapter Seven - Moonlight Swim 45

Part Two – Settling into a New Homeland 53
Chapter Eight – Starting from Scratch 54
Chapter Nine - Settlement and Homeland Visitors 62
Chapter Ten – Intruders 84
Chapter Eleven - The New Synneva 96
Chapter Twelve - Kisti and the Ho-Chunks 102
Chapter Thirteen – Talking Paper 109
Chapter Fourteen – Crisis in the Well 112
Chapter Fifteen – Old Settlers Reunion 118
Chapter Sixteen – Ho-Chunk Full Moon Ceremony 128
Chapter Seventeen – Growing Slavery Discussion and the County Fair Debacle 142
Chapter Eighteen - Uncle Tom's Cabin, John Brown, and Citizenship 147

Chapter Nineteen - Kisti Confronts Jenns   151
Chapter Twenty - River Runners and Baby Thomas   158

Part Three - The Civil War   163
Chapter Twenty-One - Enlistment   164
Chapter Twenty-Two - Eivind Steps Up   170
Chapter Twenty-Three - Letters from Ole and Aspun   174
Chapter Twenty-Four - War Comes Closer   178
Chapter Twenty-Five - Hendrick Enlists   183

Part Four - New Life Starting Over   197
Chapter Twenty-Six - Beginning Again   198
Chapter Twenty-Seven - Eivind Finds Music   205
Chapter Twenty-Eight - Railroad Passage   209
Chapter Twenty-Nine - Eivind's Decision, Randine's Dream   218
Chapter Thirty - Changes for Susan, Kisti Takes the Train to Oshkosh   225
Chapter Thirty-One - Death at the Door with New Days Emerging   234
Chapter Thirty-Two - Eivind and Martha and Kisti's Sanctuary   240
Walther Lysne's Acknowledgement   251
Walther Lysne's First Chapter   253
Biographys   256

Robin Lysne's Prologue and Acknowledgements

Hendrick and Kisti Lysne came to Wisconsin from Norway in 1854, and brought Kisti's Mother, Synneva Moe, and their three children with them. They were the first ones to immigrate to the U.S. on the Lysne side of my family.

The story of Kisti and Hendrick Lysne was first written down and brought into the world by my grandfather, Walther Herman Lysne, who was told many stories of his grandparents as a small boy. His father Edwin (Eivind) Lysne, and Edwin's sisters, Randine (named after her grandmother, Randine Hakonsdatter Stokanes Lysne - mother of their father Hendrick Olesson Lysne), Susan, and Lallie often told stories of their parents, Hendrick and Kisti Lysne, to the three grandsons of Eivind as well as Randine's and Lallie's children.

Walther Lysne's stories were first written in a book he wrote about his grandmother called Kisti. There are many amazing aspects to her story, including Kisti's connection with the Native American people in Northern Wisconsin. Kisti and Hendrick bought land outside Amherst Junction, Wisconsin, where they settled with their family after living in Chicago for barely a year after immigrating to America.

After reading his manuscript several times, I found that the story about our Great, Great Grandma Kisti was being told from a man's perspective, which was only natural, since my grandfather wrote it. He also told a great deal about the Civil War and the horrible conflict in America in the 1860s.

While all of this is historically important, my grandfather's strong focus on the war did not seem to be what the story was really about. I wanted to get more deeply into an understanding of what life was like from Kisti's perspective, and who she was and what made her such an example to so many people, both Indigenous and

European, and especially to her own children.

She was an extraordinary ordinary woman; a woman who found her way with her family in the new world of America. She found ways to cultivate relationships with the diverse group of settlers who came by wagon train through Chicago, Illinois, to settle in Wisconsin. She also learned to live peacefully with the Native people who had lived in Wisconsin for centuries.

That is why I wanted to include the story of Kisti and her husband Hendrick in my historical series of books: Legendary Ancestral Women's Series. Unlike the first two books I wrote for this series, Kisti's Royal Garden is not a novel, though we have used many fictional elements to tell the story. It is a work of narrative non-fiction that shares true stories collected and told by my grandfather, Walther Herman Lysne, and revised and enhanced by me.

Having grown up in the Midwest, in Rockford, Illinois, in Winnebago county, I traveled to Wisconsin many times on vacation trips with my parents, siblings, and friends. I feel a great bond with Kisti Lysne, especially because of her connection with Native American people in her time.

My first connection to Native American people was meeting my dear sister-friend Mary Ann Godfrey, who died during the COVID pandemic from complications. She was a key person in introducing me to the Native American Lakota ways. She was a full-blooded Lakota woman who I met in my senior year of high school at Kemper Hall in Kenosha, Wisconsin. She knew nothing about her own people's traditions when we first met, but by the end of the year, she knew quite a bit more. To answer my many questions about her people and their ceremonies, she had asked her grandfather about their family history when she was home on vacations in South Dakota. On one of her trips home, when she came back from one of those trips, she told me about how we could perform a ceremony to become blood sisters. I agreed, and we cut our fingers and exchanged blood with each other to bind us throughout our lives.

After we graduated from our boarding school in Kenosha, she went to Germany as an exchange student. She discovered that many German people were fascinated by Native

American history. At first, they did not believe that she was full-blooded Lakota, as they thought that all the Indians had all been killed in America. This shocked her, and it encouraged her to ask her grandfather more questions. She was repeatedly questioned about her people from her German friends. This interest in her Native background helped her to embrace her heritage even more deeply when she returned to South Dakota.

I went to visit Mary Ann in 1973 during my sophomore year in college. She was the first one to introduce me to a sweat lodge and the ways of her people during my visit. After she was married and had a family, I visited her and her children in Aberdeen, South Dakota before one of the Sundance Ceremonies. Later in my thirties, she met me at the Sundance ceremonies run by someone she had grown up with on the Rosebud Reservation when I became a dancer. She came to Chicago for a reunion when I was there, then San Francisco for an Indian Health Service meeting in the 1990's and we shared dinner and talked late into the night about our lives. She came to my wedding in 1998. I visited her later in Montana on my way back to California in 2014. In the last years of her life, we became even closer due to her many health and personal issues.

When I was in my thirties and early forties, I began more of my adventures with Native American people and ceremonies. Some grad school friends and I were part of the same Tiosbye, or "extended family," led by a Native American Lakota man named Buck Ghosthorse. Buck had taught us at Mathew Fox's School for social change, the Institute in Culture and Creation Spirituality, housed at Holy Names College (now University) in Oakland, California.

My friends from my Tiosbye later invited me to a Sun Dance in South Dakota the year after graduating. After my first Sun Dance experience as a participant, I had prayed for a chanupa, or sacred prayer pipe. The next year my dear friend Paul Bibbo, one of my graduate school friends, was guided to give me a chanupa. He purchased it at an Anishinaabe store in the Wisconsin Dells run by a Lakota man.

The next year I was involved in supporting Sundance

with the Lakota people on Rosebud Reservation in South Dakota. A few years later, I would be dancing with the same group on the same reservation after five years supporting the dancers. I also danced in Northern Wisconsin with the Anishinaabe people called the Ogitchidaah, after sun dancing in South Dakota. Later I attended Buck's Sundance in Washington State, after he passed away.

Because Kisti Moe Lysne had such a wonderful connection with the native people in Wisconsin, and I have had so many wonderful experiences with Native American ceremonies, I have a unique perspective from which to bring Kisti's story to life in this book.

Thanks to my Lakota friend Mary Ann, and my Great, Great Grandmother Kisti's life story, I can envision what it was like for Kisti to be among Native American people, even though she was with the Ho-Chunks, not the Lakota tribe.

Kisti and Hendrick moved to an area of Wisconsin that was previously the land of indigenous people—the Winnebago, or Ho-Chunk, the Sauk, Fox, Menomonee, and other tribes. Part of my intention is to honor the Native tribes that had previously occupied that land for thousands of years, while honoring Kisti and her family for their love for the Native people.

I also want to share this history with my sisters and their families and with the generations to come. Another intention for rewriting Grandpa's book was to honor my late sister, Kisti Heerens Beckwith, who was named after Kisti Moe Lysne.

In the first chapter of grandfather Lysne's original version of this book, he tells the story of when he watched his granddaughter Kisti walking through the cemetery where Kisti and Hendrick and several of their children were buried. I included that chapter at the end of the book.

Thank you, Grandpa Lysne for what you have passed down to all of us. Now I hope to share it with the world. Always with love and gratitude,
your granddaughter,

Robin Heerens Lysne (White Turtle Woman)

Part One

Discovering a New Land

Chapter One

Leaving the City

The wagon train moved slowly away from flat land around Chicago and crossed the border of Illinois into the green wooded hills of Wisconsin territory. Kisti and Hendrick Lysne rode in one of the wagons with their children, Ole, Randine, and Eivind, and Kisti's mother Synneva. As the oxen pulled them slowly up the trail, the wagon rocked back and forth. Kisti sat in the back nursing her youngest child, Eivind, though she knew it was time to begin to wean him. For now, she wanted to give her one-and-a-half-year-old child the comfort of a cozy breast feeding as they traveled from place to place, not knowing what lay ahead. He needed the security of breast love and so did she, as they faced the uncertainties of life on the trail.

As she held him, she recalled the day when he was born in Norway with an aching heart. Kisti knew that she and Hendrick would have to focus on what was best for their family. Not long after Eivind's birth, she and Hendrick decided to immigrate to the new land. Norway had such limited opportunities for children born during the population explosion of the 1920's and 30's that his mother Randine was caught up in as a midwife. Their boys would have to go into the military because they would not inherit any land. Ola, Hendrick's father, was a second son. His brother Knut Tomas was the eldest son, and Hendrick's cousin Tomas had inherited the farm. Tomas and his family had to stay, and the rest of the brothers and cousins were the ones who had to leave.

Kisti reflected on their travels to America. The family took a sailing ship across the ocean from Bergen, Norway, to Quebec, where they boarded a cargo sailing boat on the St.

Lawrence River, and then took a second cargo boat through Lakes Ontario, Erie, Huron and finally across Lake Michigan to Chicago. Life in the city was difficult for Hendrick and Kisti and their children. They knew very few people from Norway and the crowded tenement where they lived was full of people who sought to take advantage of the emigrants. Hendrick got work on farms outside of Chicago, and he also had a job working for some wealthy people who had settled there many years before.

At ten years old, their son Ole was already learning how to gamble with a gang of young boys, and Kisti did not approve of the friends he was making. This made her fear for his future, so after a year in Chicago, she insisted that she and Hendrick move their family to the country. Now that they were moving into forested hilly lands with rivers running through, she was feeling more herself again.

As the wagon rolled along, the baby fell asleep in her arms, and Kisti laid Eivind down in a makeshift bed behind the trunk they had brought from Norway. Kisti stepped on the trunk and climbed up to the front of the wagon to sit beside Hendrick, who was holding the reins; Ole, Randine, and Synneva were sitting on the other side of the bench. After traveling a while longer, they came to a junction on the north side of Madison, where other wagon trains had pulled into circles to camp for the night.

This was their fourth nightly stop. This time there was a large gathering of settlers traveling out west or going up north or down south. Hendrick maneuvered his wagon into a circle with the other twenty wagons. He jumped down from the wagon, and just as he had started tying up the reins, he heard a galloping horse coming up from behind.

It was Frank DuBey. He went around to the wagons to introduce himself. When Ole waved at him, he rode over to Kisti's and Hendrick's wagon.

"Mr. DuBey, wonderful to see you!" Hendrick said.

DuBey tipped his hat to Hendrick and Ole gave him a big grin.

"Please call me Frank. Welcome to the Grand Junction

gathering. Hello Ole. Nice to see you again, Hendrick. Is this the rest of your family?"

"Yes, this is my wife Kisti, and daughter Randine, and my mother-in-law, Synneva. My son Eivind is sleeping in the back."

"Nice to meet your family, Hendrick. Ole, I will see you later!" DuBey winked at him and rode ahead to talk to the leader of the group.

"Who is this man, DuBey?" Kisti asked.

"Ole and I saw him earlier on the back of his horse when we were about to leave Chicago," Hendrick said.

"Frank is a fine man, Kisti. He scouts for the army and for the fur people. He grew up among the Winnebago people, or the Ho-Chunk, as the native people call themselves. He knows all the tribes, the Sauk and Fox, and Pottawatomies. He told me many things about the native people. He says we will get along with them if we can be kind. They have all been wronged by this government, and Frank says it is sad to see them starving."

"Starving? Oh, how awful," Kisti said.

Just then Frank DuBey returned on his horse to speak to Hendrick. Randine and Kisti were setting up their part of the camp and preparing dinner with Synneva.

In the evening by the campfire, the company of travelers heard Kisti singing a lullaby to Eivind. Her rich contralto voice floating through the balmy summer air seemed to bring the promise of a bright and happy future. She was considerably embarrassed when Mr. DuBey stopped by the wagon and asked her to come out and sing to the group.

Lars Vanganess brought out his violin, and then several other instruments came out of hiding, and soon they had formed a small orchestra: two violins, a clarinet, a flute, a guitar, and Mr. DuBey with his banjo. Vanganess struck up "Ole Norway," a song that he knew Kisti could sing. He sat there, playing along, enthralled to hear her sing the nostalgic old ballad from their homeland. Many of the travelers wiped away tears.

As Kisti was singing, Hendrick's thoughts returned to the old military school at Bergen, where a beautiful tiny girl of seventeen, with long brown braided hair and a voice out of heaven, sang to the officers of the Academy. His lieutenant father, Ola, had said to him, 'Hendrick, if I was your age, the whole army of Swedes and Danes couldn't prevent me from meeting that girl,' and he slyly arranged to have the Colonel introduce his son to Kisti Moe. She was born in Laerdal and grew up in Bergen.

Here was that same Kisti, even more beautiful, more mature, with her rich voice echoing through the woods, and her flawless figure silhouetted against the soft glow of the campfire.

It was fortunate that they had left the city, thought Hendrick, as he gently squeezed Ole, who had come over to listen. Kisti belonged to the trees, the birds, and the flowers. Even the little squirrels seemed not to be afraid. Ole whispered, "Mother is beautiful, isn't she, Father?" Hendrick pulled Ole a little closer to him, acknowledging his comment without speaking.

After that evening, the wagon train group seemed to take on new life. There was more laughter when they stopped for the night, and everyone seemed to want to contribute something pleasant to the journey. They looked forward to the evening beside the campfire and it made the journey lighter, with much visiting and planning among the women in the wagon train circle.

As they traveled north, the terrain became more rugged, with frequent stone outcroppings, and there were more hills, which slowed down the oxen. They could barely travel ten miles a day. The trees were larger, the game was more plentiful, and Indians sometimes came into camp after the wagon train stopped for the night. They seemed friendly.

On the morning after Kisti first sang for the travelers, Frank DuBey rode up alongside the Lysne wagon, removed his hat, and placed it over his heart.

"I am sorry to tell you, ma'am, that I will have to leave for a few days. I have some business in Milwaukee, but I will try to rejoin you later. I want to thank you for your singing. I can truly say that I am sad to leave such pleasant company and that

I shall be anxious to return."

He also told her about Ole's carbine. DuBey had taught Ole how to use it, and he thought Ole could be trusted with it, but he felt his mother should know where he got it.

"Hendrick, Vanganess, and I talked it over with Ole. Ole wanted him to tell you himself. He won the gun after a gamble with another young city boy."

Kisti replied, "I have known this all along, but I thank you for telling me, Mr. DuBey. Ole has much respect for you and I am glad you have shown him how to care for his gun. I am sure he couldn't have had a better teacher."

Chapter Two

Crossroad Crisis

Many covered wagons were camped where the trails to the north crossed the east-west trails leading through Madison, Wisconsin, and westwards into the Iowa territory. Several families of German, Irish, Swedish, and Polish extraction, who had disembarked at Milwaukee from the Great Lakes, were on their way west to the Iowa country. Others did not seem to know where they would settle, but they seemed content to be on their way.

There was much visiting and discussion at this point of convergence of these trails. Several nationalities, especially the Poles and Germans, kept to themselves. However, in Captain O'Riley's wagon train, the Norwegians and some of the Irish families and the Danes and Swedes seemed to like this mixed group.

One of the wagons in the camp was carefully protected by a group of six men. None of them slept in this wagon or were seen to get supplies out of it. And at night it was always guarded. When one of them was questioned, he shrugged his shoulders and said, "I sleep in my brother's wagon. We don't need the things in that wagon until we build our place." They were a rough crowd. They seemed to have plenty of whiskey, and there was wild laughter and loud talk coming from their section of the camp.

There were many Indians living in the surrounding area. Several wigwams were seen in the woods near the river, so there was considerable uneasiness in the wagon train camp. Captain O'Riley cautioned everyone in the wagons to be on the alert and prepared for any emergency. Ole stationed himself outside the wagon with his carbine, and the stern expression on his young face said that he was ready to defend the entire camp.

During the second night in the camp at the crossroads, there was a terrific shriek from the woods. It was a woman's scream, followed by several shots. The next morning every wagon was searched by a group of army officers, who ordered that all the trains evacuate the area after inspection. After a roll call, and everyone in Captain O'Riley's train had been accounted for, they were ordered to proceed.

They had barely gotten started when someone rode up and said that four more wagons, all Norwegians, wanted to join them. They were from the Muskego Bay camp, south of Milwaukee, where they had broken from another trek to go up to the Plover River Portage area, after hearing about a settlement of Norwegians living there.

The four wagons were a welcome addition to the group, and the gathering that night at the campfire gave a reception in their honor. Kisti sang a song of welcome, and just as she had finished, a vivacious young woman by the name of Mari bounced into the circle and exclaimed, "There is only one voice in the world like that and it belongs to Kisti Moe! I am Mari Nederlo, from Bergen, but my name is Anderson now. I heard that you had married my father's cousin, Hendrick Olai Lysne. Where is he?"

She talked so fast and bubbled with so much enthusiasm that before they knew it, everyone was square dancing to Lars Vanganess's violin and O'Leary's guitar. Beside them stood Captain O'Riley, his strong baritone voice singing out calls in time with the music. "Aleman left and swing your partner..." echoed through the woods.

When the music stopped, the imposing figure of Frank DuBey on his horse rode into view. He was greeted with a shout of welcome across the camp. Mari ran up to him and held out both her hands saying, "I want to thank you for telling us about these wonderful people. I have found some relatives here. Hendrick is my father's cousin, and Kisti, his wife, is the one person I would cross the ocean to see!"

Frank DuBey had found these people in a camp at Muskego Bay, and in the course of their conversation, he had told Mari of Captain O'Riley's train, saying that Mari would be in good company as she seemed to belong with them.

After the greetings were over, and DuBey had talked with Captain O'Riley, everyone was asked to assemble early the next morning as soon as the wagons were ready to roll.

Frank DuBey walked over to greet Kisti.

"I heard your lovely song as I was coming up the trail. You also had quite an audience in the woods. Chief Yellow Thunder is camping just a little way from here. I stopped to talk with him. Yellow Thunder's nephew, White Fang, gunned down a white man at William's crossing two nights ago, and they are out hunting for him. He was perfectly justified in killing the man, for he was attacking Yellow Thunder's niece."

"Mr. DuBey, we are happy that you are back with us. You give us a sense of security. Tell me, was that the shooting we heard the other evening after that woman screamed?"

"Yes, it was one of the Cole boys. He was drunk and had gotten several Indians drunk. Yellow Thunder's niece, White Water, screamed when Cole dragged her into the woods. Her brother, White Fang, ran over and sank his tomahawk into the back of Cole's skull. Now, the Coles and the rest of the renegades are out after him. They may shoot anyone that looks like White Fang or any Indian, for that matter, if they get drunk enough."

Kisti shuddered. "What does Yellow Thunder say? Does he blame all of us white people?"

"No. Yellow Thunder is party to a treaty, and he is disposed to be friendly. It is fortunate that neither one of his people was injured and that Cole was killed instead of an Indian. Still, patience can be worn thin in such instances. He does realize, however, that not all whites are alike, any more than all Indians are alike. White Fang has disappeared, along with his wife and their three-day-old son."

Kisti gasped, "Three days? Why the poor woman! How old is she?"

"Oh, she is a rather young girl, DuBey said "It's hard to say whether she is fifteen or eighteen. I can remember when she was a very little girl, and that was not so long ago."

"I have grown very fond of White Fang. One cannot blame the Indians for resenting the white people. We have been a pretty shabby lot, so there is no real love for any of us."

Frank DuBey really meant what he said. His jaw was set, and his eyes had lost their kindness. Kisti now understood why his enemies feared him and why the Indians and the army trusted him.

"Yellow Thunder is quite a personality. His real name is Waukeesaukee. He was fearless at Tippecanoe, and he did not restrain too many of his braves at the Fort Dearborn massacre twenty years ago, but he had made some friends among the white people. The Sauks, the Fox, and some of the other tribes promised him that only the soldiers would be killed. Women and children and civilians would be given safe conduct. Well, when the fight for Fort Dearborn began, it proved too much for the braves. They murdered women and children right and left and forgot about their promises to Waukeesaukee."

One fellow had the scalp of a mother from a family that had been especially generous to Yellow Thunder, and he killed the brave on the spot. He kept the scalp with the blond hair as a shrine for the dead woman. He went to the Jesuit priest and took instruction after that incident and has become a devout Catholic. He is a stern chief who demands obedience."

"And what is this message we are to hear in the morning from Captain O'Riley?" Kisti asked. "Is there any real danger?"

DuBey said, in a low voice, "I am not supposed to tell, for they are afraid people will panic. But you seem capable and levelheaded. The Sauks on the east side of the lake are restless. They have burned some barns and stolen some stock. So far, they have not killed anyone, but some settlers will want to defend their property and that could lead to an uprising."

"The army out of Fort Howard and Winnebago is on the

job. Captain O'Riley was advised to move this train on the west trail. This will take us up the west side of the lake rather than the east side as planned. Excuse me."

DuBey left Kisti abruptly and was soon lost in the shadows.

Later that night, two menacing looking men stood in the light of the campfire armed with rifles and cartridge belts, their pistols and hunting knives within easy reach. They were surly repulsive characters with unshaven faces, straggly hair under their battered hats, and tobacco stains on their buckskin shirts. It was the Cole brothers.

"We are looking for an Indian and his squaw. That copper snake killed my brother and we are out to get him. When we find them, we will finish them off quick."

Kisti asked him, "What is a squaw? Do you mean a woman? Oh, what did the woman do?" She felt Ole close beside her and instinctively passed her hand over her young son's head.

Just as the man was about to answer, he saw Ole with his carbine, standing next to his mother.

"You little bastard!" Jim Cole said.

As Cole darted forward, Ole raised his carbine, cocked it, and in a shrill voice, yelled, "This is my gun, you drunken devil, and if you come any closer I'll make a hole in you. And I am no bastard!"

Cole's brother raised his gun when the clear voice of Frank DuBey was heard. "Put your hands up, Cole. Drop your guns. Keep your eye on them Ole, and if they make a move, shoot them."

DuBey disarmed them and asked, "Where is the rest of your gang?"

"I don't know," he said, glumly.

You're a liar, Cole. I know where they are. The army impounded your wagon of contraband, and your brothers and the rest of your gang are on their way to Fort Howard. Now my advice to you is to get out of Wisconsin and keep on going. I should take you back to jail with me, but I am going to send you on the trail. I hope you run into White Fang so he can finish his job punishing you. That would be about what you deserve. There are Sauks looking for you too, I happen to know."

The Cole boys without their guns were a sorry looking pair as they slumped out of camp. When they were out of sight, Kisti knelt beside Ole, kissed and hugged him, and said, "God bless my little man!"

Randine ran over and threw her arms around her brother.

Lars Vanganess was heard to say, "See, Hendrick, your little Ole saved the whole pack of us."

"Yes," said Mari, "his father and all his people before him were soldiers, so it is natural for him." She went over to Ole and extended her hand, "Thank you, Ole, for being so brave."

Ole was embarrassed by the attention and stared at the ground.

Frank DuBey came to his rescue. "Captain O'Riley," he said, "we might as well tell the folks what we have in mind tonight, and not wait until tomorrow. After this excitement, I don't think they will be sleeping much anyway."

Captain O'Riley moved into to the firelight at the center of the circle and said, "As you say, Mr. DuBey. Folks, the route has changed. We had planned to take the train on the east trail up at Fox Crossing a few miles to the north, so we could get some provisions from the farmers in the settlements. Many of them have cows and hogs to sell, and some horses. But we will have to take the west trail, which will take us to the west side of Lake Winnebago. The distance is the same, about thirty miles, a few days traveling, but we will have to skirt the swamp a ways up. If the weather stays dry, we will have no trouble. However, in the early spring it gets bad. We thought we had better tell you now, so you would not get panicky when you noticed that we were off our course."

"Sure," said O'Leary, "and would the Captain mind telling us why we must be taking this new trail?"

"I had hoped you wouldn't ask, but you are entitled to know. Perhaps Marshall DuBey can tell you better than I."

"Well, the Sauks and the Foxes are restless. There have been some treaty violations, and some incidents similar to what happened last week, which we all know about. It is only reasonable to expect there would be trouble. There has been no fighting, but the situation is explosive. There has been some livestock stolen and some horses; some fences have been torn down and some barns burned."

"There is a general dislike of the whites among them, for they were practically forced into a treaty they had no stomach for, so no one can entirely blame them. In a situation of this kind, to see another group of white people further invading their territory might enflame them to the point where they might get out of hand. If rioters such as the Cole gang give them whiskey, things could explode. And were that to happen, well, it would not be a pleasant sight to behold."

Mari suddenly danced into the circle. "Well, if we can't sleep, we can dance! Captain, get your guitar. Lasse, get your fiddle. Come on Kisti, let's sing!"

After a long day of traveling, the party rallied and was soon in full swing. An hour or so later, after dancing and playing songs together, as the pale moon rose above the trees, the camp settled down for a good night's sleep.

Lt. Hendrick Lysne, 1838

Chapter Three

Baptism, Berry Picking, and Glory of the Morning

The next day passed uneventfully as the wagons rolled along the trail. That evening the camp settled down in an abandoned Indian village. Several of the settlers living nearby came to visit. These folks brought fresh vegetables and provisions they had raised and strange foods that the settlers had never seen or tasted, like corn and green beans. In talking with the settlers, they learned about the challenges of building new homes, and breaking up the land, and the problems of pioneer settlement.

The visitors said that up near the village of Oshkosh, on the west side of Lake Winnebago, there was another trail crossing that led west to the Mississippi River from Green Bay in the northeast. This was a busy place for travelers. There was a great migration west at this time. The farmers in Oshkosh would bring cattle and horses to sell supplies to those who were moving westward. They sold a lot of housing tools and supplies to pioneers that stopped in Oshkosh on their final trek to settle in other parts of Wisconsin.

A Lutheran minister and an Irish priest from Milwaukee came to visit the camp. From these two clergymen the group learned much about the trails ahead of them. The people in the wagon train and the clergy were united in their belief that God would see them through. The clergymen stressed the importance of kindness and fair play with the Indians and said that the settlers should try to understand their feelings.

That night, there was no dancing. Everyone felt something shift in the air when the priest and the minister began speaking about their religious traditions. There was some resistance when Kisti asked Mr. O'Leary to witness Eivind's baptism along with Mr. DuBey. When a few people began to protest Mari picked up the baby and said, "I am with you, Kisti. Let us proceed."

Kisti went to Mr. O'Leary and said, "Mr. O'Leary we are both in this train, going to the same place and for the same purpose. This land has been given to us by the same God.

"Just because you are Catholic, and not Lutheran, there is no reason why your testimony should not be valid in witnessing my baby's baptism. We may have to fight in the same battles, and most surely, we will receive the same blessings."

She took him by the hand. "Come, Mr. O'Leary; all you have to do is to stand up here and say that you will lend your hand if anything happens to either of the child's parents. Will you help us?"

Michael O'Leary, his blue Irish eyes brimming with tears, said, "Our Holy Mother, 'tis a saint ye are! Yes of course, I will be there for you, as you have been there for all of us."

He took his place beside the wooden bowl that rested on a long log by the fire as people gathered around the Lysne family, the minister, and the priest. The minister asked in broken English, "What's this child's name?"

Mari said, "Eivind Hendrick Lysne, isn't that true, Kisti?"

Kisti gasped. She hadn't thought of his proper name for some time, as they called him Eivind all the time.

"Yes, that is his full name. Eivind Hendrick Lysne."

The minister proceeded by repeating his name and drizzling water on the child's head three times.

"Eivind Hendrick Lysne, I baptize thee in the name of the Father, the Son, and the
Holy Ghost, Amen."

As he took the towel to dry Eivind's head, the priest repeated, "In the name of the Father, the Son, and the Holy Ghost, and our beloved Mother Mary, Amen."

The silence around the circle felt solemn and joyful at the same time.

Michael O'Leary came forward and shook hands with Hendrick and Kisti, and then he said to Kisti,

"Aye, and it is my soul that I have saved this day!"

Kisti placed her hand on his shoulder. "God Bless you, Mike, and Mr. DuBey, you too sir, bless you and thank you for being present for our baby son."

She hugged Mari and kissed her.

The priest came forward, took Kisti's hand, and said to her, "You are a fine, noble woman. That was a beautiful thing you asked me to do."

He turned to the rest of the settlers:

"This is as fine an example of the spirit of this wonderful country as you ever will see. I thank God that he has sent people of this caliber here and we can rest assured that success will attend this party."

After baptizing several other babies, the minister left some instructions for Ole and Randine to study bible passages, so when they got older, they would be able to be confirmed in the church.

As Kisti was climbing into the wagon with Eivind, Hendrick took her hand and whispered, "How good God is that he has blessed me with such a wonderful wife!" He kissed her, and she brushed a strand of his reddish blonde hair away from his stout face and large blue eyes, and the two of them were seen no more that evening.

The next day, after traveling several miles along the trail toward Oshkosh, the sun was still high in the heavens when they reached a clearing and the drivers began pulling their wagons into the familiar circle. The wagons slowly came to a halt. The younger oxen stretched their necks under their yokes to snatch a morsel of wild oats. The old oxen, thankful for the chance to stop, stood motionless except for their tails, swishing at the ever-present flies.

This was a good place to camp for a few days. The weary travelers were relieved that they did not have to be on the move again the next morning but could stay until the final preparations were made to depart for their permanent home sites. This would give them a chance to wash clothes and rearrange their wagons. It would be good for the children, as many were showing the strain of travel. They had been traveling for more than two weeks from Chicago to Lake Winnebago.

Randine, bubbling over with excitement, ran over to her mother from the nearby bushes and said, "Can we go out and pick some berries as soon as we get Eivind down to sleep?"

"Yes, darling. I think it's a fine idea, and if we can get some sugar at the trading post in Oshkosh, we'll be able to put up some berries for the winter."

As soon as the baby was asleep and in Grandma's care, Randine and her mother set out with their baskets in search of blackberries. Randine soon came upon a tangled thicket with berries in abundance. While they were concentrating on the task of filling their baskets, Randine heard a sound like someone sobbing behind a tree. She listened again and crept cautiously in that direction.

Sitting on the ground, with her back against a tree, an Indian girl held a tiny baby to her naked breast. The mother was so lost in her grief that she was unaware of anyone's presence until Randine put her hand on the baby's head. Startled, the girl pulled away; the baby's mouth fell from the nipple. The only sign of life in the baby was the faint movement of the tiny jaw.

Randine called to her mother for help and Kisti raced over to find her daughter with the young Indian mother. Alarmed at the sight of the baby, Kisti gently took the limp little form from the mother, and expertly nestled it in her arm. She brought forth a well-rounded breast bursting with milk. She pressed the nipple between her fingers and squeezed a drop into the baby's mouth, then she worked the little jaw open and shut and with the tip of her fingers worked the little neck and throat.

Another drop came, and still another, as Randine watched, fascinated. The Indian girl was stunned to see Kisti help her baby with its first attempt to swallow.

"Randine," said Kisti, "you had better say your prayers. This girl needs her baby and we need these people for our friends."

Soon the pale little mouth made an attempt to nurse, and as Kisti always did on these occasions, she softly sang a Norwegian lullaby. The soothing effect on the baby was just the same as it was with her own. Randine was sent back to the camp with the berries. The Indian girl rubbed her flat, unproductive breast, and Kisti placed her arm, strong and reassuring, around her shoulder.

The exhausted and undernourished baby dozed off to sleep against the warmth of Kisti's body. Kisti's love and understanding and her gentle care for the baby calmed the frightened, overwrought girl, and her tense body relaxed and she fell asleep on the ground beside Kisti.

When Randine returned from the camp, she had a small earthen pitcher and a wooden spoon and an empty bowl. She placed them near her mother, and took the sleeping baby from her mother's arms, sat down on a stump, and began to sing the lullaby her mother had been singing.

The singing startled the Indian girl out of her sleep and she jumped to her feet, terror stricken. As she cried out and reached for her baby, Randine whispered "hushhhhh" and put her finger over her lips and tilted the baby so she could see its sleeping face. Then the girl remembered that Kisti had fed her baby. She turned towards Kisti, fell on her knees, and took Kisti's hand and held it to her face.

Kisti patted her head, and then she poured some broth into a wooden bowl and gave it to her. She tasted the broth and then gulped it down greedily.

Kisti knew that this frightened, exhausted girl must be the wife of the fugitive White Fang who had driven his tomahawk into the Cole renegade's skull, for he had disappeared into the brush with a wife and a three-day-old baby. They had spent five days on the road since they heard the scream, and an extra day at the last crossing, so this baby must be barely a week old. The mother would have had very little food or rest since their disappearance. No wonder her milk had disappeared.

Steadied by Kisti's arm around her waist, the girl rested her head lightly on her broad shoulder. When she raised her tired face, Kisti planted a firm kiss on her forehead, and the girl read in the older woman's smiling eyes that she understood her plight. The poor girl broke into tears, and with her arm around Kisti's neck, the floodgates opened.

"Well, Jesus, Mother Mary, now I have seen everything."

Kisti was startled to hear Captain O'Riley's booming voice. He and Frank had walked over from the camp to check the safety of the pioneers.

"Here we are, fearing an outbreak, and we see a white woman with her arms around a weeping Indian woman. How do you do it ma'am?" said Frank DuBey, standing beside the captain with a pleasant grin.

At the sound of the men's voices the weeping girl suddenly tensed up like stone. Kisti soothed her by holding her close and rubbing the girl's arm.

"Hush, hush, gentlemen, the baby is sleeping," Kisti whispered as she looked at Frank DuBey, "And you told me these people were stoics and never displayed their emotion. This girl is tired out with a starving baby!"

DuBey came closer and spoke gently in Ho-Chunk. The girl relaxed, and she seemed not to be afraid of him. She spoke her name to him in Ho-Chunk.

"Her name is Wahopekau, or 'Glory of the Morning'. I just told her that we will be back before the moon rises. You know she is White Fang's wife, don't you? The papoose is his son. Well, I have orders for his arrest, providing I find him, which is highly improbable. Captain O'Riley, here, is my deputy."

"If I ever find him, I'll give him a medal!" said Captain O'Riley.

"And as long as the Captain has the original warrant and I have the replica, you won't have to worry about your friend ma'am."

"God bless both of you," Kisti said. "You are indeed two

pillars of strength. We feel safe with you near. But this girl will stay with me. I have the nourishment the baby needs and we all have to survive. I will take care of her in our wagon."

"Please don't act too fast," DuBey said. "This camp must not know that you have found her. There are several here who have no use for Indians, and if it leaks out that you have Wahopekau with you, I will be forced to produce White Fang, and that I do not want to do, because he will likely be harmed or killed by the soldiers. I suggest that you stay here and try to get the papoose to nurse some more, and then go on about the business at camp. You probably don't know it, but you may have averted an uprising of these tribes by this little act of kindness. Yellow Thunder will see to that."

"But how would he know about it? Nobody has seen us here."

Captain O'Riley pushed his big hat off his forehead with the tip of his thumb.

"Dear Madam, every blessed move you make in these woods is watched, especially now, when everyone is on alert. Remember, the Indians are alerted, too. I wager that Yellow Thunder will know all about this delightful scene by tomorrow morning and, believe me, we are glad he will."

Then DuBey added, "It will ease the tension all around. We hoped we had friends in the circle around the council fire. Now we know that we do. With Shannona, of the Pottawatomies, and DeKorra, of the Winnebagos, and now Yellow Thunder, things will settle down, providing we don't have any more Cole gang episodes."

When the men left to return to the wagon train camp, Randine carried the baby to her mother, who was sitting on a log. The girl brought the baby to her breast for another try at nursing, and this time there was a definite response. The mother gently stroked her baby's forehead with her finger, and then she looked into Kisti's eyes and smiled. Gone was the strain and the fear; now her face glowed with love and gratitude. Kisti cupped Wahopekau's chin in her hand and kissed her forehead.

"Randine, run back to the wagon and get the red shawl.

Take the bowl and the pitcher and spoon with you. Don't tell anyone anything about this. Bring what's left of the meat we had for dinner last night. This girl needs it more than we do." Kisti began nursing the baby again.

DuBey returned before dark, as promised, to get Wahopekau and her baby.

"I will stay with her, Frank," Kisti said. "Please go back with Randine. I will come to our wagon after the camp has settled down."

Entering the camp, with DuBey behind her, Randine saw Mari with Eivind in her arms.

Mari said, "I heard him crying so I gave him some milk out of a cup, and he seems to like it. He is too big a boy to nurse now. See, he has a tooth and another coming in. Tell your mama, I'm going to keep him!"

Eivind loved the attention. Randine wrinkled her nose at Frank DuBey in an attempt to wink at him.

Ole sauntered into the circle with his precious carbine in the crook of his arm. In the game bag on his back, there was a fluffy tail of a raccoon that bounced with every step.

"Hi Ole, I see you shot a coon," DuBey said.

"I shot two of 'em, right through the head." He slipped the game bag from his shoulder and pulled out the raccoons and laid them on the ground.

"What a wonderful supper you will have tonight!" DuBey winked at Randine.

She smiled and ran over to their wagon to get the remainder of the rib roast and some bread from a tin box, which she wrapped in the red shawl. Then she scampered down the trail to where Captain O'Riley was sitting with his rifle across his knees guarding Kisti and Wahopekau. Randine unwrapped the shawl and gave the bread and meat to Wahopekau, who stuffed it into her mouth as fast as she could.

Chapter Four

Oshkosh By Gosh

The camp crossroads in Oshkosh village was a beehive of activity. This was the largest dispersal point along the northwest trek. Wagon trains were broken up and reconfigured. Those who expected to settle within a few days' journey were loaded down with extra horses and oxen, cows, sheep, pigs, chickens, dogs, and cats. Every day, some people would leave the camp for their final destination. Others would start their trek into the Sioux country of the west or head toward the Red River between Minnesota and South Dakota territories. The migration toward the north and northwest had gathered momentum.

Norwegian and German emigrants were in the majority at the crossroads camp in Oshkosh; there were some Poles and Irish, and occasionally, a Swedish family and some Danes came to the camp. Most of the Swedes were making the northwest trek to St. Paul, St. Anthony Falls, and Minneapolis. The Germans wanted to remain near Winnebago Lake at Oshkosh. The Irish folks were willing to undertake a journey to any destination that looked promising.

From early morning until sundown there was bedlam in the camp, with crying babies, crowing roosters, laughter, and singing. There was the noise of wagons, with groups leaving and groups arriving, and strange languages being spoken everywhere.

The Poles kept to themselves. The Scandinavians from Norway, Sweden, and Denmark gathered together in tight groups with folks from their own countries. The Germans and the Irish had made their camp near Oshkosh. Captain O'Riley's Irish friends stayed with the wagon train. Mike O'Leary boasted that they had the best outfit in the trek, and the Allens, who were a part of the wagon train community, backed him up.

All of them, however, shared the mutual desire to carve out a good life for themselves in the new land. And they had a common interest in Oshkosh, which offered them all the tools and supplies with which to realize their dreams. Everything essential to the pioneer home was available in that thriving little city, where, only sixteen years before, the first attempt was made at raising wheat in Wisconsin.

There had been a fur trading post at Lake Butte-Des-Morts in Oshkosh County since the 1830s. Now in 1855, there were several dry goods stores, five groceries, three shoemakers and dealers, two hotels, a watchmaker, harness and blacksmith shops, a doctor, and numerous other services. There was a great interest in the advertisements offering wearing apparel and heavy boots and shoes for outdoor wear. They looked over the ads on the store fronts: Calico was 4 cents per yard; wheat 56 cents per bushel; flour 4 dollars per barrel; ham 12 cents per pound; salt pork 20 dollars per barrel; butter 12 cents; cheese 11 cents; eggs 12 cents a dozen; beef 5 cents a pound, and potatoes 87 cents a bushel.

Vanganess was beside himself. "Look, potatoes at 87 cents a bushel, and wheat at 56 cents. We'll be rich! This is the greatest country in the world! We can raise hundreds of bushels if we all work together."

Kisti noted the name of Dr. Christian Linde in the paper. One day when she and Randine walked into town to buy shoes and fabric for curtains and bedspreads for the home they were to build, she went to see the doctor.

Dr. Linde spoke to Kisti in Norwegian, which was his native language as well, although he was educated in Copenhagen and Edinburgh and also spoke English. She liked him instantly and recognized in him a source of great strength.

He suggested that she and her family remain in Oshkosh for the winter so that Kisti could assist him with his practice. He said that there was plenty of work for Hendrick and Ole in the mills, and there was a barrel cooperage, a door sash and chair factory, that could always use workers. Miss Emeline Coog had established a public school which the children could attend.

The temptation to stay that winter and work for Dr. Linde was great. When Kisti got back to camp, she was planning to mention it to Hendrick, for she knew that if she suggested it, he would acquiesce. But something changed her mind, and she rejected the idea, and hurried with preparations to leave for their final trek to the new land. They had heard that there was a Norwegian community in Portage County a few days drive north from Oshkosh that was forming a village. It was called Amherst, and had been established as a village before they left Chicago.

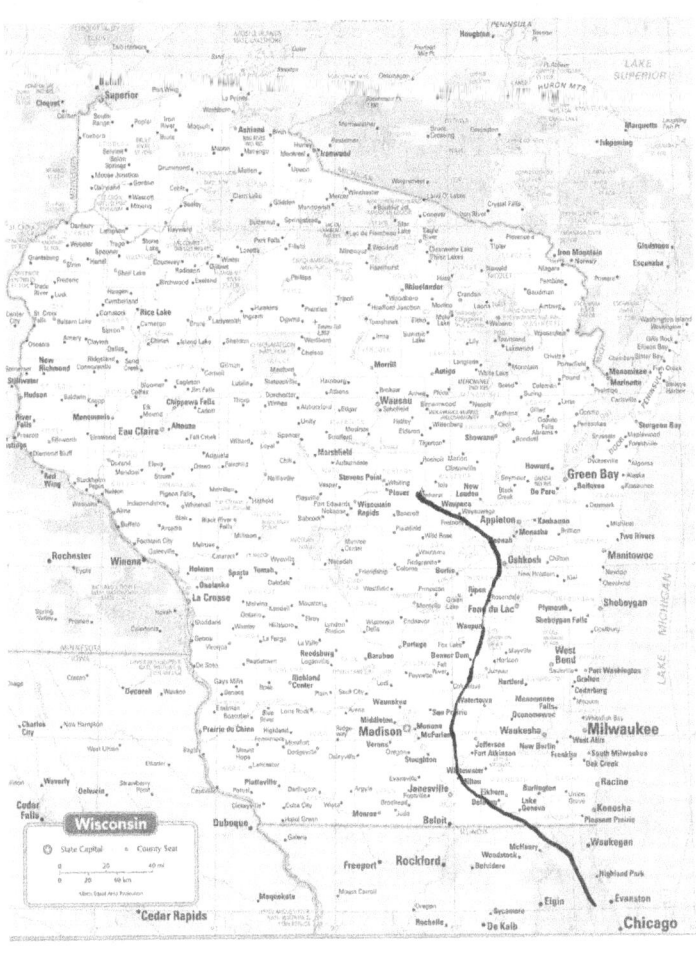

Chapter Five

Red Moon and Twigg

On her second trip into town, Kisti saw Dr. Linde, with his medical bag in hand, springing into a buckboard as she was window shopping with Randine and Synneva. She hailed him from across the street, and he waved back at her. He motioned for her to come over to his wagon.

"You are just the person I need," he said. "I hope your nerves are good, and I trust that you can stand the sight of blood because you are going to see plenty."

Kisti returned to her mother and Randine and told them the doctor needed her help, and handed them her basket, laden with store bought goods.

"I'll be back as soon as this task is over," she said, and kissed them both.

Then she climbed into the carriage and sat beside the doctor, and they drove the horses at top speed north towards Neenah.

"What are we headed for Doctor?" Kisti asked.

Dr. Linde replied, "Yesterday afternoon was payday and there is always something like this on payday. It seems there is an Indian woman who was severely injured. The white man sells the Indians watered whiskey and cheats him right and left."

"What happened to her?" Kisti asked.

"She was used as a prostitute. They get them drunk and then the women are abused. She is bleeding to death."

"Oh, how awful! What is this you mean, that the Indians get paid, and then the white men cheat them out of their money?"

"They get stocks of cheap goods and as soon as the Indian gets paid, he has to walk through a cordon of soldiers until he is off government property, and then the vultures make a grab for him. Once he is on his own, he is an open target for the exploiters. By the time he tears himself loose, he is left without a cent and won't get paid until the next quarter."

They pulled up to a one-room log hut standing in a thicket apart from the rest of the woods. Beside the sagging doorway, surrounded by traps of every description, stood Hula, a lean bronze-colored man in his mid-twenties. His shiny black hair covered his ears and his sideburns joined his straggly beard.

The features of the man presented all the attributes of the wild animal—cunning, resourceful, and fiercely defensive. He was a trapper, and if not a half-breed, then surely three-eights. He sat among his traps and pointed to the door with his thumb.

"She's in there."

The room defied description. The mud floor had probably never been swept. There were spider webs everywhere, a table and some stools constructed of small kegs, a bunk bed covered with a mangy buffalo hide, a faded army blanket, some shelves. There was a native woman lying in the corner on a pile of straw and hay, partially covered with an old patchwork quilt. It looked like she was in a coma; a trickle of blood was pooling on the floor.

Kisti hurried over to the woman and gently pulled back the cover; she was soaked with blood. "Don't move her; I must try and stop the bleeding."

Kisti pulled off her petticoat and tore it into narrow strips, which she made into small rolls. The woman had probably been three months pregnant. There was a tiny bundle on the floor, which Kisti set aside, then she placed the rolls in the woman's vagina to stop the bleeding and put one between her legs.

"God knows how many men were in here assaulting her last night," said Dr. Linde. "I'd wager that they kept her drunk, and as long as she got the whiskey, she didn't care. When she aborted the baby, she probably bled until she lost consciousness. Looks like we came a bit too late to help this godforsaken creature."

"Dr. Linde, she is a human being. She deserves our help!"

"Yes, I suppose she does, though I hate to admit it. Let's talk to the animal outside."

The doctor stepped outside. "You're Twigg, the trapper, aren't you?"

"Yep, that's what they call me."

"Is this your shack?"

"Yep, I used to live here."

"Who is this woman? Is she your wife?"

"She was with me a while this summer. She is a Fox. I sent her on ahead from Green Bay to clean up this place. I came in today and this is what I found. I don't have a horse, so I sent for you by the post rider. How much do I owe you, Doc?"

"It isn't that easy, Twigg. She might die, she has lost a lot of blood. Someone must stay here and care for her. We'll need some things to try and save her."

"Did she get attacked?" asked Twigg.

"Well, Twigg, I don't know how many men she took on last night, but she lost the baby she was carrying, and almost bled to death. We don't have much time."

Twigg went inside and touched her clammy forehead.

"Has she a chance, Doc?"

"Perhaps a slim chance."

Twigg buckled on a cartridge belt, with a holster on each side, and inspected the chambers of the guns.

"I'll go get some help. When they come, you put them to work, will you ma'am?
Just tell them what to do."

With that, he strode down the path; he had become a man on a mission, in contrast to the lethargic hulk sitting among his traps just moments before.

Kisti did what she could to clean her up, and shook out the buffalo skin on the bed, while Dr. Linde checked her fever and looked in her eyes. He left to go to the only store in the little town of Neenah to buy clean blankets, soap, and other items needed in this emergency. An off-duty soldier volunteered to get whatever supplies he could from the army surgeon.

The first of Twigg's recruits came down the path, somewhat the worse for wear, and Kisti took a wooden bucket and met them outside.

"You are Twigg's boys, aren't you? Here, please get some water."

One of the men took the bucket, and as he looked around with bewilderment, Kisti pushed him and the other boy with him in the direction of the creek in the woods.

"I think the creek is that way, please hurry!"

Others came up the path and greeted Kisti. She put them to work cleaning and fixing up the cabin. When Dr. Linde returned, the cabin was tidy and a fire was blazing in the stove, with water heating in a kettle. Kisti put clean sheets on the bed and bathed the woman as best she could. The woman was limp and still unconscious.

The workers got into the spirit of helping the native woman survive, after they got over their initial shock. They were dispatched for food, more water and wood, and more bedclothes and towels.

When Twigg returned, he had a pretty half-breed girl and a native woman with him to attend to their patient. The hemorrhaging had stopped, and she was beginning to wake up.

After giving them instructions and promising to look in on the patient later that evening, Kisti and the doctor were about to leave when Twigg said,

"Doc, I got another one in bad enough shape for you to fix. He refused to come and help out, and besides, he started the whole business with Red Moon. I winged him pretty close, Doc. I should have killed him."

Kisti went with the doctor and Twigg to see the wounded man. The bullet had gone through the armpit, but fortunately, it had missed the humerus bone and the scapula. It was a simple matter of cleaning and applying a bandage.

As they were dressing the wound, the man snarled, "Someday you'll pay for this Twigg!"

"Let me put it in plain language, Cole, if Red Moon dies, I will kill you on sight!" said Twigg.

After they left, Kisti asked Twigg, "Cole, what Cole is that?"

"He is one of several Cole brothers and cousins. Runs a still back in the woods. Sells whiskey and guns to the Indians on the sly, and sells Indian women when he can. He also runs a gambling game and is mixed up in a crooked fur deal. His brothers steal furs and anything else they can get their hands on. One of them had his skull split a few weeks ago. They said White Fang, Yellow Thunder's nephew, did it, after he grabbed his little sister. Two of his brothers were arrested, but they got off. They are around here somewhere."

"Do you think they will they catch White Fang?" Kisti asked.

"I doubt it," replied Twigg. "They are too clumsy and drunk a lot of the time. What they will do is get drunk, kill some Indian, and say it's White Fang. They are a miserable lot. After today, they will have it in for me, and I don't much care. Nobody likes them, so folks will squeal on them if anything is cooking. I'll keep an eye out ma'am, if you are worried."

Kisti was late getting back to camp. Mari had Eivind again. Randine told her mother she was worried about Wahopekau and her baby boy. The baby was better but was crying a good deal. Randine had talked to O'Riley and DuBey and they both assured her that her Indian friend was all right. Kisti found Wahopekau in better spirits inside the wagon, and the baby seemed much improved. Kisti offered him her breast and he latched on without hesitation. DuBey and O'Riley had brought the mother more food to eat, and she looked like a different person.

Kisti walked out to the clearing with DuBey and told him what she knew about the Coles and the Twigg episode and the attitude of the people dealing with the Indians.

"Mr. DuBey, what is going to happen to Wahopekau? She just can't be turned loose into the woods again. Yellow Thunder can't protect her because the Indians are not allowed to have guns. I think they are treated worse than any people in the whole world! I am so disappointed in how they are treated here that I am tempted to go back to Norway. This situation is just awful!"

DuBey put his hands on her shoulders and looked into her face.

"Listen ma'am, I know just how revolting all this must seem to a gentle woman of your makeup. Unfortunately, what you have seen is mild compared to what you might have seen."

Kisti threw her hands over her face and shook her head. She turned away and looked at the woods for a moment while DuBey kept talking. Kisti turned around and they headed towards the trail and walked slowly back to camp.

"We know it is not right, and while it may seem to you that we condone it, we really do not. There simply are not enough of us to do anything about it. It is people like you who can help to change the situation."

"Do you mean by helping the Native people?" Kisti asked, and DuBey nodded as they wandered back to camp.

It was dark when Kisti and DuBey returned to the camp circle. They joined Ole, Randine, Synneva, Hendrick, and Mari, who were seated near the fire, eager to hear what Kisti and DuBey had to say.

Hendrick stood and put an arm around Kisti, as he could see she was upset.

DuBey tipped his hat back and said, "If your kind leave, then all this trouble with the Indians will only get worse, and we will never turn this country into a fine, wonderful place to live. You have already made a difference; you have lit the first lamp."

"Yellow Thunder will never forget what you have done Ma'am, for his favorite brother's child and wife. Neither will the DeKorras of the Winnebagos, from whose family she comes. All of them together constitute the important tribes in Wisconsin, even Twigg's little Red Moon will not be forgotten."

"You know, Glory of the Morning, or Wahopekau as you call her, is not all Indian. Her people were French; her grandfather's eldest brother was Chief Chou-ke-ka and his father was Sabrevior De Carrie, who came to Canada during the French and Indian war as an officer of the French army under General

DeBroissant. He resigned his commission and went into the fur trade.

He married the daughter of Winnebago's head Chief at that time, and her name was Wahopekau. That is where this one gets her name. So, you see, your natural kindness has not been wasted."

DuBey stretched his arms towards the sky and said, "I am going to pay a little visit to your new friend and see what he knows."

Kisti said, "Wait a moment, Frank. Will you take her a small package for me?"

DuBey nodded.

She ran into the wagon and pulled a clean white nightgown out of the chest. She wrapped it in The Oshkosh Democrat, the local newspaper, and took it to DuBey.

When Kisti handed him the package, he said in a clear tone, "Don't do anything about the girl and her baby until I return. I will know then what should be done. You may have to take her with you."

Chapter Six

Preparing for Settlement

Kisti thought of her oldest son, Ole, as she lay in bed in the back of the wagon with her daughter, mother, and Waupekau and her son. She looked out at the friendly moon through the trees. Her heart was filled to bursting, recalling how Ole tried to be a man, with his carbine always at hand. Randine, bless her heart, had grown far beyond her years through her loving maternal care for others. Eivind was growing fast, and he needed the stability of a home. At almost two, with his birthday coming up in August, he had known precious little but travelling—first by boat, and then by wagon from camp to camp.

Hendrick had always been an enigma to Kisti, with his strong and silent ways. 'Righteous to a fault,' she mused. 'He is more stoic than these Indians.' He rarely laughed aloud, but he chuckled when something struck him as funny. When the Coles threatened Ole, and he had stood his ground, Hendrick didn't see the humor in it, but he laughed about it with Kisti the next day. She could always depend on him. Right or wrong, he was her champion. She couldn't recall a single instance when he had criticized or upbraided her. Even in embarrassing situations caused by her ignorance, he never censured her, but merely put his arm around her and kissed her.

Hendrick had gone to investigate land options with several other men from the camp. Men seemed to respect him. Mr. Medill, a very outspoken and wealthy man they met in Chicago, was most kind and courteous to Hendrick, as were Mr. Patterson and the people at the Custom House in Chicago. When they were leaving Chicago, John Kinzie assured him there was land awaiting them, and he unofficially made Hendrick clerk of the expedition. Kinzie had written several letters for the travelers and had given Captain O'Riley a log of the journey up to the Portage area. When Hendrick returned from his investigations in a day or two, it would be time to get together with Captain O'Riley and arrive at decisions on property that would be suited for farming. None of the land had been divided and designated as farms.

Kisti knew it was time for them to settle on land where they could build a home and cultivate a farm and raise their children. She pulled down the canvas flap of the wagon and tried to go to sleep. Life would certainly be drab without Hendrick, she thought. She had never quite realized what a place he occupied in her life. This was the first time he had been away from her for a whole night since their arrival in America.

The next day, towards evening, Hendrick and the men returned from their visit to the farming region beyond Lake Poygan, enthused by what they had seen and heard. Vanganess was so talkative the others couldn't get a word in edgewise until they plied him with enough whiskey to get him off to sleep, which was what had made him so vocal in the first place.

During their survey in Portage County, the men found out that some of the things they had originally thought would be essential were not important. There were new little towns springing up and a few homes had already been built near the land they planned to settle on. It wasn't the vast wilderness they had pictured. This added zest to their discoveries, knowing they'd be settling down in a county that was already established, and they felt impatient to get going.

When the camp folks got together around the fire that evening, after the men returned, they discussed farming versus the other trades. Everyone was interested in breaking up the land for farming, but no one seemed to take an interest in lumber, fur, mining, or any of the other opportunities the new country had to offer.

Mari observed, "These people wouldn't be riding in ox wagons if they weren't farmers. They would be on the stagecoach, with gloves and fur coats, or dusters so they wouldn't get their clothes dusty."

The men laughed at her comment and that seemed to settle the question as to whether they'd take on any other kind of work.

Everyone agreed that a one-room house would have to do for the first year. They pledged to help each other get their places built as soon as they secured the land that was available and arrived in Portage County. Mari and Anders, Hendrick and Kisti, O'Leary, Lars and Lasse Vanganess, Ashbjorn and Randi Roe, David and Ingeborg Boe, and a Pole from Milwaukee named Mike Kozickowski made up the group. A number of settlers in their train had already left the camp, but a wagon train was no longer essential for protection from Indians and thieves, since most of them would reach their final destination within three days or so.

Mari and Kisti drew up a list of food supplies; flour for bread, sugar for baking, deer or raccoon meat from the woods, a barrel of pork that would get them through the winter, vegetables, and household provisions, such as sifters, knives, and tableware. The men's lists included livestock and tools, everything that would be essential for the building of their homes.

The next day the stagecoach from Chicago came in, and great loads of merchandise were arriving in Oshkosh. The Chicago Tribune was the most highly prized newspaper in the region and it made the rounds of the camp when Hendrick went into town to get some of the supplies they needed. He loved reading it because it spoke of the changes and politics that were going on around the country.

That night an itinerant preacher walked into the circle and began to preach to them. He talked about sin and described the punishment designed by God for those who failed to cleanse their sins before they died. He was fascinated by his own description of hell and mentioned the kind of people who would end up there. Among them were the slave owners of the South and rich people like Augustine Grignon, John DuBey, John Kinzie of Chicago, and Joseph Medill.

"Whoa!" said Hendrick, stepping into the circle, "You

are taking in a lot of territory here and consigning a lot of my friends to hell. From the way you have described it, I think you must have been there. Maybe you are from hell yourself. But we are done listening to what you have to say. Maybe the slave owners are wrong, but are the slaves treated any worse than our Indians here? I don't believe in slavery, but neither do I believe in cheating anyone.

"You can say what you please about your precious hell, but I won't allow you to stand here and attack my friends who are not here to defend themselves. As to maligning a loving God, you and He will have to straighten that one out between you. If you need food to eat, we will feed you. Otherwise, GIT out!"

The circle applauded Hendrick. "Hooray for Hank!" someone shouted. Hendrick blushed and began to walk away. Mari giggled, "Gee, Hendrick-Hank- I mean, I didn't know you had it in you!"

Kisti's eyes sparkled with pride. She squeezed his arm and said, "So you have a new name now, Hank. That is the longest speech you have ever made, and I loved it. Let the rest of them call you Hank; that shows you are one of them. But to me, you will always be my darling Hendrick, the soldier you were when I first saw you."

Hendrick took her face in his hands and kissed her forehead. Kisti saw a tear on his cheek.

The minister tried to argue with Hendrick, but no one would listen to him. Mari set a plate of food on his lap, and he left as soon as he had finished eating.

Many were ready to start breaking camp the next day. Some folks had decided to cast their future with Oshkosh, others left for Neenah north along Lake Winnebago, and still others chose to go to Algoma, which was on the coast of Lake Michigan. Most of these people were German. Except for a few Swedish families, most of the Scandinavians chose not to stay behind. The original wagon train under Captain O'Riley was still intact, due to the unity of this community and the affection they felt for each other. Mike O'Leary boasted, "We have the best outfit in the Wisconsin trek!" They had to plan their path to Amherst, so they were one of the last groups to leave the following day.

The wagons got crowded with supplies and had to be rearranged to make room when a barrel of pork was added, and then a barrel of flour, bolts of materials, tools axes, adzes for scraping wood logs, augers, mauls for wood and stone, draw knives, and other tools used in the construction of cabins and the clearing of land.

There was much excitement when the stagecoach arrived that morning, and a passenger alighted and began to hand out copies of the Waupaca Spirit. The editors were the Redfield brothers and some of the advertisements carried the name of Wilson Holt, General Merchandise, which was also in Amherst, just a few miles from Waupaca. Mention was made of the flourmill of W. C. Lord and Wilson Holt located between the two tiny towns. In the news items there was a mention of Silas Miller, pastor of the First Methodist Church, and of Circuit Judge Cate, who would hold the first circuit court session in the new Methodist church after they arrived. There was mention of a missionary, who also was a physician, with a British name of Cutting March, and of Miss Dora Thompson, who would teach the district school for another year. All of this was happening near where they were planning to settle.

This was wonderful news to the people at camp getting ready to depart. Much of their fear and trepidation about the unknowns of the future vanished when they read the Waupaca Spirit. They learned that there was a mail route, with a post office at Waupaca Falls; the mail was sent from Green Bay to Plover to Waupaca. Captain David Scott was the postmaster. There was a church, a school, stores, and law offices, so everything was in place and ready for them. Kisti's heart sang with the promise of a bright future and that same joy was felt throughout the camp.

Wagons were pulling out every day now, singly, in pairs, in threes and fours. They were told that there was no need to keep together in a wagon train for safety's sake, as the Indians were subdued and disposed to be friendly. However, Captain

O'Riley advised taking the marsh route.

"It has been quite dry, and the trail is pretty good, but if it begins to rain the trail will turn to mud soup and make it tough going. Time to get on our way.

"I would suggest that we leave with what we have now. We'll be able to get more provisions at Waupaca Falls. I understand there are goods available at the store in Amherst. Don't burden yourselves by taking anything more than you need."

They discussed the route as a group, and decided to go to Winchester the next day, with their wagons greased and loaded, and the oxen well fed and rested.

That night, the circle of folks around the campfire began to grow as other travelers came to gather for the last time. Strangers, never noticed before, began to appear and joined the circle.

Mari danced out into the middle of them and called out, "Lars, get your fiddle! Come on all, let's dance."

Soon there were enough musicians for a makeshift orchestra, and the music began. With her auburn locks flying in the breeze, and her quick vivacious movements, Mari's dancing was so exciting that hardly anyone could sit still.

She grabbed a bashful giant by the wrist and pulled him to his feet. Even Hendrick danced with Kisti and others as the night went on. Two musicians from Chicago joined the group, a fiddler and a flute player. Kisti sang her song of Norway, and then she asked Jacobs if he would sing a couple of slave songs from the South. He obliged, and sang "Swanee River" to a round of applause. Then he sang, "De Campton Races," and many others joined the dancing.

Kisti saw Randine standing at the edge of the circle beside Wahopekau, with her baby strapped on her back. She seemed unafraid and fascinated by the music. Back in the shadows stood Frank DuBey, and Kisti's anxiety about Wahopekau vanished when she saw him. He nodded to her and motioned with his hand for her to come talk to him, and so she left the dancing and walked over.

"I am glad we came in time to hear you sing. I guess you have undertaken a responsibility you hadn't planned on," said

DuBey.

"Oh, Mr. DuBey, we are all in this together!" Kisti replied.

"There are other Coles here besides the man over in Neenah. The agent at Fort Howard let the other two go. Some settlers were robbed on the trail leading off the Green Bay Road, and I suspect that they are from the same gang."

"Oh dear, should we watch out for them on our way to Amherst tomorrow?" Kisti asked.

"No, but be careful. One of Twigg's cronies came to town yesterday. He is quite a frontiersman and will hang around Cole and get what information he can. He knows all about the White Fang affair and he knew Wahopekau, as does Twigg. You will have to take her with you. Until you get to Winchester, keep her out of sight as much as possible." "Thank you for letting us know."

"It is best to take Glory of the Morning, Wahopekuu, with you when you go to Amherst, or wherever you are headed. O'Riley will see that Wahopekau gets to Plover. She has some powerful relatives there who will see her through. Her husband is there now, in hiding, though she doesn't know about it. It will be a happy surprise for her. These people are quite well to do. They are intermarried and live respectably. Most people accept it as a matter of course in Plover. In fact, this young lady, Glory of the Morning, is the legal interpreter for the Winnebagos, and she is smart enough to arrange a lawyer for them when she gets to Plover."

Wahopekau walked over and stood next to Kisti and leaned against her. Kisti put her arm around Wahopekau and extended her other hand to Frank DuBey.

"Frank, how can I ever thank you for what you have done for all of us. I am grateful to you for training Ole with his carbine, and for all the protection you have given us. And thank you for the concern and care for this young girl and her baby. It is no burden to have her with us, it is a pleasure."

"You will hear plenty about my Uncle John. He is a hard man, as one gets to be in this country. In his youth, survival depended on being the strongest and the first to act. I came from

Montreal to help him out after he was a trapper, but he was hard on the Indians. He demanded the Chippewas, the Menominees, the Winnebagos, and some other tribes sign treaties. In one case he knocked out a Chippewa chief with his fist because the Chief refused to agree with the treaty. I kept books for him, but I could not stand how he treated the tribes. He thought I would make a good priest in Montreal, I guess."

"You are a wonderful scout for both the tribes and the U.S. army," Kisti replied.

"I went on my own and it has worked out well, as I am still a U.S. Marshall, and I have done my uncle greater favors than I could have by working for him. Now I am the apple of his eye. You will hear much grumbling about John Kinzie, Augustine Grignon, and many others. But remember they had a job to do that was different than today. All they have done has benefited us, and while probably not gentlemen, it will undoubtedly prove to have been the best thing for the settlers. Time will tell. You will be reimbursed for your trouble in taking care of Wahopekau, for they have the means."

"But I want to do this. I don't want pay for it," Kisti said.

Don't refuse their effort to do something for you, for that is like depriving them of a chance to be your friend. That is important, Kisti." Frank blushed. "I beg your pardon, ma'am, I called you by your first name."

"Please believe me, Frank, it is a real compliment and I appreciate it."

Frank looked at her with loving eyes, though he knew his life was not made for having a woman in his life. And of course, she was happily married to Hendrick with several children.

"You are a wonderful woman, Kisti. I am glad you are choosing to settle in this country with your family, as you have far better values than my uncle and many other whites."

Kisti smiled at him and took his hand. "May you be safe Frank, wherever you go."

The next morning, as they were arranging the wagon to start their journey to the Amherst area, Kisti wondered out loud where Wahopekau and her baby were to sleep. She turned to Hendrick, and he took Kisti out of earshot and said, "Ole and I are going to sleep in Lar's wagon, and Randine will be with Mari, so there will be plenty of room for you and the girl."

Kisti was astonished. "You knew about her? I thought it was all a secret!"

"Well, Ole saw you when you met her in the woods. DuBey and Captain O'Riley told us the whole story when you were in town. They said that we would have to take her with us to save her life. We felt we had better treat it as a family affair."

"Incidentally, your Indian patient over in Neenah is on the mend and wants to see you. We are going close to that area when we get on the trail. Dr. Linde will meet us in town. You are to ride with him, and he will drive you over to take the wagon train."

Kisti put both her arms around Hendrick's neck and kissed him. "I have, without a doubt, the finest family in the world. They all do things for me behind my back, but I love them all the more for it. That goes for my wonderful friends, too. Oh, we will be a grand people in this great new country."

Chapter Seven
Moonlight Swim

By sunrise, the three wagons that were to stop at Winchester had a fourth wagon join them; Vanganess was now in one of the wagons. Captain O'Riley got them moving through Oshkosh, and then took the route that would go past Butte-Des-Morts Lake to Winchester.

As they were passing through the towns, Wahopekau watched their progress through a gap in the canvas covering as she sat in the back of the wagon with her baby and Synneva. Randine had joined her mother, Eivind, Ole, and Hendrick on the bench seat. They saw Dr. Linde drive up alongside their wagon, and Hendrick pulled the oxen to a halt. The doctor asked whether Kisti would join him to say goodbye to the young Indian girl, Red Moon, whose life they had saved. Kisti agreed and hopped down from their wagon and climbed into the doctor's carriage and off they went to Twigg's cabin.

The young Indian girl that was staying with Red Moon met them at the door and let them in. Red Moon was sitting up in bed, clean and wearing the white nightgown Kisti had sent. She looked very pretty as she held out her hand to Kisti.

"I wanted to see the kind white woman who helped me."

Kisti took her hand. "I am so glad to see you are getting better."

Red moon said something to the girl in Indian words that Kisti couldn't understand, and the girl went to her pack and pulled out a string of beads, worked in a beautiful design in white, blue, and black. She put the strand around Kisti's neck, and it reached her waist. Tears came into Kisti's eyes.

"It's beautiful. How proud I am to have it!" Kisti said.

The girl said, "The beads say, 'This white woman has a kind voice, a nice smile, and a big heart. She is a good mother to Indian women.'"

Kisti thanked them through smiles and tears.

Red moon said, "You wear these. Indians see them, they will know you are Indian's friend."

Kisti hugged her, and after checking on their supplies and making sure they had enough to eat, Kisti and the doctor left. Dr. Linde was quite impressed.

As they drove along, he said, "This is really an occasion of honor. Most white people think Indians are stoics, but this shows they have another side we never see. I guess they understand love and kindness as we do. We just haven't tried it out on them, which is wrong. It will be a lot easier for many of us around here now, for this news will reach the Indians and the white folks."

Kisti murmured to herself, "I feel as though I have been sanctified with these beautiful beads. I'll never forget this."

"You keep on being as you are, and you will do well in this country. I only wish I could convince you to stay here and help me. You don't know how much we need people like you," Dr. Linde said.

"But I know you will be going to Waupaca Falls south of Amherst. I have a colleague there, a missionary and physician, by the name of Dr. March. He will appreciate you as I have. You will no doubt be a great help to him."

The wagons followed the trail to the northwest along the lakes and up to a town called Winchester. Most of the women wore their hand-woven dresses from Norway and the men had caps that were clearly not cowboy hats, but more like hats a sailor would wear. The sight of another group of wagons with Norwegian dressed settlers entering their town caused two brothers to remark, loud enough for everyone in the passing wagons to hear, "We might as well call this 'Little Norway.' When we started there were seven English families, now all the rest are Norwegians. Where do they all come from?"

As Ole rode by in the wagon with his family he said with

a smile, "Norway."

The brothers laughed. Ole jumped off the wagon and went to chat with them. They learned from Ole that they had come from the Chicago country and that Captain O'Riley was the one who was leading them to the Amherst Junction area.

"He is Irish, like you!" Ole smiled at them. "We are going to church here today, as it is Sunday," Ole said as he walked alongside the slow-moving oxen. "Come join us if you wish!" Ole ran to catch up with his family's wagon and jumped up on the bench. Hendrick smiled at him and chuckled.

That Sunday there was such a crowd in the Winchester Lutheran Church that the benches were filled and there was hardly room to stand. The pastor, Rev. A.C. Preus, read scripture from the book of Nehemiah, the ninth chapter, emphasizing the protection the Lord had afforded the Israelites in the wilderness, even though they had broken the original commandments on several occasions.

Everyone agreed that the sermon was very appropriate. More wonderful by far, to Ole and Lars and the children, was the excellent dinner that followed. There was much reminiscing between Hendrick and Kisti about their old church in Norway and how lovely it was to be in a real church again. The minister gave them considerable information about how to start a church in Amherst. When the gathering broke up, produce and food was sent along with the travelers for use on the road. The people of Winchester had done well to welcome the new pioneers, and they were all proud of their success.

Fresh meat, eggs, milk, and all the things that testify to a well-established home, inspired them to build a good life for themselves. Kisti and Mari managed to take some of the fresh meat to Wahopekau. Mari had gotten it from people in Winchester who were from Valdres, Norway, where her husband Anders was from. They said she could have anything she wanted, but Anders stepped on her toes, so she settled for milk, bread, and meat.

Wahopekau was more than grateful for the food, as she had to remain hidden all day. As soon as night came and the other friends were settled into their wagons, Randine, Mari, Kisti, and Wahopekau took the babies and went out for a long walk in the moonlight.

Their friend Wahopekau led the way through a patch of woods where they heard the wild nostalgic cry of a whip-poorwill. She led them down a little path to a small lake with a sandy beach. Without a word, she laid her baby on the clean sand, got out of her clothes, and waded out into the clear water to swim.

"We aren't going to be outdone, are we Kisti?" smiled Mari, removing her blouse.

Kisti saw that Eivind was sound asleep in her arms. So she laid him next to Wahopekau's baby on the sand, and put her shawl over them. Then she slipped out of her dress.

Within moments they were all skinny-dipping in the delightful water. Wahopekau came ashore, took handfuls of white sand, and rubbed it all over her body. The others did the same and reveled in the warm flow of heat on their skin. After one more dip in the water to wash off the sand, they walked along shore while the warm breeze dried their skin. All of them felt refreshed.

Wahopekau held one of her dark bronze arms against Kisti's and Mari's pale skin and they laughed at the contrast. Mari took a strand of Wahopekau's coarse black hair and held it against her own auburn locks and the four of them laughed again. The babies were still sound asleep on the warm sand. After getting dressed, they sat on a sloping hillside overlooking the moonlit lake. The mellow soft summer breeze and gentle night inspired Wahopekau, and she began to sing a soft crooning love song of the Winnebagos.

Kisti, Randine, and Mari sat there spellbound in the moonlight as they listened to her haunting voice. With her wild beauty silhouetted against the moon, Kisti thought she had never seen anyone quite so beautiful.

Suddenly, she stopped singing and listened attentively; she listened again, and then darted down the hill to the edge of the lake. She let out a little wild cry and disappeared into the thicket. Moments later, she came back, picked up her baby and whispered, "White Fang!"

Kist grabbed her arm. "Listen child, come back to the wagon before daylight. I will leave food on the back of it for him. Tell him that we are leaving for Waupaca tomorrow and that we will be in Amherst in three days. Also, Captain O'Riley will take you to your relatives in Plover. Tell him that the Coles are in Neenah. And for God's sake, do be careful."

Wahopekau smiled and nodded. "Me tell." She picked up her son and disappeared into the bushes.

Mari shook her head, "Kisti, you sure have a gift for getting into things. Nothing exciting ever happens to me, but around you, it sure does. I hope those dirty Cole devils don't find White Fang and hang him. And I hope Ole doesn't run into those Cole drunks without his gun."

Kisti prayed, "Please God, protect Wahopekau and White Fang, and all of us!"

The next morning, Wahopekau and her baby were back in the wagon sound asleep when Kisti awoke. The food they had left on the back of the wagon for White Fang was gone. Hendrick decided to get on their way without waiting for Captain O'Riley and the rest. They had been assured the road was in good shape as far as the Landing, and left word that they would camp somewhere nearby the trail when the others followed later.

They had just bedded down for the evening when the others appeared from their wagon train. There was much laughter and talk among them. There was not much danger as far as White Fang was concerned, since the Coles were drinking it up in Neenah and probably would stay there until they ran out of booze, or as soon as there were furs to steal.

Captain O'Riley speculated that this year they would begin to steal lumber, which would mean that they would relocate near the DuBey Falls, up on the Wisconsin River. Between Captain O'Riley and the trapper, Kisti was made to feel that there was no danger anywhere within a thousand miles.

Towards the end of the following day, the party forded

the shallow Tomorrow River, and at last they were in Tomorrow River country. They pulled up their wagons within eight miles of Waupaca Falls, and Captain O'Riley led them through the little town to the western outskirts, where they would make camp for the last time as a group.

The men went to Waupaca Falls, and the women and children busied themselves with evening chores. There was an abundance of food remaining from the Winchester Sunday potluck and it looked as if this was to be the land of plenty for all of them.

As soon as it grew dark, Wahopekau emerged from her hiding place with her baby and Randine and got out of the wagon, and she and Mari walked along the trail to the river. After a refreshing swim, Randine left Wahopekau to go back to the wagon, as she sang her Winnebago love song to her baby. After the baby was asleep Wahopekau returned to the wagon too.

The men returned later that night, charged with anticipation for the morning, when they would go and see the land they had bargained for. The people were restless in the camp. Before the first streaks of light appeared in the east, the yokes were already placed on the oxen's necks and the smell of coffee and frying pork filled the sweet morning air. This was the day!

By the time the sun had risen, they were moving up the Tomorrow River trail towards Amherst. Wahopekau walked alongside the wagon with her sleeping baby in the stiff little cradle on her back, his dark head bobbing with her every step. The beaded band around her forehead, from which the cradle suspended, was different in colors and patterns from the one Red Moon had placed around Kisti's neck. Hendrick walked beside the oxen with his hands behind his back in deep mediation. Still, he could hear Mari and Kisti as they chatted.

Mari's voice was raised to a high pitch complaining about her husband and Kisti laughed. "Never mind, Mari, this is what you are here for, to be with Anders."

"But I hate his damn big feet and the damn boots that cover them."

"Mari, Mari, honey! Why hate his feet and boots? I have never heard such a funny gripe about a man. You don't hate him Mari, Anders is your husband!"

"I don't hate him. I love the big clumsy ox. I wish he was an ox!"

"Mari honey, it's quite wonderful, really. I have two oxen and I wouldn't part with them or any of the five members of my family, not one of them! Here you have only one family member and you storm about him! Are you worried about the new baby?

"But why should it happen now? No home, we are living in the woods among animals, and me bigger than the pork barrel? I can get along with this one but not two of them!"

"Oh, come now, if children were only born when it was convenient, there wouldn't be any. They always come at the most inconvenient time, and they say and do the most inappropriate things, and we love them anyway. The more they are in the way and the more they embarrass one, the dearer they become. The more Ander's feet and his boots annoy you, the more you will love him, too!"

They were nearing Amherst when Captain O'Riley approached them on his horse. He dismounted and fell into step beside Hendrick.

"Well, everything seems to be in order, Hendrick. You don't have to go to Plover to register your land. We can make out the transfer at Amherst and I will go out with you and show you where your property is so you can begin to get settled. I am sure you will be well pleased. I will also relieve you of your burden of the Indian girl and her baby. Her people are around and will take her to Plover with them. They are influential and wealthy on the white side of her family. A lawyer is being retained by the Winnebago tribe to help them."

"She has been no burden to us, Captain. She is perfectly welcome to stay as long as she wishes."

"Hendrick, there is one thing that I am going to warn you about right now. Be damn careful who you invite into your house to eat. You Norwegians have a failing in that you are too hospitable. Up here, that just doesn't go well. Remember, you will have hardly enough to live on as it is, and you cannot be cleaned out of your provisions by serving guests. The best way to avoid trouble is not to begin it. Invite no Indian to your house, or they will all come."

"Thank you, Captain O'Riley. I will tell my wife, but I doubt that it will do any good. She gave much of our food on board the ship to a stowaway. The sailors were about to put him in chains, but she kept him fed, and so we did help him. She has a philosophy that everything will work out for the best, and sure enough it does!"

I have seen that Hendrick, and I know it works with her. I can only tell you what I have observed. You will get on well, no doubt."

"There is a man by the name of Rice who will process our papers and take your deposition and register your claim for you at Plover. I will go back to the others now. When you arrive, just wait for me."

Hendrick nodded and tipped his hat, and then he took in a deep breath of the fresh air of his new land.

Part Two
Settling into a New Homeland

Chapter Eight

Starting from Scratch

As Hendrick and Kisti and their family approached Amherst, along with Lars, Mari and Andres and the others in their wagon train group, they passed an old sign that said Groversburg. Hendrick had heard that the Grovers family owned a large percentage of this land at one time. Adam Uline, a settler who lived there, had renamed the town after General Amherst, a famous Revolutionary War soldier who was a native of Amherst, Nova Scotia. Members of the growing town had decided to call it Amherst rather than Grovesburg, and they raced to make it official with the state in 1853, just two years before the Lysnes arrived.

The group of settlers stopped short of the river and turned north. Here the trail widened and divided in several directions. Hendrick and Lars decided to drive their families and wagons into town to wait for Captain O'Riley. While there, they went to search for William Rice, the first clerk of the newly organized town of Amherst.

When they met O'Riley in town he had everything arranged, and the title guarantee was signed and sealed before witnesses and delivered to Hendrick and Kisti. The deed was subject to final recording of the county records from the Department of the Interior of the United States. Captain O'Riley processed titles for several others in the group as well. The captain had also brought with him the mail from Waupaca Falls, and Hendrick was thrilled to receive a letter from his father Ole in Norway. He hadn't heard from him since they left Chicago.

Hendrick, Anders, David, and Asbjorn set out from Amherst with their families to see their new land. Driving through the northeast section of the township, they headed south and passed several substantial log houses that were built by Norwegian settlers. The trail was well worn from Amherst to the north and northeast, with several new homes along the way. They passed Lasse with his wagon, who had already arrived at his land. Captain O'Riley was there, along with a county man, who helped them identify boundaries by the surveyor's plots.

"Keep on this trail until you hit the Scandinavian Trail. When you reach the fork, which runs to the southwest, wait there for me," Captain O'Riley said.

Captain O'Riley caught up with them on his horse and showed them their plots. The Lysne's land was heavily wooded on one side with a beautiful meadow at the top of a slight hill. This is where the house could be built. Looking down from the hilltop, the meadow was bordered by forests, thick with trees. An archway in the center of the trees made a beautiful entryway into the woods. They had about eighty acres of land, plenty of acreage for farming.

O'Riley knew that White Fang was following their wagon through the forests to meet them when they arrived at Kisti's and Hendrick's new property. Wahopekau heard White Fang calling to her inside the wagon. At last she was safe now on this land, so she jumped out of the wagon with her baby. Hendrick saw her jump out and pulled the reins on the oxen. Then Kisti, Hendrick, and Randine escorted Wahopekau and her baby over to White Fang. They greeted him for the first time. Speaking to them in broken English, White Fang thanked them for taking care of his wife and child. Randine and Kisti hugged Wahopekau goodbye.

"We will miss you, Wahopekau," Kisti whispered, holding her close.

After they let go, Wahopekau placed her hand on Kisti's heart and took Kisti's hand and placed it on her own. "Kisti my new Mother."

White Fang and Wahopekau and their child disappeared into the woods. Hendrick saw two men from their tribe greet them beyond some trees.

As Kisti, Randine, and Hendrick walked back to the wagon to join the rest of their family. O'Riley greeted a man named Knute Blasky, who came over to introduce himself. Blasky owned the land to the south of the Lysne's new property. He immediately offered his help with any construction needs. He was an excellent carpenter and cabinetmaker, and his services would prove to be invaluable.

Knute suggested that the Lysne cabin be built with poplar logs like his own house. Poplars grew there in abundance, and they were easier to cut than the other hardwoods and could be smoothed and matched with the least difficulty.

Over the next few days, as soon as sufficient clearing had taken place, the Blasky brothers came with their axes and adzes, saws and hammers, and began to construct the new Lysne log cabin, which would be 12 feet by 16 feet, with a kitchen complete with a fireplace and windows. The beds would be installed near the fireplace, and there was also a sleeping loft, which Ole claimed for himself. The loft was reached by cleats nailed beside the chimney that led up to a small opening in the ceiling.

Kisti was happy as she watched their house being built. She sang the whole day through, while discussing the plans for the kitchen and fireplace as they were being constructed. To her, Synneva, and Randine, the cabin was a palace. After three days, the house was almost done. They arranged the bed locations, and installed the kitchen cupboards, and Knute built a dining table where the family could enjoy meals together. The men also built a picnic table outside where they could eat in the summertime when it was too hot to sit inside the house. Guests could join them too.

After the house was finished, Kisti and Hendrick invited the Blaskys for dinner along with Mari and Lars. Many secrets of the neighborhood would be revealed to Ole as he lay in the loft with his ear near the hole when neighbors came to visit, as he did that night. Hendrick and Ole were out before dawn the next morning, clearing away oak trees and underbrush and preparing the ground to sow the winter wheat for the next year's harvest. They helped their neighbors build their cabins, too. The community of new settlers became like family to them, and they would help each other whenever needed.

As the fall approached, Ole and Hendrick helped Knute harvest the wheat on his farm. Knute gave Hendrick the seeds from his own field. Soon the Lysne farm was prepared, seeds planted, and wood cut for the winter's use. Hendrick and Ola erected a barn for the cow and her calf and the oxen, with a hayloft and all things necessary to prepare for the unpredictable season ahead.

Kisti wondered how harsh the winters would be in these parts. They had a barrel of pork and a barrel of flour in the barn, and Ole could hunt for deer, or bears. One of the neighbors had told them about a new flourmill near Amherst. She had faith, so she refused to worry about their future, yet she and Synneva and Randine prepared everything they could for the coming winter.

When the fall leaves were turning, Mari came over one day and told Kisti about the meeting to organize a congregation being held at the home of Amund Brekke. Rev. Preus of Winchester would be there, so they decided to go to the meeting that afternoon.

The crispness of the air on that clear fall morning, and the crunch of the leaves underfoot brought a thrill to Kisti's heart as she, Hendrick, and Mari walked to the Brekke home. Here and there a huge oak or a maple tree blocked their path, and in some places, a boulder so large that it was easier to make a path around it than climb over it. When they reached the Brekke home, Mari and Anders, and the Boes and the Roes were already there. The new settlers were united in an important mission: to establish a congregation in Amherst. Kisti and Mari had similar ideas for the congregation, including confirmation, Sunday school for the children, and potluck suppers to build community.

Meanwhile, Ole and Aspun were busying themselves tracking down the big bear tracks they had discovered on a path through the woods. Randine had stayed at home with

Eivind and Grandma.

Six other families of northeast Amherst were represented at the meeting with the new settlers, and twelve from Scandinavia Township and Iola. Reverend Preus welcomed the vision for the new church and offered his guidance and support. It was decided that a church be built at once, and that it be placed above all other matters of importance. It was agreed that since the Hellestads wanted to donate their timber for the building, the church should be constructed on their land.

The folks at the meeting were highly elated when they left the Brekkes. They had established a congregation and were now part of the community. As they were coming through the woods together in the brilliant moonlight of the October night, their voices were raised in a song of thanksgiving "Love, Thanks and Eternal Glory," and the sound of their voices echoed for miles around.

Ole and Aspun had tracked the bear over the hills and followed the tracks down along the course of the river. The camp was less than a mile from the Lysne house. The two boys soon came upon a camp of Ho-Chunks at a small clearing in the bend of the little river. The reception of the Indians was cordial and some of the boys Ole's age showed them their bows and arrows. They were fascinated with Ole's carbine and Aspun's muzzleloader, and elated when they were invited to shoot the guns. The Indian boys showed them their bows and arrows. They told them that the bear they were tracking had been killed.

The Indians had butchered the bear and roasted it on the fire pit and were now having a feast, to which Ole and Aspun were invited. Ole thanked the chief and his wife for their hospitality and invited them to come and visit his new home. Aspun felt that Ole spoke for him also, so he just bowed and smiled. When the sound of their mothers' singing in the woods reached their ears, they hurried home to find out what the singing was about.

The very next day, all the Indians from the Ho-Chunk camp lined up in front of the Lysne house and sat on the ground. Hearing the commotion, Kisti came out. The Chief arose, extended his right hand skyward and said, "We come to enjoy a feast. Yesterday, young brave enjoy feast in my tepee. We come to yours for feast. We heard you sing in moonlight."

Kisti smiled and bowed, but she thought, 'Oh Lord, what will I do?'

Randine tugged at her skirt and said, "Put on your Indian Waupun. Wahopekau said you should wear the beads when the Indians were around. Red Moon said it would show that you are one of them."

Kisti bowed again and said, "Please, sit down, I will prepare the feast."

She thought of the pork barrel they had stored in the barn. Ole came into sight and was greeted with cheer and amiable words from the visitors. Kisti called to him.

"Come in here son. See what you have gotten us into? Go out and build a fire where we boil the kettle for clothes and fill the kettle with water. I don't know what we will feed this crowd, but I won't turn them away, because God only know what could happen."

Ole took some coals from the fire in the kitchen and he and a few of the Indian boys built a fire then set the kettle on it, after filling it with water. Soon the water was boiling and cooking began. Kisti used all the pork and added many vegetables to make a stew for their guests. While this was going on, the boys busied themselves with target practice and the Indian boys instructed Ole and Aspun on how to make a sturdy bow. They showed them how to select wood for the bow and arrows and what bird feathers to use. The time sped by, as the aroma of the feast cooking floated in the air of the bright October day. Kisti and Synneva had cooked several loaves of bread as well. When all was ready she came out to serve the guests.

"Herre Gud, Kisti!" exclaimed Mari as she came down the road to visit. "What in the name of Heaven are you up to? Have you started a congregation of your own?"

"Oh Mari, you don't know how welcome you are. I am so glad to see you. Ole and Aspun wandered into the camp of these people while tracking a bear yesterday and they invited them to eat with them. Afterward, Ole did as I have taught him; he thanked them and invited the Chief and his wife over for dinner. When you invite the Chief, you invite the tribe, and here they are, the very next day!"

"I have never seen such a gathering. Scolding Ole isn't going to help. But one thing is sure, Kisti, you aren't going to have any pork left for winter, or anything else, either. This group will clean you out."

"I know it, Mari, but I am going to feed them what I can. I don't dare to do otherwise."

When the feast was over, the pork barrel was empty and the flour in the barrel was almost gone. The Chief arose and thanked Kisti, and then he called attention to the beads Kisti wore. He told his group that she was one of them, and they should treat her and her children as such, and that the day had proved her heart was right.

Kisti thanked the Chief for his visit, and then she walked over to sit on the stone near the fire and burst into tears. Ole told the Indian boys that the reason for her tears was that all the food stored for the winter was gone. One of the boys ran to the Chief and whispered to him. He came over to Kisti and pulled her to her feet and said, "White sister can dry tears. She will have meat when we have meat. She will not be hungry. All Indians promise."

Hendrick came home after dark that evening, carrying a sack of freshly ground meal on his back. Kisti told him of the day's calamity with tears in her eyes. Hendrick sat down and pulled her onto his lap, recalling that Captain O'Riley had warned them about extending hospitality to the Indians. Well, Ole couldn't be blamed when his elders didn't know any better.

Still, Hendrick was sure that it was all for the best. That evening, the Blaskys came over and they talked long into the night.

The next morning, Kisti looked up from her sewing to see one of the little Indian girls, about the age of Randine, watching her through the window. Kisti went out and took her by the hand and showed her where Randine was shelling hazelnuts. There was another girl outside, too shy to come in, but soon the shyness was overcome, and the girl's merry laughter rang out as she helped Randine with her task.

The social encounter with the Ho-Chunks proved valuable, as Hendrick had predicted, for the Indians would teach them many things. Whenever they killed a deer, they would bring part of that meat to Kisti and her family. Ole learned from them how to make partridge traps, and fish traps, how to spot deer, and where the bears hibernated. They trapped muskrats and mink, otter and beaver, and the Indians showed them how to tan and cure buckskins. All members of the Lysne family now had buckskin jackets, and so the first winter passed without much discomfort. They had made friends with the people who had lived in this land for many centuries.

Chapter Nine

Settlement and Homeland Visitors

On the first Thanksgiving in the new land the members of the original wagon train held a reunion. Everyone converged on Amherst at a field outside town where great tables were set up and everyone contributed to the event. The O'Rileys came, too. Mari led the dancing and there was much singing. Many new acquaintances were made that day. When the party from the northeast township left Amherst, their wagons were loaded with many supplies bought at the stores. Ole had a new supply of cartridges for the carbine, and Aspun had a supply of powder and caps.

On the trip home, Kisti suggested they all meet at Mari's and Ander's and help them finish building their house so their family could move in before the winter. Anders had been busy clearing land and planting winter wheat for the settlers. He had been so generous with his time that they were still living in their wagon, plus a small shelter.

On the appointed day, Knute, the Blaskys, the Boes, and the Roes descended upon Anders and Mari, and by nightfall, much of the house was finished. It was considerably larger than Kisti's and Hendrick's house, having two rooms besides the kitchen. A wonderful large fireplace had been provided, and the home looked spacious and grand.

Ole and Aspun had killed a large buck for the occasion. That evening there was singing and dancing, with a promise that on Christmas Day the Andersons would host the official housewarming.

Mari was now many months along in her pregnancy. With this being her first baby, she seemed more reflective and quiet than usual. Even though she was still full of joy and loved the gatherings, she thought about the change that would be coming to her and Anders with a newborn.

David's wife Ingeborg confided in Kisti that her time would be in May. Aspun's mother Randi said she was expecting in the spring. Mari had two or three months to go, and it was obvious that Mrs. Blasky would be delivering in May at the same time as Ingeborg. Kisti invited them all to visit her home the following Thursday afternoon.

When they arrived, she brought the conversation around to their babies, and it was soon clear that everyone in the gathering was expecting a new baby except Kisti. She said to the ladies that it would be nice if they all agreed to help each other during their special time and share clothes and any other things that might be needed. It was settled that they would meet again in two weeks. At every meeting someone new was introduced and made welcome. Randine loved listening to the women who gathered, and she loved taking care of her brother Eivind.

One of Randine's native girlfriends brought her an Indian cradle for Eivind, so she wouldn't have to hold him so much of the time but could wrap him snugly in the cradle and place it against a tree while the two of them played.

The Christmas housewarming at Mari's was a wonderful event. The snow was very deep that day and it was bitter cold, but everyone stayed warm inside the house. Although food was plentiful at the potluck, there was never much in reserve for Kisti and Hendrick. Kisti often remarked that the larder they had built on the north side of the house to store their meat, flour, and vegetables was like the widow's oil in the bible story; it never quite ran out completely. [1]

The time came soon after Christmas when Mari was about to deliver. She had become a bit wistful of late, but her lively spirit still sparkled in her eyes. On the path through the woods to Mari's house, they met Anders, who told them that

---

[1] Widow's oil comes from the bible; 2 King 4. 89

Mari had brought him a big boy about two hours before. When Kisti walked in the door, Mari called to her from the bed.

"My big boy beat you here, Kisti! I don't see anything so terrible about having a baby."

"Mari you are a wonderfully lucky woman. It is your sweet, buoyant spirit that makes things come easy for you."

It was wonderful to have an established address, for now letters came from Norway. Sometimes Hendrick received mail from Chicago. They heard from William DeWitt, and from Joseph Medill and Mr. Patterson. Captain O'Riley stopped to visit several times that winter. Frank DuBey came by one day and gave them news of the Cole trials. They were finally prosecuted on several charges: their attacks on women, their illegal dealing with liquor, stealing from others, and taking wood from other people's land, were just a few of the charges.

Wahopekau was reunited her husband White Fang. He had a trial in which he was absolved of murder, and they were happily established over on the Portage River.

DuBey and Kinzie had extended their lumbering operations and there was an opening for a bookman at DuBey Falls on the Wisconsin River, which they offered to Hendrick. He accepted the job, even though it was north of Amherst and would take over an hour on horseback to get there. The lumber company loaned him a horse. Riding again for the first time since Norway gave Hendrick a new interest in owning a horse himself. He would arrive home from the lumber camp on Friday evenings and return on the Sunday afternoon or evening. The pay afforded them many comforts, and Hendrick always returned home loaded down with food from town.

Grandma Synneva was busy with spinning, weaving, and sewing. Kisti helped her with the sewing when she could. Before she knew it, Synneva had made new covers for all the trundle beds in the house.

Ole and Aspun were sent Lutheran catechisms from Rev. Preus in Winchester, which they were to memorize for the first confirmation meeting at the new church the next year. This pleased their mothers greatly, but of course, Ole and Aspun preferred to be out in the woods with the carbine and Aspun's big muzzleloader rather than indoors studying. The boys spent many a wonderful evening before the fire, molding lead bullets. Often times, they were out looking for bear tracks around the lake. But with proper coaxing and patient tutoring from their mothers, Ole and Aspun mastered the commandments. They also learned several hymns by heart, and studied the meaning of the Lord's Prayer, the Apostles Creed, and the sacraments for both baptism and communion with the Lord's Supper. And they learned the significance of church terms, including the litany, the altar, the declarations of Lutheranism, and other matters designed to impress upon the young mind that would enhance a Lutheran Christian life.

There was also the study of the church history concerning the persecution of the Christians and the martyrdom of the saints, and, of course, the struggle of the reformers, up to the time of the reformation. Reading of Luther's trials in his biography, the boys were especially surprised to learn that Luther threw ink and his own waste matter at the wall to scare away satanic spirits while writing his sermons.

Through the winter, the silence of the snowy woods and hills around their cabin was interrupted only by gusts of the north wind, the occasional wolves howling, or a cry of an eagle flying overhead. Sometimes they could hear drumming from the Ho-Chunk people camped along the river.

On still, moonlit nights, after the children were snug in their beds, Kisti would sometimes go out to visit her neighbors who lived just down the road. She would walk down the path on the heavy cushion of snow to the Boes, or tromp through the woods to visit Mari or the Roes or the Knutes. She loved to hear the crunch of the snow under her feather-lined moccasins made by her Indian friends. Sometimes when the snow was too deep, she would wear Ole's old boots instead.

Her neighbors often scolded her for venturing into the woods at night with the timber wolves howling. But Kisti thought it great fun and the woods were so beautiful on moonlit winter nights. Oftentimes, she would go out to the clearing behind the cabin and sit on a stump to listen to the sounds of the night. There was a tree behind the stump that served as a backrest. This quiet place was where she held her devotions and did her praying. She called it her Königs Garten, or Royal Garden, although there was only snow and sparkling stars shining in the night. She loved watching the moon rise over the forest.

The first winter passed, and at the sign of the first thaw in March, the Blaskys began tapping the sugar maples. This was a fascinating process for Kisti and her family to watch. The Blaskys had learned how to do it from friends out East in Vermont and New Hampshire, who had learned it from native people before they ventured on to Wisconsin. Ole and Aspun were very willing helpers when it came to boiling the sap into syrup. The maple syrup and sugar were a wonderful addition to the lefse and pancakes as they moved into spring.

The days in the spring and summer for Ole and his friends were filled with working from sunup to sundown—planting, cultivating, and harvesting wheat and corn and vegetables. They also hunted animals, cared for the oxen, milked the cows, and fed the calves, and cleared fallen tree branches after storms to use for firewood. They chopped wood and gathered kindling and bark to start the fires. When the weather warmed up, and the ice had melted on the lake, they would plunge into the lake for a cool swim at night.

When they planted the new crops in late spring and early summer, the wheat showed much promise, as did the potatoes, corn, and garden vegetables. Hendrick came home from the lumber camp to find that a new calf and piglets had been born on the farm. In July the hen, that they were sure had found its end in a fox den, appeared one morning with twelve little chicks. All the world was bright and full of abundance for the Lysne family that first summer.

The Blasky's baby was born in May. Kisti had tried to

lend a hand, but a German midwife from Plover was in charge, so Kisti and Mari fed the men folks while they awaited the birth. Other members of the family had things well in hand. This was the fourth baby for the Blaskys, a chubby little girl.

The womenfolk and the minister prepared for the first baptisms. Everyone from the church congregation was invited to celebrate the event. Early on a Sunday morning in June, a caravan of ox wagons creaked through the wooded trail to the service at the Scandinavian Church seven miles away; it took most of them two to three hours with the oxen. All had come with picnic baskets, and when the service was over, a feast was spread out on tables under the trees by the river.

The Boes were unfortunate with their baby. Ingeborg had a severe fall and miscarried their child. Only through the constant care and devotion of the women of the neighborhood could Ingeborg be brought back to health. It was not until midsummer that she was able to take part in the activities of the ladies' group, which had become a strong arm of the church in East Amherst Township.

The Roes received their baby daughter without much ado. Aspun Junior was excited about having a new sister, but he confided in Ole that he was afraid she was an Indian. Aspun was naïve about how babies were conceived. So was Ole.

"Ole, she is redder than any Indian in this whole country."

"Shucks, Aspun, all white babies are born red! My little brother was red as a beet. He isn't red now." They decided to keep an eye on her just in case.

There was also a new baby at the Adam Peterson home, named Carl Adam. He was baptized later that year. The community began to grow as this new generation was being born.

The Norwegian community around Amherst rapidly populated as more and more new people settled there. There were two families of Lobergs—Jon and Johan; big, buoyant, enterprising men who had previous experience in the new land, they had moved north from southern Wisconsin. They came with ample building equipment and knew that their homes and barns would soon become the showplaces of the township. Hendrick was appointed by Judge Cate to fill a vacancy as a supervisor. His duty was to handle the county affairs in Amherst Township. Hendrick took it upon himself to inform the property holders of the lands bordering on main section lines that they would eventually be obliged to relinquish a strip along the border for public roads and possible railroads.

He began steps to establish a school district and offered the land on the northwest corner of his quarter section for a schoolhouse. This land was deeded to the district unencumbered and in due time the schoolhouse was built. Randine was an apt student, but Ole and Aspun were reluctant ones. However, they progressed well, despite their desire to be out hunting and exploring.

The following year, Hendrick was elected to the supervisor's post and elected chairman of the school board as well. There was much activity in establishing the new township, especially with others who were moving to Amherst. Anders was elected town Constable; Asborn was elected Assessor, and David Boe, Justice of the Peace.

There was a great gathering at the home of Johan Loberg on June 24th, the ancient Norwegian holiday of Midsummer's Day. In honor of this occasion, a young minister named Rev. Duus was introduced as their new pastor, because Rev. Preus at Winchester was preoccupied with the congregations in Oshkosh and Algoma. The Scandinavia Church was lucky if Rev. Preus could hold church services once every five or six weeks. Traveling ministers were common, and Rev. Preus was in high demand.

Johan was a talented violin player and several others in the gathering were also musically gifted. The evening was enlivened by the music and dancing; although young Duus did not openly approve of dancing, he knew better than to try to impose his narrow views upon this hardy group. He knew that, while they subscribed to the church of their heritage, there was greater liberty in this new country. It was a bit difficult for a foreigner to grasp this until he too became infected with the desire for freedom.

Rev. Duus decided that diplomacy called for tolerance at this point. Later, when the homes were completed and prosperity began to weaken the natures of these sturdy people, he figured that a suggestion here and there would bring them to realize that the old church values were a desirable restraint upon their children.

This church would be the inheritance of the children. It is only natural to want to use the power of religion to influence the minds and souls of the next generation, young people without memories of Indians and broken treaties. What difference does it make now if they dance, sing, and even imbibe a little. There's so much potential for the next generation. Yes, he thought, if I am called to dedicate the new church, this will be the subject of the first sermon.

So the idea of dancing and frivolity no longer disturbed him. He joined the merriment, except for making excursions to the barn, where some of the men went to observe an exceptional bull and share homemade beer. The bull's salient points were analyzed and documented among the men, and it seemed to require many trips to the barn. Mari finally asked Anders, "How many gallons of that stuff are there?"

Midsummer night festival lasted until the wee hours. Duus suggested that they sing the nostalgic hymn, "Now Rest beneath Night's Shadow." They entered into the spirit of the song with a sincerity that convinced the young clergyman that his vision for the future generation was the right one.

> Now rest beneath night's shadow
> The woodland, field, and meadow;
> The world in slumber lies.
> But you, my heart, awaking
> And prayer and music making,
> Let praise to your Creator rise.

On the Fourth of July, the neighbors gathered again to celebrate. There were speeches, games, and contests throughout the day. In the evening there was square dancing, singing, and activities that brought people together.

There was talk among the townsfolk that a fair should be held after the harvest with prizes for the finest wheat, the nicest potatoes, the best bread baked, and for other farming endeavors, including the animals being raised. This would stimulate the people to do their best in everything around the homes. Many Norwegians had held harvest festivals in Norway. They were accustomed to having such festivities in their home communities. Now they would start county fairs in the new land like the festivals in Norway.

The town of Amherst was growing fast. There was already a flourmill, and new people were coming daily. There was talk that the railroad was building its way north from Chicago. Changes were taking place rapidly and everyone felt how important it was for them to be a part of the emerging new town.

The Lysne barn was enlarged that year to accommodate the increase in animals and a problem arose with the wheat and potatoes. With the technical advice of Knute and the help of willing neighbors, a cellar was dug on the sunny side of the house. To Kisti this was like adding another room, for it gave her space to store food and keep it cool.

Ole and Aspun had studied hard through the winter and following spring with the confirmation book they received from the minister in Winchester. Reverend Duus was aware that they were studying. The time finally came when Kisti and Aspun's mother Anna decided their sons had learned enough to entitle them to stand for confirmation. The boys were close to the same age, now twelve and thirteen years old.

Reverend Duus examined both boys and declared them fit as far as their learning was concerned, but he said they were too young to assume responsibility for their own moral actions and were advised to wait another year or two. Confirmation was a rite of passage into adulthood. Kisti objected to the pastor's advice and told him about the many responsible tasks the boys had done for their families. Anna also disagreed with the minister, and by the time they got through talking with him a second time, he had agreed that the boys were ready for confirmation.

Randine was a child who loved learning new things. Randine, now ten, was devoted to her brother Ole, and she loved listening to him recite his confirmation doctrine. With Kisti's coaching, Randine had learned the lessons more readily than Aspun.

During their second winter, in 1856, they were snug and comfortable in their home. Hendrick worked again for the Kinzie interests up at the falls. In the spring Ole would assume the status of a man through his confirmation. No longer would he be treated like a child, but as a responsible young man, with friendly counsel from his parents and pastor.

Ole had willingly taken on more responsibility. Now as a thirteen-year-old, he took care of the livestock and cleared the fields, but he still had time to hunt with Aspun and the Indian boys. Many of the deer he killed were given to the Indians, keeping only enough of the meat for a meal or two. This was also true of other game he shot. He helped them plant their corn and potatoes, and they reciprocated by making moccasins for his entire family and buckskin shirts with beautiful, beaded designs for Randine and Kisti.

Ole was given a special shirt with the Ho-Chunk tribal insignia on the back. He didn't fully appreciate its significance until he was a bit older. Even little Eivind wore moccasins and leggings made for him by the appreciative native people, who were proving to be good neighbors and liked to live in peace with Kisti and her family.

The winter warmed into spring earlier than usual that year. Hendrick received a letter from his father Ole in Norway saying that he would be coming through their area that summer and would like to visit with his family. Hendrick was excited that his father was coming to visit. He had so many children now with his second wife, Anna. He invited his father's second family to stop and spend a weekend on their way to Minnesota. To accommodate their visit, Hendrick cleared a special room for them in the barn, and Kisti made beds of hay and straw, as they did in Norway.

According to his father Ole's next letter, they would arrive by a wagon train that was heading towards Minnesota and would stop for a weekend at Kisti and Hendrick's home. He wanted to see the land where they had settled and meet their friends from Norway.

Kisti had never seen Hendrick so nervous and excited about anything before. She tried to calm him down, but he was set on making his father's visit special. He was so excited that he cut flowers from the fields and put them in vases in the barn where they would sleep, and covered the straw beds with special woven blankets the Ho-Chunks had made for Hendrick and Kisti.

When the day arrived for the visit in mid-summer, Ole and Hendrick went to town to greet Grandfather Ole and Anna and their children. The wagon train was an hour later than they had anticipated. When the wagon train finally came into view, Hendrick saw his father driving a wagon at the latter part of the train. There he was, standing up above the oxen and waving his hat to Hendrick.

The train slowed down just outside of town and drove into a field where the wagons pulled into a circle and stopped. Ole handed the reins to his oldest son, jumped off the wagon, and ran to Hendrick to greet him and his grandson and namesake.

"Gooden Dag, Papa!" Hendrick shouted in Norwegian, as the two men embraced and held each other for a long moment.

"My son, so wonderful to see you!" Ole said in Norwegian.

He saw young Ole, and just as he stepped forward to greet him, the rest of his family jumped off the wagon and rushed over to greet Hendrick and Ole. There were three Oles; the grandfather, the son of Hendrick, and the son of Ole, who was five years older than Hendrick's Ole. There were several other children that Ole had had with his wife Anna, who came up slowly and stood beside him with their two youngest. She was stout, and had aged quite a bit, as had his father. Hendrick could see that the traveling had been hard for them. It had been two and a half years since he had last seen his father and Anna in Norway before their immigration.

As they chatted and hugged each other, Hendrick suggested they bring their wagon out of the circle and follow them to their home. It seemed the wagon train would be camped there for several days to replenish food and supplies, along with ammunition.

Hendrick and his father jumped on his wagon so they could chat on the way, while Ole's son Ole took the reins of the oxen to drive the wagon to the Lysne home. He reached out a hand to help his mother Anna get up into the wagon, and one of the small children nestled between her son Ole and Anna. Some of the children jumped in the back of Hendrick's wagon, while others jumped into the covered wagon.

On the way there, Hendrick pointed out the land where the new church would be built eventually, and the homes of their neighbors. As they approached the log cabin and the large barn behind it, Kisti and her mother came out of the house waving, with three-year-old Eivind beside them.

The children jumped out of wagon and ran to greet their Aunt Kisti, who was now pregnant. As they circled around her and hugged her, Anna sat in the wagon looking rather frozen; she had not expected her children to be so overjoyed to see their Aunt Kisti again.

After the two families had greeted each other, Anna and Ole followed Hendrick into the house, where he showed them the inside of the house he had built for his family. Then he took them to the barn to see the lovely space with flowers he had prepared for his father and stepmother and their children.

Kisti was wearing her moccasins and Anna asked her about them in Norwegian, as she did not yet speak English.

"Where did you get those shoes? Did you make them yourself?" Anna asked.

Kisti smiled, and said softly, "No they were made for me by the Ho-Chunks who live close to the river. They made moccasins for all my family. They are a peaceful people, and we are like family."

Anna looked at her as though she had been slapped in the face with the reality of living in America. "You are like a family with Indians? How can that be?"

Kisti smiled and said kindly, "It is how we have learned to survive together here, as white people settle and take more of their lands. I will share some stories of our experience with the Indian people with you Anna, not just the Ho-Chunks, but the Sauk and Foxes."

Anna looked surprised. As she helped Kisti prepare the feast while minding her many children, Ole and Hendrick went for a walk along the edge of the woods.

Kisti and her son Ole and his friend Aspun set up the table outside for the feast and brought out the food when it was ready for their family guests.

Winona came out of the house to join Randine, Synneva and Eivind. Anna was shocked to see an Indian woman come out of their house. She looked rather uncomfortable.

When Kisti saw her response, she put her arm around Winona and introduced her as if she were one of the family. "This is Winona, from the Ho-Chunk people. I would not know what to do without her. She comes every day to help us out with Eivind, and she is such a wonderful sister to all of my children." Kisti looked Anna straight in the eye, so that she knew how serious she was about her statement.

Anna nodded to Winona to greet her, and said to Kisti. "How can you have these people in your house? We heard terrible stories about murders and rape on our journey across the ocean, in Chicago, and on the way here."

Kisti kissed Winona on the cheek and asked her to go help Synneva and the boys get ready for dinner. Then she sat down with Anna and spoke to her in Norwegian.

"Anna, we were wisely told, as we were heading up here from Chicago, that if we treated them kindly, we would be treated well by the native people. We took that advice seriously, as it was, and still is, a time of great tension with the Sauk and Fox.

"When we reached Madison, some white men tried to rape a young native girl and they almost killed her. We heard her screaming in the woods and then a gunshot when we were camping outside of Madison on our way up here. One of the white men, named Cole, was murdered for that horrible act by the brother of the girl, named White Fang, and we learned that his wife had just had a baby three days before. He had to flee, and his wife was left on her own to fend for herself with the newborn child. His sister was taken in by the local tribal people.

"Randine and I found his wife, Wahopekau, in the woods as we were collecting berries, and I nursed the child, who was almost dead. We hid the two of them and we fed his starving mother. If we had ignored them, both would have died. This was the best thing we could have done. The Ho-Chunks helped us get through our first winter, after we fed them our winter stores. They taught Ole how to hunt creatures we do not have so abundantly in Norway. Believe me, they have become family to us. Please respect them. We certainly do."

"Anna was stunned. She looked at Kisti. "Why, I never thought this is how it would be in America. We thought the land was free."

"The land where we settlers make our homes was taken away from the Indians. They were forced to move from their land and sign agreements that only benefit us white folks. The treaties are broken over and over again by the U.S. government. The Indians have been treated terribly by this government, but some tribes are kind to us if we are kind. Others, like the Sioux, are not as friendly, and they are fighting for their land in Western Minnesota. Be careful when you settle there, if that is where you are headed.

Honestly, I cannot blame the Sioux or any of the tribes. We have taken their land. We will talk more about this tomorrow, as we will have plenty of time to share our stories. We are glad you arrived safely." Kisti took Anna's hand and squeezed it.

Anna's youngest tugged at her dress and she picked up the little girl and held her. Anna looked frightened and uncertain about living in this strange new land.

On their walk around the farm, Hendrick told his father

Ole how he and Kisti had established themselves in this town along with other settlers they journeyed with on the wagon train. They had become friends with these folks, as well as with the Indian people in the area.

Hendrick asked Ole about his relatives back in Norway.

"Your sister Anna and cousin Thomas send you their love and best regards. They are all doing quite well, regardless of being the ones who had to stay. Neither of them will ever leave Norway. Of course, we are the ones who had to leave."

After Ole told him all about cousin Thomas, who had taken over the Lysne farm, and his sister Anna, and other extended family members, Ole paused and was silent for a moment. Then he said:

"Before I left home, I want you to know that I laid a wreath of lavender and daisies on your mother's grave. I miss Randine, she was the love of my life. She worked so hard helping others in her midwifery and caring for our family. She took care of so many babies, our babies and the ones of others."

Ole had turned sixty before their trip across the Atlantic in September, and Anna was twelve years younger, born on the 5th of April in 1809. Most of their children were approaching their early teens, except for those who were born in the last few years.

The two men walked in silence for some time. Hendrick remembered his mother Randine as one of the kindest women he had ever known, though she did have a temper. Kisti was very much like her, though Kisti was less prone to get angry without letting people know it. When Kisti got angry it felt like a flood of water let loose. His mother Randine's anger was more like a smoldering flame.

When they returned to the farm, Ole turned to his son and said, "Please do not repeat anything I said about your mother to Anna. She must feel that she is the only woman I care about now; she witnessed my terrible grief after Randine's death. Then with my brother Knut's passing four years later, and mother's passing, your grandmother, soon after, I felt such grief for so many years from those losses. Anna and I became a family because we had so many children to take care of from both our families. Our love came later, unlike with your mother. I fell in love with Randine at first sight when, as a young teen, she was nursing you after your birth mother, Ragnild, died."

Hendrick nodded, "Don't worry father, I understand. Randine was the only mother I knew. I will never forget her, though I was barely fourteen when she died. You have told me many times about her, and Ragnild, God rest their souls."

"Randine was meant to be your mother, Hendrick. No doubt about it," Ole said, putting his arm around Hendrick's neck as they walked into the yard between the barn and the house.

A huge table made of boards on sawhorses had been set up in the yard outside the house by Ole and Aspun and was ready for the family feast. Everyone gathered and found a seat on the chairs and benches. Hendrick stood up and said a prayer of thanksgiving for his family and his half siblings—many sisters, and two, much younger, brothers. He was thirty-six years old. Hendrick's oldest, Ole, was born just five years after his father and Anna started having children, six years after his mother Randine died. Hendrick looked around the table at his half siblings, who were almost the same age as his own children. His father and Anna's children were: Ole age eighteen, Johan sixteen, Jens thirteen, Brithe eleven, Metta (Mettie) ten, Christine nine, Anne seven, Julia four, and Britta was just two. Kisti's and Hendrick's Ole was thirteen, Randine twelve, Eivind was about to turn four. With Grandma Synneva, that filled the table with twelve children and six adults! Winona joined the feast too, of course, and was seen as an adult because she helped so much, though she was young.

For the feast, Kisti and Hendrick served their family venison and pork, as well as potato lefsa, vegetables from their garden, and potato and spinach pies. They only made lefse and potato pie for holidays, and they wanted to honor their family on this special occasion. After the feast, Mari and her husband came over with a cake for dessert. Other friends and neighbors stopped by, as they had been invited to come and greet Hendrick's extended family. Ole and Anna were happy to meet and speak with other Norwegians.

Some of Winona's people had also come to greet them. Ole was very kind and welcoming to the Ho-Chunk people. Anna was quite formal with the tribal guests. She had never seen people with such dark skin before. However, she did learn from Kisti that they were humans, just like themselves. She also learned from Winona, whose words Kisti translated, that the Dakota tribe and the Ho-Chunks were archenemies. The Dakotas were less peaceful toward the white settlers.

That Sunday morning, the entire Lysne family went to the church in Scandinavia, Wisconsin, a few hours away by wagon. After church they showed them the new gravesites. Ole and Anna met many new settlers that day and were encouraged to find a church community near the land that they planned to homestead in Minnesota. The weekend with Kisti and Hendrick and their family was so helpful for them before they traveled to their own territory. By the end of the weekend, Ole and Anna and their children had a better picture of what it's like to settle in this new country.

On Monday morning, Hendrick with his son Ole beside him, drove their horse carriage with his father Ole, Anna and their children to meet the wagon train on the other side of Amherst. Their oldest son, eighteen-year-old Ole, drove the oxen wagon with his sixteen-year-old brother Johan. When they joined the wagon train and said goodbye, Hendrick realized that this might be the last time he would see his father and Anna and his half siblings. Hendrick's tears welled up as he and Ole drove the horse with an empty carriage back to their farm.

One day, not long after Hendrick's father and his family had left, Winona came over to sit with the Eivind. Kisti noticed that she looked sad and asked her what was wrong.

"The white man's customs are strange. My Ho-Chunks are trying to get along with the white man, who forced us from our lands and our homes."

Kisti hugged her and said, "I know that the white men's agreements have not been kept. You make an agreement with us and then another one is thrust upon you. It is unfair to violate these agreements. I am so sorry. We will do whatever we can to help your people."

Kisti and her family accepted the Ho-Chunks (Winnebagos) as they were. They shared their land as much as they could. She and her family were accepted by the Ho-Chunks in the same way. Their mutual admiration was based upon respect, equality, and human dignity. They helped each other whenever they thought it necessary and never imposed a request for favors.

Kisti and Hendrick learned early on that a locked door was viewed as an unfriendly act and could terminate friendship with an Indian. Many a night Kisti was startled, almost into a panic, to hear loud snoring from a sleeping Indian stretched out before the fire. Eventually, she became used to it, and actually felt safer, knowing that the Indians would defend her home if any armed robbers came onto the property.

The Indians were taught many new things in Kisti's home. She made herself understood about such matters as muddy feet, spitting on the floor, and other uncouth habits of the Native people, since they had never been in a wooden house before. The idea spread and soon there was a new code of conduct among them. They respected Kisti's home policies, much to the amazement of the other settlers, most of whom kept their doors barred and forbid Indians to enter.

There was a time when some criminals were roaming the settlement and terrorizing Indians and whites alike. Then everyone barred their doors. Chief Oshida told his people to knock twice on Kisti's door and say, "OSHIDA." He advised his people to stay near camp until the criminals were apprehended.

Chief Oshida appealed to Judge Cate for the protection of his people, and the judge commissioned Hendrick to notify the Constable and the Justice of the Peace to take the proper measures. The neighborhood was deputized to help, and because of her knowledge of the Indians, Kisti was asked to inform them what the other settlers were doing. She arranged for a meeting with the Ho-Chunks and that meeting did much to ease the tension between the settlers and the tribe.

Chapter Ten

Intruders

One morning, as Ole was clearing underbrush on the east forty, he heard someone chopping trees in the poplar grove where he had cut the trees to build their house and barn. He went to investigate and found a man and his son with axes in hand. Eager to welcome new friends and neighbors, Ole rushed forward to meet them.

He was surprised by their cold reception. The person he had presumed was a boy turned out to be a little man with a beard that covered his face, in an unbroken line to his eyebrows almost hiding the small piggish eyes that did not meet Ole's open blue-eyed stare. The larger of the two growled at Ole, "What are you after, Bub?"

"I was working over the hill and heard the chopping. I wanted to see who was cutting down our trees," said Ole, expecting for him to ask if they could cut the timber.

"Your trees? His trees!" he said to the little man, who cackled in a high thin voice. "You had better get off my property. I won't have you running around trespassing on my land!"

Ole was livid.

"Your land! This is our land. I have cleared our land for farming and we built our house and barn with the logs from this forest. You are cutting down our trees."

"Thanks for clearing some of my land. I didn't ask you to. As long as you can pay for the logs I don't care. Now get off my land, I have work to do!"

Ole had never hated anyone before, in all his life. The time when he aimed his carbine at the Coles he was angry, but he hadn't felt hatred like this. He was glad he was unarmed, for he would have been tempted to kill this man; it would have been as easy as shooting a buck or a wild pig. Ole stood there stoically without moving.

The larger of the two roared at him: "You heard what I said! Now get the hell out of here before I split you in two!" He raised his double-bladed axe over his head while Ole glared at him with anger.

The man lowered his ax when a shot was fired from the woods; the bullet hit a small branch from a tree and it landed on the ground between them. He lowered the axe and growled.

"You seem to have friends!"

Through clenched teeth, Ole spat out, "You bet, I have lots of them!"

Johan had been following bear tracks from the marsh up through the woods. As he came closer, he heard voices and came upon the scene.

"Squatters!" he muttered. "This had better be nipped in the bud now, or it could become an ugly mess." He had seen the results of squatting near Koshhonong and Atkinson, and it wasn't pretty when the irate settlers got finished with them.

When he saw the upraised ax, his first impulse was to shoot the hand holding it. Then he remembered that his gun was loaded for bear hunting and the shot would sever the hand from the arm; and there was the danger of ricocheting bullets.

The man with the ax looked scared when he saw Johan and his rifle in the woods, but he said to Ole, "Git off this property!" Ole stomped out of the woods.

When Ole reached home, Johan was already there ahead of him, telling Kisti what had just happened. Kisti was furious. She set out briskly in the direction of the poplar grove. Ole grabbed his carbine and was about to go with her but Johan restrained him.

"Ole, if you had your carbine this afternoon, what would you have done?"

Ole looked down at his feet for a moment, and then looked in Johan's eyes, "I might have shot them both. But if I'd had my gun with me, they wouldn't have dared to talk like that, and I'll bet they would have been off the land by now!"

Johan chuckled. "Maybe you're right, Ole. Let's walk back over there and see what your mother does with them."

They walked in silence along the path and circled around so that they were downwind from the grove. They heard a sound like a cat screaming! Kisti had taken the little man by the ear and pushed him towards his partner. The little man fell down screaming at the other man's feet.

"There are some things I can't stand, and you are all of them. You two are evil. If you ever speak to anyone in my family like that again, it won't be this easy for you."

She tore off a willow branch to use as a switch and began to whip both of them with it. "Now get off this property! Both of you! If you think you have a legal right to be here, defend yourself like gentlemen, show us your deed, you rats!"

The cowards rushed out of the woods, leaving their axes behind.

Kisti called, "Don't forget your tools!" She threw the axes toward them. "Now you don't have any excuse to come back here!"

Johan and Ole, who had watched the whole event unfold, were laughing out loud. "Oh Mom, you were wonderful. When you pulled the little devil's ear he squealed like a rat! I never wanted to hit anybody so bad in all my life!"

"Hush. This thing isn't over yet. If they are squatters, we will have to act quickly and take the appropriate measures, or there will be trouble. I will go to the Justice of the Peace and to the Constable and get this thing settled. When Hendrick gets back, he can see Judge Cate. In the meantime, stay out of this grove. Let's not do anything to cause more trouble."

Johan went down to the Boes and sent a note by Ole up to Constable Anders. Johan went home and returned with his brother, Jon, and Knute, along with Aspun and his father. Anders appeared with his brother-in-law, and the Blasky's came a short time later. Kisti shuddered when she saw Jan Blasky with a coil of rope on his arm. They had guns, but he said they were for defending their sheep and calves from raids by predatory animals.

Kist appreciated their clumsy attempt to put her at ease. When Johan and Ole looked at her and grinned, she resolved to make the best of it. However, before they departed, she said, "I hope God will give all of you the sense of justice you need. I would first hear their story and bear in mind that they are looking for a place to build a home just as we were. Please do not forget that we are good people, entrusted with the destiny of this great country, and we must act accordingly. God be with you and guide you."

"Well boys," Johan remarked, "If you had seen her in action a few hours ago, you wouldn't have thought we would ever hear these words. If I live for a millennium, I will never forget her leading that squealing ape by the ear!" He shook his head and laughed until the tears came. "But she is showing us the best course to follow!"

Blasky explained to Kisti that a rope always came in handy in the woods and he was rarely without it. Aspun's father observed that it was especially convenient where there was a trial in progress. It helped the one on trial to tell the truth, and often was great assistance to the judge in helping him make up his mind.

The men walked to the poplar grove and came upon a camp wagon. A fire was going and a sprightly little man with a pointed cap on his head was moving around it. He looked like something out of Norse mythology.

"I think we ought to kill it and put it in a bottle!" Aspun said, poking Ole in the ribs.

Jan Blasky cut in. "Don't waste your bullets on him. I'll find you a stick."

The men's laughter startled the little man. He turned around to face the group of men.

"What do you want? You don't belong here. This is my land. Get away from here!" His voice was high-pitched with a nasal twang, and he bounced as he shook his little fist at the men.

Over at the wagon, they saw a gun barrel poke through a flap of canvas, and a gruff voice demanded, "Better get moving.

You have no business here."

Jan Blasky went around the wagon when the gun appeared, he and grabbed the gun by the barrel and said, "Let's see your gun, feller."

The man offered no resistance when he saw the group of men, every one of them with a gun in the crook of his arm.

"Come out, stranger, and meet the folks who live here. Nice gun, army gun, is it not? Were you in the army?"

"Won't answer that or any other questions. You ain't got no right!"

"Oh, stop preaching about your rights. That's why we're here. Might as well introduce ourselves. You can call me Johan. This is Asbjorn. This is David and my neighbor Knute. What did you say your name was?"

"I didn't say, and it's none of your business."

Johan's face hardened.

"We were in pretty good humor up until now. We came here to be neighborly, because we are here to stay, and we are in the majority. Whether you live here depends upon whether we want you here and how you act. I'd start thinking quick if I were you."

Constable Anders stepped up. "Your name, sir?" He took a book and pencil out of his pocket and prepared to write.

"Wait a minute. I don't want any trouble."

"You are going about it in a poor way. I'll ask you once more. What is your name?"

"Petter Pettersen."

"That's more like it. Where are you from?" Anders said.

"Denmark. Two years ago, we came to Milwaukee, then to Columbus. Came here with Jenns. He had taken this land and I came to help him build a house so he could bring his wife and child up here."

"Where are they?"

"Oconomowoc."

"Were you in the army?"

He looked embarrassed; his face turned red.

"How did you get your army rifle? This is your business.

Whether you deserted or got kicked out, isn't any interest to us, either. But I would say you are using pretty poor judgment to act the way you did. I take it he's paying you to help him?"

"Yup," Petter said.

While his partner was being questioned, the little man, Jenns, was stomping the ground, berating the Constable in Danish.

"You are invading our privacy, you bloody ass! How dare you question us?"

The men knew enough Danish to know what he was saying but acted like they didn't understand. David asked him if he planned to actually settle down among them, and whether he had been raised in a place where people lived together with shared community interests. When David spoke to him in his own dialect, Jenns realized that they knew what he'd said. David finally came to the question of boundary lines and property. Jenns became agitated again, and it was only when they informed him that they were interested in every man obtaining and keeping his own property that Jenns settled down.

He produced his surveyor's plot, and a description of the forty acres upon which he was standing at the present time, with some penciled notes describing the forty acres to the west and south, where Ole had found him earlier that day. They explained to him that this plot of land belonged to Hendrick and Kisti Lysne and he was advised to make no more trouble.

"And," said David, "to prove our good faith, we will help you erect your cabin, if you will show us where you want it built, after you get the paperwork checked with Judge Cates in Amherst. Get the ground ready and begin cutting your own poplar logs, and we will come a week from today."

His shifty little eyes glinted, and he stammered, "How, how much?"

Johan cut him short. "It won't cost you a measly penny."

The men withdrew and walked back towards the Lysne home.

"I still say we should have kicked him off the land," said Blatsky. "He'll make a hell of a neighbor."

"Well, Blasky," said David, "he may not be so bad once he finds out he can't get the best of us. I am willing to give him a chance."

"So am I," said Johan, "but in the meantime, I am going to get me a nice big lock for my hen house. I'll bet you a pint of the finest whisky that we will find things missing, and then he will report to someone that Indians have stolen his chickens or a pig, or that he has seen an Indian do this or that, to cover up for himself. I am bringing this up now because I have seen the likes of him before. He isn't going to change just because he escaped getting hung. I'll bet he has had close shaves all his life and that is the reason he's come to America. But I'll accept him, along with the rest of you, for the sake of his wife and their unfortunate youngster."

Kisti resolved that, the following week, she would be the first to meet with the men and supply them a portion of food while they built another new home for Jenns and his family. She was determined to wipe the ugly incident of this day out of her life. While she knew that her actions were justified, they went against her principles, and she felt disturbed by it.

Ole and Randine sensed the burden on their mother's heart, and they did what they could to lighten her spirit. Ole brought in water from the well without being asked, filled the wood box, and did so many out of the ordinary things that Kisti had to laugh despite herself. Randine did the dishes, and took Eivind out for a walk, and swept the house, which she usually did only if asked.

Kisti drew both of her children to her and said, "Bless your dear, sweet hearts. You know your momma is unhappy, don't you? I am sad because I let my temper get away from me today. You must help your mother never to do that again."

Ole lit up. "You should have seen her, Randine! She had that little man by the ear, and he squealed like a rat in a trap. All the neighbors thought you were wonderful, Mom. Johan told them all about it and you should have heard them laugh!"

"Ole, don't make it harder for me. I am not proud of it."

"We are proud of you, Mama," said Randine. "I can't see

anything wrong in your trying to protect our property."

Grandma Synneva, who was knitting by the fireside, chuckled quietly.

The next week, Mari came over to the Lysne's with her bouncing baby Albert. Randine was to take care of him and Aspun's baby sister Anna Marie. David and his wife Ingeborg Boe, who was again pregnant, but in much better health, came too. Ashborn Roe and his wife Randi came along and, of course the Blaskys. Johan and his wife Wilma, and his brother Jon Loberg, were also ready to help build the cabin. They had arrived there early in the morning to help erect Jenns' house.

The summer outdoor fires were started, and the kettles hung. The whole neighborhood was assembled. The men had pitched in to build the house and the women fed them and cleaned up after the construction. The house, a two-room log cabin, rose out of the ground like magic. Much fun and ribaldry went on among the workers and by evening, the cabin was complete, including the roof and window trim. Finishing was a matter of personal taste and they let Jenns decide on the details.

Kisti carried on as if there had never been anything unpleasant with Jenns. She refused to talk about it, so people stopped questioning her. Jenns avoided her at first, but Mari contrived to have Kisti fill his coffee cup, so he had to meet her face to face.

Kisti smiled and said, "I am so glad we are to be neighbors, Jenns."

Her kindness and sincerity so startled him that he spilled his coffee on the ground. She smiled, took the cup from him, poured it full and handed it back. He stammered appreciation by nodding his head and said thank you to her under his breath. Kisti nodded and got on with pouring coffee for others in the group. She was unaware that many folks at the gathering had stopped eating to watch this performance.

"People who work as hard as you do need more food," she said pleasantly. "Let me fill your plate again."

Mari shook her head.

"Kisti, I swear, I can't figure you out. I should think you would want to cut his gizzard out and you have that bum eating out of your hand. But I love you for it!"

She had her arm around Kisti's waist and patted her tummy. She nearly screamed.

"Kisti, you are either awfully sick or you are pregnant." Her eyes were opened wide. "Ladies come here and feel Kisti's belly. I bet it's triplets!"

"When is the big event? We hope you will count upon us to be of help," said Anne Marie. She and Johan extended their arms and gave her a hug.

"This is, indeed, a day that calls for a good old time tonight!" Mari said. "We must celebrate the new house, and if Kisti's new baby doesn't rate a party, then no one does. Johan, get your fiddle. Anders, you and Halvor get your accordions. Gee, I wish Captain O'Riley was here with his guitar."

And what a party it turned out to be.

The early summer moon glowed softly through the branches of the trees; the smell of fresh chopped wood and shavings mingled with the scent of early June roses that grew in abundance. Their friendliness and camaraderie of the neighbors bound them together as a growing community. Even Jenns mellowed under the spell of the evening. Petter was like a new person.

After the construction was done and everyone had gone home, Petter walked over to the Lysne's. Kisti and her family, who had already returned, heard a timid knock at the door. There stood Petter.

"Ma'am, I just had to talk to you before I leave. I was all wrong."

Kisti stepped outside and closed the door. "Let's go over there and sit down, Petter. I want my children to go to sleep."

She led the way to a log near the well and motioned for Petter to sit down beside her.

"I haven't seen a woman like you since I last saw my mother. I had forgotten that there are such people. I got into a scrape in Denmark and went to sea to escape the law. I came to America and joined the army, and I was in the Mexican and then the Indian wars. I got drunk and slipped away from my unit, planting evidence to lead them to believe I was dead. I think I probably succeeded.

"I got to Saint Louis and met some of the river men that came off the log drive, and they told me about logging and lumber in the Wisconsin territory. I came up here as far as Columbus when I hired myself out to Jenns. The incident a week ago was nothing new to me, but I want to tell you that I am sorry for it. I feel ashamed for the first time I can remember, and I don't feel good about it."

Kisti put her hand on his. "What a compliment that you confess to me your secrets, but I cannot understand why. Aren't you afraid I will divulge them and you will be apprehended?"

"No, I am not. I believe you would help me and right now, I need some advice. Tonight has done something to me. To see people get together and return good for evil is something I thought existed only in the Catechism. I only hope that Jenns sees it the same way I do. Maybe he will, if he lives here long enough, but I doubt it."

"Why do you think he is incapable of change? If you can, why can't he?"

Petter shook his head. "No, I don't think so. He is rotten all the way through." He stood up and walked a few steps and came back and sat down again.

"You see, ma'am, what I am trying to tell you is that his wife is going to be your neighbor. Well, he isn't going to let her be a neighbor to anybody; that I can tell you, and I'd watch the boy. If he didn't think there was money in keeping the boy alive, he would not have lived this long."

"Do you realize what you are saying? Those are frightful accusations you are making, Petter."

"What I say is true, and the reason why I tell it is to be sure the poor woman will have a friend when she gets here. I know you are the one to tell. I am very sure she won't tell you for her boy's sake, but I feel you should know her story."

"You must be very fond of her, Petter."

"I have never felt so sad about anyone in my whole life. I knew her people and they are a very fine family. Jenns does not know that I knew her, or I never would have been here. Her name is Anna; she is a lovely girl with beautiful brown eyes and dark hair. She has a heavenly voice and is a wonderful person. She worked in the Amalienborg palace in Copenhagen. Just what she did there I don't know for sure, but it wasn't in the kitchen or cleaning the palace. She did a lot of writing and was always with some of the palace women when they went places. Well, Anna and one of the family's royal sons fell in love, but she wasn't from a good enough class to marry him. They call her a commoner. She kept her condition quiet and cried her eyes out. I saw all this because I worked as a guard at the palace before coming to America. I witnessed her sadness."

"The police learned of it, then they got a hold of Jenns, who they wanted to get rid of anyway. They told him to marry her and get out of the country. They paid that rat $700.00 and free passage and gave her the choice to marry him or suffer the consequences of an unwed mother. And in the old country that is the end of a woman's life."

"So Jenns got himself a gorgeous slave, and he is low enough to enjoy it. I know when he gets himself settled he will try to ask for more money, and that is why he couldn't afford to have anything happen to that youngster. He will never let her forget that he was paid to marry her, and he will hold that over her as long as they live."

"I am so glad I could find someone to tell. I am sorry about the other day, and when you threw him down in a heap, I felt like stepping on him and squashing him like the worm he is. Well, I have told you, and I am glad. I will have to go now."

They rose and Kisti gave him her hand. "I am so glad you told me, Petter. I am sure Anna and I will get along. The poor dear, I shall do everything I can to make her life as happy and easy as I can."

"I am sure you will, I feel better now."

Petter went off, and Ole appeared out of the night.

"What did he want, Mom? Did he bother you?"

"No, dear. He did me a great favor. He really is a very fine person when you get to know him."

"Yea, he looked fine when he held the ax over my head, very fine I should say."

"Well, I know this now, Ole, he would never have hurt you. Of that I am very, very sure. Come son, it is time you were in bed."

"Wait, Mom, I want to ask you something. Are you going to have another baby?"

"Yes, Ole, dear. You will have another sister or brother!"

Ole Lysne - Hendrick's Half-Brother

Chapter Eleven

The New Synneva

The summer passed rapidly, and the corn grew fast, reaching undreamed of heights; the wheat heads were full. A bountiful harvest was evident everywhere. Hendrick and Ole took turns at the cradle scythe, cutting the grain, and Kisti and Randine raked and bound the bundles of stalks, as they stood thick. During the harvesting, Grandma did the cooking and looked after Eivind, who wandered far and wide and got into everything. She kept him out of the broiling sun and out of the well.

The weather was clear and the sun was hot, ideal for the harvest. The grain dried just right, and in another day, if the weather held, it would be cut and hauled in for the threshing.

Kisti worked hard to keep up. As Randine raked, she looked towards the end of the row and calculated.

"Six more stalk bundles, Mom." Then we'll go get a nice cool drink and something to eat."

"Oh, Herre Gud!" Kisti stooped over, crying, and sank to her knees.

Randine screamed and dropped beside her, and cried out, "Father, Ole, come quick! Something has happened to mother."

Kisti grabbed Randine's hand. "Hold still, darling. I will wait just a minute, and then maybe I can get to the house. Run and tell Grandma to get the bed ready."

Hendrick stood beside her.

"Kisti, darling, are you all right?"

"Oh Hendrick, I thought it would be in September, but I guess it is to be born now, and soon. Here, give me your arms, both of you."

Hendrick and Ole supported her as Kisti walked to the house and fell exhausted upon the bed.

Ole ran down to the Boes to ask Ingeborg for help, and when he returned a short time later, Randine came out with a bundle in her arms.

"Ole, we have a little sister!"

Ole peeked at her. "She's too small to live," was his only comment.

There was no doubt about it. She was very tiny. The nails on her little hands and feet were incomplete, and for a few days Kisti fed her by dropping milk into her mouth.

Jon and Johan came the next day with Knute and his son, Isaac, and the harvest was completed more quickly than they had anticipated. That evening Knut appeared with a rocking cradle which he had made when he heard that Kisti was pregnant.

In due time the new baby was able to nurse, and even though she weighed less than five pounds, she made as rapid progress as any other baby. Grandma was so constantly in service that Hendrick said one day, "She is so much like you and in your arms so much of the time that I guess we better call her Synneva to honor you for all your hard work."

So, Synneva it was.

One day while Kisti was still resting in bed, she heard a gentle knock on the wall beside the open door. There stood a lithe young woman with a lovely kind face, big brown eyes, and a wealth of mahogany-colored hair that hung in two great braids. In her arms was a boy, about a year old, with large blue eyes. Kisti extended her hand.

"You must be Anna, aren't you? I have waited for so long to meet you."

The timid, shy young woman smiled gratefully at the pleasant greeting. Kisti liked her immediately, and when she left, they promised that they would get together again soon.

It was hard to believe that anyone could be so cruel to such a lovely person. She hadn't yet told Hendrick what Petter had told her, and she was the only one who knew Anna's secret.

She often wondered whether Petter had informed the girl that Kisti knew her story, but she never betrayed her vow of secrecy.

"Someday, sometime," thought Kisti, "she will tell me of her own accord. I only hope it will not be a drastic situation that prompts her to tell me the truth."

Fall came and went. The Bancrofts arrived at the Lysne farm one cold day in November and asked Kisti and Hendrick if they could hire Randine to come and care for their children, while Mrs. Bancroft helped her husband with legal issues and needs for people in the county. Randine's face lit up with excitement. Kisti looked first at Hendrick and then at Randine. They spoke together about what the change would mean for all of them, and when her parents agreed to her new position, Randine jumped up and down. She gathered some clothes in a travel bag, and then rode off in the carriage with them to Plover, where they had established a home. Mr. Bancroft served as a lawyer for the Kinzie interests, and Grignon and DuBey also needed his assistance as an attorney, so he was well situated at Plover, which had become the county seat.

The house seemed empty after Randine went to work for the Bancrofts, but little Synneva, Eivind, and Ole kept the household busy enough. Hendrick was back at the falls again in the lumber industry, and so the household revolved around the Saturdays when he would be home and the Sundays before he had to leave again. Sometimes he would return on Friday evenings, and over the Christmas holidays he was home for a whole week.

Johan was also employed as a lumber man, and Jon took care of both his and Johan's livestock while his brother was working in the woods. The Blaskys were cutting trees in the woods as well for the winter. Ashbjorn Roe, Aspun's father, and several of the men availed themselves of the opportunity to help expand the lumber activities.

Ole and Aspun attended school sporadically because they felt out of place with the smaller children in the one-room schoolhouse. It was decided between them that when the next winter came, they would find a way to be in the woods themselves.

Ole and Aspun had heard some of the men tell romantic stories of the log drives on the river. All winter long the two of them talked about how they would practice spinning logs in the river and try to stay on top of the logs without falling off. They had their hearts set on joining the log drives, and never lost an opportunity to hear men talk of the romantic danger-filled adventures as they floated the huge rafts down the Wisconsin River and into the mighty Mississippi to St. Louis.

The winter warmed into spring earlier than usual that year, followed by a hot summer and autumn season, but by Thanksgiving time, the snow was deep and the weather was bitter cold again. The harvest had been unusually good, and there was a sense of abundance and plenty for all the farmers. Little Synneva was developing rapidly in her own tiny way. She was a very small child, with tiny hands and feet, but her body was perfectly formed, and presented no problems. She was healthy in every way, even though she was born prematurely.

Anna and her boy Hans frequently visited, but Kisti noticed that her visits were always timed for when Jenns was away. She was also very careful about timing when she invited Kisti over to her own house to visit.

Mari was pregnant with her second child, but this time, it didn't dampen her spirit. She was as happy and vivacious as ever, animating everything around her with her infectious laughter. To Kisti, Mari was the bright light in their country neighborhood.

The women neighbors managed to meet during the winter days, first at one house, then at another, while their menfolk were busy with the logging work. Aspun and Ole had found work nearby at a sawmill established by Lieutenant Jerome Nelson on the Tomorrow River. There was also a new blacksmith. They called the sawmill Nelsonville. While this was a far cry from the log drive the boys dreamed about, it was better than nothing, and they would learn more about lumber. They decided that as soon as the ice broke, they would float some logs down from the woods to the mill.

Toward the end of the winter, Kisti realized that she was pregnant once again, and the coming autumn would bring their fifth child. She was happy about it but felt puzzled that it should have such a mild impact. The news didn't fill her with the same kind of anticipation that she had felt with Synneva and Eivind, or with Ole and Randine. It seemed almost as if she didn't care whether the baby came or not. Eivind was growing like a weed; he was asking questions and in constant motion. Grandma was a very capable, and the household weathered the winter smoothly.

Chapter Twelve

Kisti and the Ho-Chunks

The Ho-Chunk people were frequent visitors at the Lysne home, and many a morning Kisti awoke to find a couple of them asleep on the floor near the fire, or she would be aroused by the smell of smoke and see the silhouette of an Indian hunched over, putting sticks on the fire. She never ceased to be startled by them, but it was comforting to have them nearby, especially since Hendrick was gone most of the week in the winter.

Their presence was not unwelcome, except that they always seemed to show up unexpectedly. They had a burning curiosity about everything the white man did and couldn't understand his objectives in life. To them the only important things were the essential needs: a fire, a shelter, and meat. Aside from the necessity to make clothing to cover their naked bodies, there was no point in working beyond the effort required to subsist. They fished, trapped, and hunted. Occasionally they played games of skill, such as shooting arrows at a target and hiding near wild animals where they grazed. Some of the rougher games like Lacrosse, that required great effort and much activity, were becoming a thing of the past, since the sport designed for training warriors and was not as necessary. These days, the white man promised them protection, and even food.

None of them wanted to work for hire. That was beneath the dignity of the stalwart male. Mother Earth provided food and shelter, and they listened for her guidance in hunting and in protecting their people. The women planted corn and tanned the buckskins from deer, and used bear pelts, fox, wolf and otter fur for warmer clothing. The men were avid traders, and would trade pipes, furs, moccasins, ponies, and dogs for supplies they needed for their camps, such as iron skillets, or axes that were made of metal.

There was never any trading between Kisti and Hendrick and the Indians. They shared generously and seemed happy to bring the family food, such as venison or bear. They learned that Kisti never accepted dog, skunk, or crow meat, and stopped offering it.

Ole often went hunting with the Native boys, and he had learned how to make bows and arrows in several Ho-Chunk camps. Sometimes he and Aspun remained there for the night when they were stalking game.

Guns were forbidden for Indians, but Ole and Aspun found some guns for them to hunt with and no one in the community seemed to notice. They shared the fruits of the hunt with each other, and often when Ole returned from town, he would bring red ribbon and trinkets for the Indian girls and fishhooks or fishing line for the boys.

Hendrick would bring some items for the Indians when he returned from the falls. There was rarely any conversation between Hendrick and the native people, except for Oshida, and their discussion concerned affairs that were of mutual interest. They had deep respect for each other, but their relationship never proceeded beyond formality.

Kisti, however, would laugh and joke with them, and they would laugh with her and seemed to appreciate her attempts at fun. They loved to hear her sing, and she taught them several songs.

One day when Kisti was ironing, Otwana, the sister of Winona, and one of Randine's special friends, who had just been married came to visit. They had given her a red shawl as a wedding gift. That day, she was wearing the red shawl, and she had brought some new moccasins for Eivind and baby Synneva. She was a fussy baby and wanted to be picked up all the time. Grandma, who was down at the Boes, was not there to give her the attention she wanted. As Otwana sat on the step beside the open door, she seemed concerned that the baby was trying to get out of the cradle. So, Kisti picked up Synneva and gave her to the young bride. She held her in her arms and gently rocked her. Kisti sat beside her and sang the little lullaby. She carefully formed the words, as the Indian sisters wanted to learn the tune and the words. Otwana sang it over and over again, and Synneva enjoyed it immensely.

> "Two small mice,
> cheese a half a slice,
> two pieces of fish,
> I stole behind a dish.
> 'Now I'm dizzy, I will sleep,'
> said the kitty.
>
> That was long ago,
> he kept on doing so,
> Now he's big and fat,
> just a lazy old cat.

The next day Otwana came again and asked to hold baby Synneva. Mari was visiting Kisti with her own two babies at the time.

"Good Lord, Kisti, do you let her hold your babies? Don't you know that Indians are dirty?"

"Well, Mari, a little soap and water will get them clean. She was married a short while ago and wants to practice caring for a baby. She likes to come here because I also teach her English words."

The girl began to sing the lullaby with a remarkably beautiful voice and she almost had the words right. The melody was perfect. Soon Kisti, Mari, and Otwana were all singing together. Winona joined them as she walked up the trail from the Ho-Chunk camp.

A few days later, when Kisti visited the Ho-Chunk camp, they would pay her the supreme compliment by singing the lullaby she had taught Otwana, the young bride and sister of Winona. Several of them lined up and sang her the lullaby.

When they had finished, Kisti placed her hand on her heart and wiped away her tears with the other hand. They stood together in a semicircle, grinning from ear to ear.

Day after day, the young bride, Otwana, and Winona came to visit Kisti, and baby Synneva became very fond of Otwana. Winona was fond of Eivind and spent much time with him. Otwana's patience and concern for Synneva's welfare endeared her to the household. Kisti did not realize how much she had become a part of their family until she announced one day,

"Come new moon, Otwana no come no more."

"But, Otwana, why? Don't you like it here with us?"

Sitting in the doorway, as was now her custom, with little Synneva on her lap and her cheek against the baby's head, she took Kisti's hand.

"My heart I leave here. We go to white man's school. My husband say you make me a good wife. He want to be like white man. He ask army man to go to school. Army man said yes he could go. Yesterday he go to Indian Agent, he say go next new moon. We will learn to read, write, we can be like you and your friend Mari."

Kisti sat down beside her and put her arm around her. Synneva was half asleep in her arms. Winona was holding Eivind on her lap. She was sad to see her sister leaving.

"Otwana, you are our friend. See, the baby trusts you and loves to be in your arms. It will not be any different when you are a great lady, you will always be Otwana to us. We love you. I hope you will come and see us and that you will be very happy. Also in school, they may teach you about our loving God."

"We both got same God, that's why we go. Winona you come and hold little one when we go? She likes to be with Randine's mother and little sister. She come?"

"Of course she can, she is always welcome. She is like Randine in many ways. They are great friends. Randine will see her when she comes home."

"I see Randine. I go to Plover with husband. We see Wahopekau, she say she come to you."

"Oh," Kisti said, "how I would love to see Wahopekau and White Fang."

"She come see you, she see Randine all time. White Fang go to white school, too."

In a few days Wahopekau appeared at the door, just as Otwana had said, and Randine had come with her. This was Randine's first trip home in a long time and Kisti was surprised at how much her daughter had grown and matured. Mrs. Bancroft had given her a new dress and she had pinned up her braids to form a crown of mahogany hair around her head. She did not look like the little girl that had left them at Christmas; Randine was a young lady. She was to be confirmed in the summer, as she was twelve years old and growing up so fast.

Wahopekau seemed much more mature than when they had parted with her on the trail. She had been tutored by her aunt and had learned to read and mastered the English language wonderfully. Kisti also saw a new a grace in her movements.

Wahopekau had lost much of the wild look of four years ago. While there was no mistaking her tribal origins, she was indeed a shining example of what her aunt had taught her.

The little boy was a sturdy child, well fed, with a ruddy face, piercing black eyes, jet-black hair, and strong white teeth. Kisti brought him to her and hugged him tightly as he laughed and squirmed and she nuzzled his soft brown neck.

Wahopekau told Kisti, "We call our baby Frank because Frank DuBey saved White Fang's life. While you saved his life and mine, if we ever have a girl, we will name her after you."

Her little son Frank and Eivind were much taken with each other, and they became the best of friends almost immediately. Moments later, as they played outside in the dirt, it was hard to tell which child was the darkest.

Wahopekau told Kisti that she and White Fang and Otwana and her husband, Spotted Deer, and little Frank would be going to this school so they could learn more about white people, and how to keep the peace with them.

"How are you going to this school? Is someone sending you there? Is it the government, or the army?" Kisti asked with concern in her voice.

"No, we are being sent by a well-known, wealthy fur trader and businessman from Kaukauna. He and his family live between Appleton and Green Bay. His name is Augustine Gringnon."

"Oh, I have heard his name," Kisti said.

"He learned our languages, and over many years of working with our people, he sympathized with the Indians, as he had worked with many tribes throughout his life. Through an arrangement he has made with several tribes, he offers anyone who wants to obtain an education to be sent East to a government school. We see people like you, Kisti and Randine, being kind and so loving, and we want to learn more about white culture. Others were not as nice as you, but soon we learn the differences and some of our people want to be with good white people."

Kisti learned from Wahopekau that Frank DuBey had been sent out into the Minnesota territory and that no one had heard from him for some time. There had been rumors of Indian trouble in the west, but information was meager, and no one paid too much attention to what was going on outside of their own area.

Ole and Hendrick were pleased to see Randine and Wahopekau there when they came home. Hendrick was so glad to see his family again, and spend time with Kisti.

Later that evening after dinner, Ole and Randine walked with Winona, Wahopekau and Otwana to their camp. Ole went with Winona ahead of Randine and Wahopekau. Just before they entered camp, Winona tugged at Ole's sleeve. "Set gun down," she whispered. "Hurry, put hands out." Ole did so. Winona stood in front of him with her arms outstretched and pressed her firm breasts and small body against his chest. She wrapped her arms around him and hugged him tightly, then let go and skipped away before the stunned boy could say a word.

Winona ran ahead of the others and disappeared into

the camp. Ole's heart was beating so hard and thumping so loud in his ears that he could scarcely speak to the others. Randine and Wahopekau caught up with him. He had brought ribbons to give to Winona and some of the other girls when they visited the camp.

That night Ole couldn't sleep, and he tossed and turned in his bed. He finally got up and went outdoors to sit on the log by the well; he tried to understand the strange emotion he had felt when Winona suddenly put her arms around him. Until that night, he had never noticed how pretty she was. There was still a warm sensation radiating from the place in his chest where her body had touched his. He had never felt anything like that before. Soon the darkness gave way to light, and a gentle breeze stirred the trees as the red ball of the sun began to shine through the poplar grove.

Chapter Thirteen

Talking Paper

The crops were planted in the ground and the hay was harvested and put up in stacks. Randine had been confirmed that summer and was back in Plover with the Bancrofts. The two Ho-Chunk couples, Wahopekau and White Fang, and Otwana and Spotted Deer, were at school. Two letters came addressed to Kisti. One was from Wahopekau, the second letter was from Otwana who had written to Winona. Kisti sat down with Winona to read them to her.

Wahopekau's letter talked about life at school. She said she missed her sister Winona and her father, mother, and brothers, and that she was learning the white man's ways, and many things that would make their lives easier and happier.

Winona listened wide-eyed, unable to fathom the idea of the "talking paper." Even though they weren't there, she could feel Otwana talking to her. The next day, she brought the letter over again.

"Otwana say more to Winona?"

Kisti smiled, careful not to ridicule her for the question.

"No Winona, the same as yesterday, and many years from now this letter will say the same words. Here, I will show you."

She brought over a pencil and paper. "Look here, Winona, this is how your name is spelled in English. See? Winona looks like this on a talking paper."

Kisti slowly wrote down each letter of her name. "You see, it looks just like this on your letter." She held the printed words on the page beside the letter. "See, just how Otwana wrote down your name. Here, Winona, try it."

Winona took the pencil from her hand and slowly and carefully began to copy the letters of "Winona," beginning at the wrong end, with the "a." Kisti put her hand gently over Winona's hand. "Winona, you make pretty patterns with beads. We have twenty-four beads that we call letters to spell words—I will make them for you."

She printed each of the six letters of Winona's name separately and then wrote them together in one word. The girl was fascinated, and in a short time she had the letters arranged in the proper sequence to spell her name. She then asked for the rest of the letters and how to spell names of other things. She learned how to say the alphabet, adjusting her lips to make the sound for each of the twenty-four letters, and now understood how they were formed into words.

Winona learned to spell her name and several other words. Kisti was amazed at her receptivity and rapid understanding of the English language. She was so eager and willing to learn that Winona's lessons became a daily affair, and she soon was a regular presence in the household.

Winona's desire for knowledge would not be limited to writing but she wanted to learn how to read as well. She also wanted to learn how to sew and cook like Kisti and Synneva and the other white women. She was thrilled when Kisti scrubbed her hands and showed her how to make yeast and knead bread. Everything domestic, including the care of the baby, was very important to Winona.

Kisti taught her how to make tea and to serve it properly. One day Mari came to visit when Winona was there with Kisti. They went out to sit at under the big oak tree, and Winona brought out a tray neatly laid with a white cloth with a pot of tea, teacups, and some little cakes that she had helped Kisti bake the day before.

"Well, I never," exclaimed Mari. "Kisti, how do you do it? These people don't even come on our land. They never speak except when they are spoken to and here you have them working for you. I just don't understand your power over them."

"Mari, do I have power over you?"

"You sure do, there isn't anything I wouldn't do for you, you know that, Kisti. Well, I guess that is where the power lies then. You love these Indians, and I guess they feel it. I don't love them, Kisti. I wouldn't hurt them, but I don't care to have them near me. I guess that is the way they feel too. It's funny. Things work out pretty much the way we think and feel. Are you having trouble with the little ape to the east?"

"Anna, his wife, comes up to see me every so often, but I never see him," Kisti replied. "Eivind likes her little Hans, so the children play while Anna and I visit."

Winona saw Ole come up from the field and he waved to her. He sensed her nervousness whenever he was in her presence. But since that night in the woods, neither of them had spoken about what had happened—and there was no sign of anything personal between them—until that day. Ole was at the well with his shirt off washing himself, as he often did after returning from the field for supper. Just as he was about to reach for his shirt, Winona jumped out from behind the well and held up a shirt with fringes made of soft doeskin with the Ho-Chunk insignia on the back in beautiful beadwork.

"Put this on, you wear for Winona?"

He extended his arms, and she slipped the shirt over his head, and after she pulled it down, he caught her and held her close to him and kissed her lightly on the lips. Winona relaxed and utterly melted in his arms, then gently pushed him away and sat down on the log with her eyes on her moccasins.

"The women in our village all helped to make the shirt," she said softly, her eyes still on the ground. Her neck and face were flushed a deep crimson. They make you one of us one day. You come?"

"Sure, I'll come Winona." He sat down beside her on the log. She put her hand over his mouth.

"No talk now."

They looked towards the house as Kisti with Eivind were going through the door. Ole wondered how much his mother had seen.

Chapter Fourteen

Crisis in the Well

As Hendrick and Ole were preparing the grain cradle and scythe for harvesting wheat in the barn, the sound of horse's hooves reached them. Someone was riding at breakneck speed. When they ran out to see who it was, the rider stopped, and they recognized him, but couldn't remember his name. There was no time for pleasantries.

"Wilhelm Bobbe is down in the well," the man shouted, "the walls have caved in. He is still alive and we need help to dig him out. Bring your shovels and ropes," and away he sped.

Ole grabbed the spade with the long handle and started running to the Bobbe's place three miles to the south. Hendrick called after him, "I will come later this evening."

There was much panic and excitement at the Bobbe's. Mrs. Bobbe was wringing her hands and the men were digging frantically without any system or order, just throwing the dirt in every direction. Johan had heard the news on his way to town and was just arriving as Ole appeared on the scene.

"It looks like we have a job to do here. I am glad you brought your spade. First, let us help Mrs. Bobbe."

Johan went to her and said, "Now Mrs. Bobbe, this is a time when you will have to be bigger than you have ever been. Crying will do nothing to help; it will only unnerve those that are here trying to help you."

"Oh, I am so worried about Wilhelm, he is all I have," she responded. "What can I do, how can I help?"

"You go put on the coffee pot and get all the food ready that you can. The other women will be here to help you soon and the men will work all night. We won't leave you. Come, dry your tears. We will get Wilhelm out very soon."

He went to the well and saw an iron pipe protruding out of the ground. The men were trying to wiggle it loose and were striking the pipe with their shovels.

"What are you doing? That is what is keeping the man alive down there." Johan said. He called down into the pipe, "Wilhelm, this is Johan. Are you alright?"

"Yes, I will be alright if they would quit pounding the pipe."

"Are you hurt?"

"Not much, it is pretty snug here, but part of the casing is around me and I can breathe alright, but I cannot move my legs. I am alright if you fellows can dig me out."

Johan turned to the men. "I don't want to be the boss here, but it is obvious that there must be some kind of order if we are going to get anywhere."

"Tell us what to do, Johan, and we'll do it," Amund said.

"Amund, you have horses, go get them to haul the stones out. They could be a great help. Send someone over to get Knute and Lars. Have them bring their tools. We have heavy construction to do here. Lasse, you used to do timberwork. Take men with you and fell some of those trees in the grove over there. Cut them no more than six inches through. Leave the length intact until Lars and Knute get here. Andes, keep these men digging. Get the dirt over to one side. Leave three sides vacant around the well so we can get to it. Keep two men digging, change off every fifteen minutes, and keep shoveling the dirt away so it won't clog up around the pit."

Johan called down the well. "How are you Wilhelm?"

Through the pipe came the answer, "I am alright. Are you getting things going? I am comfortable but it is dark as pitch in here."

"Don't worry, Wilhelm, relax and save your strength."

Lars Vanganess drove into sight with a brand-new team of horses and harnesses. In the back of his wagon was a keg.

Johan called to him when he spied the keg. "Pull your team up here, Lars, and you can have a job. I'll help you."

As he got into the wagon, he said to Lars, "For heaven's sake, let's hide the keg and dish it out after we finish this job. If the men get wind of it, I am afraid poor Wilhelm will be a long time in the well."

So, they drove behind the barn and hid the keg in the hay after having a sip to test its flavor and potency. "Yes, okay, we will have to keep this hidden for a while," Lars agreed.

"Lars, you used to build ships, didn't you, in Norway?" Johan asked.

"Oh, ya, you betch ya. I can cut and lay a hull for schooners or sloops. You name it. I'll lay it."

"Well, Lars, Knute will be here and will let you know what is required. We will have to cut some timbers to make a casing that will hold Wilhelm."

Blasky appeared. "I was a timber man in the mines in Silesia."

"Fine, we'll have to shore this well up as we go along."

Knute and Lars came over. The men kept digging in relays. The women of the neighborhood appeared with food and coffee and set it out. Now and then, a chosen few men who had found a source of much inspiration in the hay behind the barn, went out for refreshment.

When she saw them felling the trees, Wilhelm's wife called out, "Those are the trees that Wilhelm had saved for the new barn."

Lasse came close to her and said, "Better get him out of the well first or he won't need the barn. He will be able to reuse the wood after we get him out."

She began crying again, and the women came running out to comfort her.

The carpenters banged together a makeshift derrick with a swinging boom so that the soil could be hoisted up and swung out of the way, which would be needed as soon as it was competed.

The neighborhood team was organized; everyone was put to work and had their jobs to do. Wilhelm was cheerful despite the predicament he was in. He talked to his wife now and then, encouraging her the best he could when he heard the tears and anxiety in her voice.

Everyone remarked what a lifesaver the iron pipe had proved to be. Wilhelm could communicate with them and it gave him air.

The men worked through the night. Hendrick had joined them early in the evening. Some slept in the hay; the night was mild and the weather was dry. The digging went on and on. Vanganess went home to do his chores but reappeared the following morning with extra supplies of food, and there was another keg well hidden in his light wagon.

The boom was working, they were down quite a few meters, and the casing was laid as they proceeded to send the shaft deeper. There were those who argued against such a substantial casing, but conceded it was wise when Johan explained the reason for it:

"If the original well casing had been substantial enough this would not have happened."

The derrick and boom were praised as a work of art. The loudest praise came from those who went most often to inspect the hay behind the barn.

The food provided in abundance was good and the men were cheerful despite their hard work. Wilhelm seemed to be of good cheer, even though he was thirsty and hungry and could hear the constant commotion on the ground above him. Someone asked Wilhelm if they should call the preacher. Wilhelm's responded, "Sure, tell him to come, and have him bring a shovel."

The women of the neighborhood were there in force, working in shifts. A huge iron kettle swung from an oak log suspended between two forked timbers over the fire pit. It was filled with water for boiling soup. A long, improvised table was set up outside, and the food appeared and disappeared as empty bowls were refilled as the day wore on.

On the beginning of the third day, a Sunday, people began to gather early, many of them having been up most of the night. Wilhelm was getting weaker from his long confinement. Those who had assumed the responsibility of digging him out were nearly exhausted. Hendrick came for a while and went back home. Ole stayed on and shoveled and sawed timber when it was needed. He and Aspun worked together.

Around eleven o'clock the iron pipe commenced to move and the men shoveling became more cautious as they started to remove the crushed casings. Everyone was tense. The womenfolk began to gather, and Mari marshaled them into the kitchen and assigned them tasks to keep them occupied and out of the way.

Soup was ready to feed Wilhelm. Water was ready for his bath. Clean clothes had been laid out for almost three days now, and all were in a state of excitement. At twelve fifteen, Wilhelm got his head out from under the casing that had imprisoned him in a half sitting position. He could hardly speak.

"Water is what I want most," he said with much congestion in his dry throat.

The rope was slowly dropped down to him with a tin cup of water, and he was able to get the rope around his chest as he freed one arm and then another. The boom and derrick crane pulled him slowly out of the rubble, and the men were careful to extract him without injury. Someone brought him a cup filled with the beer from the keg. He gulped it down. As he emerged the men cheered.

The minister was there, and so was most of the congregation. There had been prayers said for him that morning in church. Everyone who gathered said a prayer again now, and a hymn was sung as Wilhelm emerged completely from the well. Finally, he got cleaned up and fed. The minister came out and spoke to them and asked them to thank God for having delivered Wilhelm out of the well.

Vanganess tipped his hat back on his head and said, "Well, I'll be damned, and to think we wasted three days of our time to get him out when he would have gotten out anyway. Well, he got the best well curbing this side of Milwaukee for sitting there anyway."

The crowd hooted. "Well," said Anders, "It was a pleasure to work for the Lord anyhow. We were instruments of God, brother, no doubt about it. Anyway, I think we should be happy about it."

Wilhelm and his wife appeared. "I can't thank you all now, but I want you to come back here next Sunday and be my guests so that I can thank you properly. Maybe the minister will have the morning service here, and then you can stay the rest of the day."

All of them cheered and the kegs were brought out. They relaxed and consumed the remainder of the kegs. The crowd celebrated together and then one family at a time slowly left for their homes.

Chapter Fifteen

Old Settlers Reunion

Kisti drove her cart home from the Bobbe's with Mari and Anna Marie, and left them at their homes along the way. It was a great satisfaction to them to have helped with Wilhelm's rescue and they were proud to be members of this wonderful community.

That night, Kisti walked out to her Königs Garton in the clearing where she went to sit and contemplate her life. She sat a long while and offered thanksgiving prayers, as the whippoorwills called to their mates, and Johan's hound dog bayed in the distance, and the crickets heralded an early fall. The late July moon reclining on a downy cloud filled her joyous soul with a blessed peace.

Someone approached her in the stillness of the night. She was startled at first, but then she saw it was Ole.

"Can't you sleep, son? I should think you would be exhausted. You have been up for three nights, haven't you? What's bothering you?"

"Then you have noticed? Well, I slept pretty good at the Bobbe's house, but I was tired from the work. I am troubled by something, Mother, and I don't know what to do about it."

"Sit here beside me, my Hjerte (heart). You have become such a man, all of a sudden, it seems like. You have had to be a man, haven't you? You never have had much of a chance to be a boy. We have moved about so much, and sometimes I wonder if we have done you wrong."

"Done me wrong, mother? Never! This life here is wonderful. We are building a home together in our new country. Eivind is growing up in it. Synneva was born here in our new place and now there will be another baby. No, mother, nothing wrong at all, everything is RIGHT!"

"But I can't help but think of Winona. They want to take me into the tribe. I like those people, mother, they are honest and fair, but I don't want to be an Indian. Although I like being with them, I couldn't live like they do."

"Well, Ole, my precious heart, you don't have to live with them or be like them. They are giving you an honor because of all that you have helped them with, and what you have learned from them too! They want to show you their love, appreciation, and admiration. You cannot turn them down. They would never recover from the hurt, and it would hurt you too, son, if you didn't accept their generosity. It is a respectful award, you know, an extraordinary honor. You had better accept it. As for Winona, she is a precious spirit, one of the forest if ever there was one, and I could love her like a daughter."

She hugged Ole close to her. "Little nubbin', you and Winona are both young, so very young, although you have grown into a strong man before my eyes without me realizing it. I can't tell you what to do with Winona, I can only love you and pray. You will do what you are supposed to do. That I know.

"In Norway there would be certain rules, and it would not be impossible for a white man to be in a relationship with a native woman. Here I am not so sure. We know what the bible says about love. We are supposed to be guided by what it says. But what does your heart tell you? What does your heart say, Ole?"

"It says plenty, Mother, but I don't understand all of it. Sometimes it says, 'Ole you are a damn stupid animal.' Then again it says, 'When did you get to be so mighty?' Then I think of Winona. I want to hold her in my arms and then I get mad at myself for wanting her. And then I think of Aspun, and I can just hear him splitting his pants laughing."

"Does your heart tell you there is any reason to decide right away? There is no hurry, you know. Why don't you stop worrying about the things you don't understand, and thank God for every day, and be happy? It is said that all things work together for good. So let us believe that, son, and take things as they come. I have placed you in God's care and nothing can happen that is not supposed to. That I know. Ah, the lovely moon is going to bed. We should too, don't you think? Don't you worry about Winona, son. Things will work out for the best for all of us."

"I don't fancy being a squaw-man though."

"Hush, who said you were going to be such a man. If you love her, you will not treat her in a disrespectful way. You will love her as your partner. This is not like that terrible word. You will find a way to unite with her in your heart. There is no rush. You are still so young. She is a wonderful young woman, Ole. Give yourself time to ponder your feelings."

The next Sunday the entire neighborhood assembled outdoors at the home of Wilhelm and his wife Inge Bobbe for a day of festivities. Pastor Duus and the congregation held the service there, as suggested the previous Sunday. The choir had practiced on Thursday evening and sang their hymns flawlessly. To begin the service, the minister took his text from the Apostle Paul, Act 14:11 11 When the crowd saw what Paul had done, they shouted in the Lycaonian language, "The gods have come down to us in human form!" Then he added the Hebrews 2:14, "Because God's children are human beings--made of flesh and blood--the Son also became flesh and blood. For only as a human being could he die, and only by dying could he break the power of the devil, who had the power of death." The minister tied in the message with Wilhelm's narrow escape. He made his sermon mercifully short, and then honored the help from the community as the spirit of God moved through them all.

The spirit of the occasion was one of fellowship and good will. All of the old timers were there, and they reunited with many groups who had become separated during the great migration.

At the gathering after the sermon, great plans were laid for the Amherst Fair that everyone was excited about. Food was ample and there was a good supply of the beer for which the Germans were rightly famous. Those who had met just a few years before shared their amazement at the changes that had taken place The number of new children that had been born and were now part of the community was a wonder to them.

Mari made the suggestion that they reunite for a settler's picnic every year on that day or the Sunday nearest August 8th, to which everyone agreed. Mari was elected secretary of the "Old Settlers Reunion," as they called it.

Mari stood up in the meeting and said, "Since we are going to share each other's troubles, we might as well share each other's joys too. Let us bring out coffeepots and something to eat; a little music would help, and maybe we could dance away our troubles."

Pastor Duus walked out of the meeting with Hendrick and said to him, "Hendrick, I don't believe in dancing, so I can't sanction it!"

Hendrick replied, "Neither do I care for it, particularly. It would be easy for me to forbid my family to dance, but I do not wish to impose my will upon them. Besides, they are doing no one harm. We danced all the time in Laerdal. So why not let them dance here?"

The pastor's wife Sophia came out to join in the conversation. "Darling, I remember when we danced in Norway, outside Bergen. It was part of every gathering. I know your teachings say not to participate in dancing, but we have a diverse community. Dancing is part of the Native ceremonies after all. Come on back in, dear one, and let us put aside the dancing rules. People need a way to forget the troubles of this time."

Pastor Duus stood there stiff and anxious, but he softened as his wife Sophia spoke, and she put her arm in his and led him back into the community group meeting.

"I cannot sanction dancing, but if this is a community meeting, I have no say in it. Do what you wish, while I distribute the food and clothing for those in need. Those who wish to help me are welcome," said the pastor.

Sophia smiled and kissed him on his cheek, then she joined the other women in laying out the baked goods.

The question of dancing was not brought up again, and

Pastor Duus was very well liked as time passed. His charming wife softened his stern demeanor, and she engaged people with her warmth and sympathy.

During the building of the church, the services were held in homes throughout the community. Many of these homes were simple log cabins, not very large, and they were jam packed with worshippers on Sunday. Almost everyone had trusted dogs and guns as part of their pioneering equipment to defend their livestock against bears, wolves, and foxes, and to keep Indians from stealing their chickens and cattle for easy meals. Wherever there were settlers, there were guns and dogs at worship services. This was accepted as normal.

At the Brekkes place, Nils was sitting directly below Pastor Duus, who was standing up trying to talk above the noise of the children. Jacob's dog made a pass at Nil's forearm, while Nils had his dog Spot by the collar, and while trying to get him out of the room, he knocked several people off the planks that served as their seats.

"Jacob, get your damn dog off my arm!" Nils hollered.

Jacob grabbed the dog's collar. He ain't no God damn mongrel like yours is!"
Jacob shot back.

"Come on out and I'll show you."

Jacob let his dog go. "Sick'em!" he shouted and with a joyous yelp, and the dog caught Nils by the seat of the pants and tore one of his pant legs off completely. The service was in pandemonium, as youngsters cheered the dogs on.

Nil's wife was wringing her hands. "Why the poor, poor man, that is the only pair of pants he has! What shall we do!?"

Pastor Duus soon supplied him a pair of doeskin pants, although no one knew where he got them. The service was postponed until a more favorable time. The doeskin underwear pants that Nils wore that day was cause for much speculation. Several people asked his wife how Nils had come about them, and how practical they were.

Sophia ushered the dogs and the noisy children cheering out of the house. Returning with grace and a smile, she said, "Well, we shall have a service next week, but please leave your animals outside so we do not have another such event. Thank you. Now let's get the food ready to share."

Pastor Duus's wife, Sophia Charlotte Lorentz Duus, as a native of Norway, was especially friendly to those from her home country. Everyone loved her.

One day she and Kisti walked through the new graveyard, where an attractive plot was laid out, and there were already three graves in the newly hallowed ground. She said to Kisti in Norwegian, "Someday I will be happy to die in Norway and nowhere else. I so miss our native land, and I want to return someday."

Kisti was stunned, as Sophia was a beautiful healthy woman. She thought, 'Why is she thinking of her death?'

About a month later, when the church structure was almost completed, Sophia became ill. She was able to be present at the dedication, when two of the Herman Preus Lutheran ministers were there; both were from Norway, and served the Evangelical Synod that was being established in Northern Wisconsin. Two young men were also present; one was a missionary by the name of Brandt; the other, named Mikkelson, was already ordained.

Everyone remarked on how Sophia was looking rather ill and were concerned about her health. She revealed the awful news that she did not expect to recover. Several of her closest women friends who were with her throughout her illness gave varied accounts of her beautiful death that occurred within a month of the dedication. The favored story was that she called her husband to her side and requested that he remove from her finger their betrothal ring and wedding ring, for she would have no further use for them.

Pastor Duus tried to administer the last sacrament to his wife, but he wept so much that he was unable to proceed. A white form appeared to him at the window, and from this he received strength to continue. When he finished, she pulled him to her and whispered, "Farewell, my dear, in Jesus' name."

On her tombstone in the new cemetery was written: "Lovingly erected in memory of the pastor's wife by the women of Scandinavia congregation: Sophia Charlotte Lorentz Duus, Born in Kristiania, June 28, 1828, died July 25, 1858, Farewell in Jesus Name."

Pastor Duus tried to remain true to his call, but the haunting memory of his precious Sophia prevailed upon him all his waking hours. He would sit for long periods by her grave in solemn reverie and would often neglect his meals. In his fierce loneliness, he decided that he could better serve his vows in another locality where new scenes would help him to forget the past and move on.

He tried another call in the southern part of Wisconsin, but at the end of the following year, his closest friends received letters from him postmarked from Norway.

Reverend Nils Brandt filled the vacancy, and he was very well liked. He had a pleasing personality and a way with the young people and the Indians. He had done a lot of missionary work with the Pottawatomies with a friend of their Chief Shabbona, and worked with Yellow Thunder and Shawnee Waukee, or John Kinzie. The Indians called the Kinzies Shawnee Waukee people, or "The Bearer of Silver," because while John was the Indian agent at Port Winnebago in the early days, he brought them silver coins provided by the government in payment for their lands, as called for in the several treaties.

With the new church, there was much activity in the congregation. It was already understood that sooner or later there would have to be other places of worship built, and so a plot of ground was set aside on the Nils Larson place in Iola Township called the Krogness farm by some.

On the Kankrud farm in New Home Township, there was another plot of ground set aside as a burial place by the Kankruds for the day when a new church was to be erected on that site. The owners stated that nothing could dissuade them in their wish to donate the land, even though other families criticized their generosity. And so, the dead were buried in the plots before a church was built there.

It was the new summer season, and the annual community gathering would be held at the County Fair again that August or early September. Kisti was startled when she realized that August 10th was Eivind's birthday, and Synneva's was on the 17th, and soon there would be another August birthday. What would they call the newborn? There should be a Hendrick, there should be a Thomas named after Hendrick Lysne's grandfather, there should be an Anna, after his grandmother. Well, Hendrick named the other two. She would name this child.

One rainy evening, on the 5th of September 1859, having been to the County Fair that day, Kisti felt pangs that were too substantial to be ignored. She called her mother Synneva, as neither Ole nor Hendrick were at home. Together they made the preparations. Grandma was about to go get someone from the Boes to help when Winona appeared at the door.

"You are just in time, my dear," said Kisti. "Will you take the two youngest and care for them, please? Mother you stay with me. This is not going to take long, I can tell."

Within the hour the new baby boy was born. Hendrick and Ole returned from the fair shortly after. They were astounded to see Grandma holding the new baby.

"See your new brother!" said Grandma, as she placed Thomas beside his mother; he was the fifth member of the growing family.

The baby seemed healthy, and Kisti did not feel as depleted as she had with the others. She had plenty of nourishment for him and his appetite was as normal as any child. Hendrick agreed to the name of Thomas, as his father, Thomas Lysne, had not yet been honored in the naming of the children. Randine was pleased to learn the news, but in the letter sent to her mother, she asked her when she planned to retire from making babies. Kisti was surprised, though she realized that Randine did not yet understand the reality of being a woman; pregnancy and bearing children was women's uncontrollable role in families. She noted to discuss this with Randine the next time she returned home.

Winona had made herself so indispensable to the family that Hendrick offered to pay her for her work. This made her very sad. She was usually awestruck in Hendrick's presence. Later, she confided in Kisti that it was such a privilege to be at their house that she could never accept pay for anything she did for them.

Fall came early and the Indians predicted a hard winter. They pointed out the signs that this was so—the early frost and the flocks of birds migrating earlier than usual. Ole and the rest of the family doubted the truth of this prediction but, as Kisti said,

"They have been around here much longer than we have, and they should know."

She had talked to Oshida and his people who were all preparing for a hard winter.

Mari also had heard the prediction, and as the women of the neighborhood were discussing the prophecy she was heard to say, "Well I would much rather have too much this spring than get caught at Christmas with too little."

And so, the settlers prepared storage to make it through a hard winter. It had been a fine growing season that year; the crops were plentiful, and the harvest was bountiful. Ole and Aspun had stacked ample firewood by the house. The spinning wheels and looms were much in evidence in many of the settler's homes. The cellars were filled to the brim, and Kisti saw to it that plenty was put by for Winona and her family.

The native women were laying by a considerable amount of corn in storage and Kisti wondered why their able-bodied men did not do that work instead of the women. She was wise enough not to mention it, however. Winona summed it up by saying:

"Our people are very funny. Your people all the time; work, work, work. Our people only women work to make clothes, baskets, blankets from skins and we enjoy talking with each other while doing this work. Men hunt, sit, fish, sit, sleep, sit, smoke, sit, eat, sit, all the time sit, sit. Their work has been to provide food for us, and they do, they are always ready to find us food. Today, they do not see what else to do."

Oshida, who overheard them speaking as he approached, came over to Winona and Kisti and said to them, "Our men listen to the spirits of the forest for guidance on their next hunt. They also listen for bears and wolves that might attack our people. They do as the Great Spirit wishes them to do. They are not disregarding the women and their work; they are protecting them."

Winona said, "No one has told me that before, Chief Oshida."

Oshida smiled and said, "Now you know."

Kisti smiled at Oshida. She was delighted to learn how very different their cultures were. Yet her husband and the men in his family had served as soldiers to protect their people, and they protected their families. Perhaps it was just a different way to care for the women and children.

When Oshida turned to go back to his camp, Winona leaned up against Kisti and hugged her.

Kisti laughed, "Dear Winona, you like to work, don't you?"

"I like to be with you," she answered.

Chapter Sixteen

Ho-Chunk Full Moon Ceremony

During the last moon of October 1859, many native people began to gather. This included Fox, and Sauk, and Ho-Chunk. Every day two or three new faces would be seen around the countryside and in Amherst. When Ole entered Oshida's camp one morning, he saw many new wigwams. Some structures were not like the Ho-Chunk wigwams. He asked one of the boys, "How come many strange Indians are here?"

"We have big feasts come full moon. You come?"

"Sure, I'll come, but if there are too many Indians, soldiers will come from Fort Howard. I am worried for you."

"Not many come, just few Fox and Sauk for holiday. Yellow Thunder come to see your mother. Spotted Deer come. Otwana, White Fang, Wahopekau, come from white school. All come, big feast. You come?"

"Sure, I'll come. Aspun, too?"

"No, Aspun no come. You come."

"Sure, I'll be there. When is it? Sunday?"

"No Sunday." He counted on his fingers and held up three of them. "Three days, full moon, big moon."

Two days later, Wahopekau, Spotted Deer, Otwana, and White Fang came to call on Kisti and her family and invited her and Ole and Hendrick to the big feast.

Winona, who was standing beside Kisti and Ole, sidled up to Ole and said, "You wear Indian shirt?"

"Yes, I will wear it. Mom, will you wear your beads?"

When the day of the full moon arrived, Kisti, Ole, and Hendrick were dressed in their best native clothes. Ole, in his doeskin shirt, Kisti wearing her beaded necklaces, doeskin dress, and moccasins, and Hendrick with his moccasins and the doeskin shirt made for him in the first year of their settlement. The three of them entered the camp together. They greeted Wahopekau with White Fang, and Otwana with Spotted Deer. Yellow Thunder, seated with great dignity and wisdom, was the Chief of all of them who were present. The men wore headdresses, and the women were dressed in doeskin dresses with beaded necks.

Wahopekau, who kissed her, greeted Kisti with unreserved affection. White Fang shook hands with her, as did Spotted Deer. Yellow Thunder rose to his feet and extended his hand, which was unheard of at their Native gatherings. Chief Yellow Thunder usually nodded in acknowledgement to his white guests, but rarely gave anyone such a warm reception as he did Kisti.

Otwana showed the effects of the short sojourn at the Eastern school among the whites. She was well groomed, wearing her doeskin dress, with her hair in two long braids, and she moved with a grace that equaled that of Wahopekau. Her beauty and charming manner made Kisti very proud of her. These people seemed less like strangers to the little party of visitors than some of their own people.

The surprise of the evening was when Frank DuBey came into camp with Twigg and Red Moon, looking well and healthy. Red Moon timidly approached Kisti. Sensing her embarrassment, Kisti quickly stepped forward and took both her hands. "Red Moon, how glad I am to see you. And Mr. DuBey, it is indeed a treat to see you, too."

Shaking hands with Kisti, Hendrick and Ole, DuBey said. "I hear that you are well settled and the community is thriving. Amherst has become quite a town. These people in the native community tell me that you are following the policy that you started out with to be friendly toward Indians and it is evidently paying off, like I told you it would."

"Mr. DuBey, tell me about yourself. Where have you been all this time? Wahopekau said that you were in the Dakota and Minnesota territories," Kisti said.

"Yes, there has been quite some trouble there. I will tell you all about it later. Tonight, you will hear many Indian speeches and you will be impressed by what great orators these people are. By the time we are through, which will be almost morning, you will know more about them and the state of affairs than you ever dreamed you would."

"Frank, it is wonderful to have you back in our community to help us understand what we can do, and what we need to leave to the tribes," Hendrick said.

"Hendrick, you are doing fine without me! I want to congratulate you on your oversight of the school and road program. Judge Cate told the command at Fort Howard that you and your people here have the situation under better control than anywhere in the state. Your policy to leave these people alone and help them when you can is the wisest one and the least complicated. There is some concern about this gathering from the military. I maneuvered things to give me an opportunity to be here as an observer, and I am happy to see that it is working for all the people."

"Why should they be concerned about this event?" asked Hendrick. "This is a friendly feast of the Medicine Dance."

"Yes, but it is a treaty violation. There are Sauks, Foxes, Oneidas, Menominees, Stockbridges, and Ho-Chunks, here. As you know, there is to be no assembly of the tribes as we see here. They are supposed to stay on their reservations in Iowa. Yellow Thunder came back, as did others. The Sioux are their natural enemies, and the Menominees and other tribes had a field day massacring them. So since then, the powers that be have taken a little softer view of their plight.

"The records of battles can be dangerous to the U.S. Army. Those who influence Indian affairs in Washington that go by the biased records of the uprising twenty to thirty years ago have no idea of the present state of affairs. I will say that the army has done a commendable job in many instances. They are trying to do the right thing, but they are not political in their thinking, only realistic as far as security is concerned."

"We all thank heaven for you, Frank DuBey. I would like to see you in charge of these affairs in Washington!" Hendrick said.

"Thank you, Hendrick. I have been called to Washington on two occasions upon the suggestion of General Harney and was received with polite attention by President Buchanan. While some of the harsher policies have been modified to a great degree, the President is from the East and has the New Englander's perspective. I do believe that if he were properly informed, he would do something more constructive about this matter."

"But who advises him on this situation?"

"Well, there are several advisors. There is pressure on the President to secure private gain for those who want to make money off the land. Rarely are the Indian's interests at heart. They have no representative to protect their interests. Those who wish to exploit the Indians have plenty of representation and they often present a picture in Washington that is neither factual nor has any element of truth in it but is purely designed to take advantage of the Indians' holdings and get him out of the way."

"But what can we do about it, Frank?" Kisti asked.

"Well, I wish I knew for sure. I have thought about it quite a lot. It would help if we had strong representation from this area besides those with lumber and mining interests. We could try to elect a president from this part of the country. Yes, and that is a distinct possibility with some representatives from Illinois and Wisconsin.

"Oh, look they are moving the drum to the center of the circle. The moon is beginning to rise. Let us be seated while the Medicine man greets the moon and offers up the Indian's prayer. It is very sacred time for them.

"The Chief will soon announce the opening of the Hitch-E-A-Yum in Chippewa, that is the Medicine Dance. It is a far cry from the Sioux version, I can tell you. Wha-kau-zee-kau is

Yellow Thunder's official Indian name and he is official chief of this ceremony. Some of the lesser chiefs are here according to rank. The important chief next to him will be at his right. Oshida, the host Chief, will be at the left. Hendrick, you are to be the Important Chief and be seated next to him. He has the privilege to name them."

Kisti looked at Hendrick and smiled with pride. "You have done so much, dear Hendrick, and so quietly."

"You are the key to it, Kisti," Hendrick replied.

The drummers seated themselves around the mother drum in the center of the large circle. Some of them kneeled and others sat on logs around the drum as they pounded in a steady heart rhythm together. Each of the men took turns beating the drum when his turn came. The moon was rising in the east to the rhythmic cadence of the drums. As Chief Waukauseekau, Yellow Thunder, stood up and extended his arms towards the rising moon, the pounding of the drum softened and he began the prayer. The feathers of his headdress touched the ground as he raised his face towards the sky. Frank translated the prayer from Ho-Chunk to English for Ole, Kisti, and Hendrick.

"Oh, Great Spirit, the same now as in ancient times, descend upon us from thy habitation, which we are permitted to see in the reflection of the moon. Dwell among us with thy presence and grace our festivities with thy presence as we bring honor to those whom we would have you bless and protect. We wish to have them as one of us. Those who, through the example set forth by thy son Jesus, have merited our confidence, our trust, and our love, and we look towards thee for the sanction of our act. Grace this occasion with thy presence, we offer this prayer in the name of all the tribes assembled here, Amen."

The drumming increased its volume. Kisti, sitting beside DuBey, whispered to him, 'That was a Christian prayer, spoken with such beautiful words and language. I am truly amazed."

"Waukauseekau is a zealous Christian. He embraced Christianity after the Fort Dearborn massacre. When his trusted friend was killed by some of his own men, his remorse was so great that he turned to one of the priests and took instructions. He has been uncompromising in his religion ever since. He has been quite an influence among the tribes, and I might add, he has influenced some of the whites too. Your kindness toward his people has strengthened his resolve for peace with the whites. If there were any doubts, you surely dispelled them forever with what you did for his brother's son and Red Moon, and by the way you treated Oshida's group."

Oshida came forward and extended his hand to Hendrick. "Welcome. We wish you to take your place among our Chiefs."

"I-I..." Hendrick began to decline the honor, but a jab in the ribs from Kisti and a punch in the back from DuBey kept him silent. With all the dignity he could muster, Hendrick was presented to Waukauseekau-Yellow Thunder, who, standing erect, extended his hand. Hendrick, a product of generations of military breeding, instinctively responded with a click of his heels, snapped to attention, saluted sharply, and extended his hand.

DuBey whispered to Kisti, "That did him no harm here. Look at the other Chiefs."

A murmur of approval was heard throughout the assembly. "The Ho-Chunk nation, 'the people of the sacred voice' are proud to welcome you."

Hendrick bowed politely. "The great pride is mine to be welcomed by the eminent Ho-Chunk nation and their illustrious Chief Waukauseekau."

"Wonderful," whispered DuBey. "Couldn't be better."

A headdress of the Ho-Chunks was placed upon Hendrick's head by two of the lesser chiefs and he took his seat of honor beside the Big Chief Yellow Thunder. Frank DuBey was seated near Hendrick.

The Mother drum was now beating loudly and steadily at a rapid pace. Everyone sat in a semicircle opposite the chiefs to complete the circle.

Yellow Thunder rose and addressed the assemblage. Beginning with Hendrick, he called everyone by name, introducing each person after he motioned for them to stand; the Chief announced the names and the tribes they represented. There was enthusiastic recognition from the tribes with chanting and words of praise as each one of them stood and bowed.

"Noble chiefs, friends of the Ho-Chunk, many winters and summers have passed over the head of Waukauseekau, and this could well be the last time I will address you as your chief. Soon they will call for me and say, 'Waukauseekau, take your blanket, your pipe, and your headdress of eagle feathers. Give the sacred bundle to your son.' We are going on a long journey to a pow-wow with other great chiefs of all the tribes, the Great White Fathers of long ago, and the great chiefs from across the big waters. We will go to Supreme Council Lodge where we will discuss the fate of all people. There all of the records will be told, there we will see our mistakes, our wrongs, and what we have done right. So before I go, I want to leave with you my council and review my actions before you so it will appear in the record that I said it to you while I am still Chief. I wish to be judged by what I say tonight. I will speak in Ho-Chunk then English so all of you will understand what I am saying.

"I have addressed you before with the council of war while I have fought with my many brothers, with the Foxes and Sauks, with the nations of the Iroquois. Many winters ago, I changed my council because it gave the wrong advice. I have seen what it has done for us as a people and I can see, and so can you, that there is another way rather than being without women, without husbands, and without fathers, without food, with cold winters, without covers and shelters for our bodies.

"I remember the many promises of the white man to the Indian that have been broken. I have seen our people taken from their homes and moved to new grounds which had no hunting, no fishing, no shelters, and many of our people became sick and died, sick in the heart from being lied to and sick in the heart with longing for our ancient family lands, and sick in the body because we were sick in the heart. And many are not here tonight for they died because of this.

"But in spite of all this, I bear nothing in my heart against the white people. I have seen those with forked tongues, who have told us one thing and done the other. I have seen them with stone hearts mistreat our people. I have also seen among my brethren many scalps with golden flowing hair, many with flowing black hair, and many with red hair, and the scalps of children that did not fight the Indians. I have seen babies in arms taken from frightened mothers and swung by their feet and their heads dashed against stones. I have seen as much lying and cheating among our own people with forked tongues making false promises as white men.

"So we are not to blame, all of us, they are not to blame, all of them. So it must be that we live with each other in friendship and trust and then we will have all we need. The Great Spirit, the maker of all things, has made enough for everyone and there is plenty. He is too wise to make more people than he can provide for.

"We have learned to change our ways. We don't like to do this, but maybe it is His will that we change. We have met together tonight to give honor to a true example of what I say. You have heard what occurred at William's Crossing when my daughter was attacked. That white renegade was an evil man. You have heard how Wahopekau and White Fang escaped and how he defended his sister. You have heard how her baby was almost dead and how a white mother nursed him at her own breast and saved the child and mother's life, when there was danger to herself. You have heard how she saved the life of Red Moon, and how many times she has shared food here with Oshida's people and how her son had shared the fruits of the hunt with these people like brothers and this Chief has made it possible to let them live here in peace even though they were forcibly moved against their will.

"We want to do these people honor tonight, we want to make them one with our people. We have many witnesses to hear of these things they have done, and we will hear them before you will decide in this council to honor them with us.

"Now, I want to say that in my heart there is a peace. I

know that my Great Spirit, whom I call Jesus Christ, wishes me to do this, and I know that it is His will. This is my last council and advice to you. Let us learn to live with the white man. Learn to live their way and meet them as brothers and sisters. I am glad to say this."

With that, he sat down. Silence prevailed for a long time afterwards. The drumming had died down until scarcely audible. Soon the tall imposing figure of Oshida rose from the semicircle. "We will hear witnesses, now."

Wahopekau came forward. "Women are never heard before men in council, but I feel I have a right to bear witness to what has been so truly said."

She told about that awful night; the narrow escape, the horror that her baby was dying, the exhaustion, and how Ruudine and Kisti had found them and nursed the baby back to health and hid them in the wagon until they were safe to leave. She told them that Kisti was like a mother, so kind, with her heart filled with love and compassion for all the native people. Wahopekau continued in the Ho-Chunk tongue. She said that she wanted the Indians to make an exception and have Kisti be known as the Mother of the Ho-Chunks.

Others followed with their testimony . . . White Fang, Spotted Deer, Otwana and Winona. Oshida asked whether others wanted to speak. Frank DuBey rose and spoke to them in the Ho-Chunk tongue and wound up in English; he talked about how they had met, and praised Ole's courage and Kisti's compassion, and that she had threatened to return home when she saw the things that were done to the Native people. He told them the story about Ole and the Coles.

Red Moon followed, speaking in the Sauk Language. As she was talking, she went over and drew Kisti to her feet; then she walked gracefully into the circle with her arm around Kisti. When she had finished, she led Kisti back to her place.

The testimonies were finally over. Some of the other chiefs made speeches and spoke proudly of their people's experiences. Two chiefs withdrew many scalps from under their blankets and said they wished to bury them. One of them said,

"They burn in my hands and they cry out at me when I sleep. I can no longer kill, I want to be free."

So, after the vote was taken with sticks, they claimed Ole, Kisti, and Hendrick into the tribe, and made Kisti, "Mother of the Ho-Chunk," as Wahopekau had suggested.

Ole was brought before the fire. Oshida's son was brought next to Ole. They were turned face to face. Yellow Thunder approached Ole, and said, "My son, you are about to be made a true blood brother of all the Winnebagos. Is this your wish?"

Ole bowed his head. "It is a great honor to be a brother to the Ho-Chunks."

"Put your hand on his shoulder."

Ole put his right hand on the boy's shoulder.

"Now you do the same."

The young Oshida put his right hand on Ole's left shoulder. Yellow Thunder bared Ole's left arm, drew his knife, and deftly made a small incision on his forearm. He did likewise on the Indian's arm. Ole's arm was placed diagonally across the Indian's chest and the Indian's arm placed across Ole's chest so that the wounds were touching and the blood of the two boys mixed. The boys tightened their embrace with the other arm, while Yellow Thunder chanted the old blood brother ritual in the Ho-Chunk tongue. The drumming grew louder, and the boys remained embraced as everyone in the circle gathered around them chanting Ee-yi-ee-yi-ooo-yi-oo-yi, over and over again. When the drumming faded with a signal from Yellow Thunder, the tribal people backed away and broke up the circle and the dancers returned to their place in a widened circle.

Yellow Thunder came towards the two boys and separating them, he said, "The blood of the candidates has now been merged, Ole is now one of us by blood."

A cheer went up from the assemblage and he called to Oshida to bring forth the sacred bundle, which was wrapped in the finest doeskin with beautiful beadwork and the insignia of the ancient Winnebago tribe, and had many strings of wampum and beaded streamers.

Yellow Thunder brought the sacred bundle to Hendrick

and motioned for him to stand. He told Hendrick before the gathering that this was the sacred bundle of the Ho-Chunk containing all the sacred symbols of the tribe.

"It has been in our possession for centuries and has been handed down for many generations from one chief to another. In order to be a true and trusted brother of the Ho-Chunk and one of us, it must be that at this time when necessary this symbol of authority may be entrusted to you. This bundle holds the spirit and the secrets of all the Winnebago nation and its friends, which includes the Pottawatomies, the Sauks, the Foxes, the Kickapoos, the Stockbridge-Munsee, Mohicans, the Oshidas, the Chippewas, and all the other tribes of our great nation. When holding this bundle you will feel your responsibility for the welfare and wise rule and council of all these tribes that constitute the great Winnebago nation."

The mother drum began to beat more loudly as Hendrick closed his eyes and he felt the power in the bundle. Tears fell down his face and he humbly bowed his head. The drummers beat more gently.

"Now, we want you to place it in the hands of the mother of the candidate. Wahopekau came over and took Kisti by the arm and led her before Hendrick and he placed the sacred bundle carefully in her arms. Kisti felt the power and vibration of the prayers in the bundle, and she held it like a sacred newborn child. The drummers pounded loudly as she held it. Then the drumming faded, and she turned towards Yellow Thunder, who continued.

"This is to show and demonstrate that this family is united and that they have been brought into the Winnebago tribe and that she has been entrusted with the sacred bundle. She, in turn, will give it to her young son, the newly made brother."

Kisti turned to Ole and placed it gently in his arms. She planted a firm kiss on his cheek. Then she kissed the forehead of Oshida's young son who was inducted with Ole. Ole looked at his mother with widened eyes, feeling the vibration of the bundle, and held it carefully, as his mother had done. The drummers beat the Mother Drum more loudly.

A murmur of approval went around the assemblage and the women clapped their hands and chanted their approval. Yellow Thunder raised his hand to the drummers, and they faded into a gentle drumbeat. He approached Ole and commanded him to raise his right hand to Heaven and to take the following oath:

"I, who from this point on, will be recognized as Tuan, Tuan of the Ho-Chunk, make this promise before all chiefs that I will, when entrusted to me, protect this bundle with my very life. I am now a true Winnebago. You have seen my blood spilled in Winnebago cause and mingled with Winnebago blood. From this point forward, I am a trusted member of this tribe. I and my family will always protect your people."

The assemblage returned to their places when the ceremony for Kisti began. Ole was asked to bring her and the bundle before the Chiefs. Yellow Thunder received the bundle from Ole and made a long and touching speech.

"Women are part of the council, as they support their husband's decisions. We love our women, and honor what they do for our tribe. We respect them for their wisdom, and we love the mothers of our children, and take care of them and protect them.

"On this special occasion this evening, you have all heard the testimony of Wahopekau and Red Moon, and of Otwana and Winona. You heard Spotted Deer and the man Twigg corroborate the testimony of these women along with Frank DuBey. Tonight was a sacred occasion in the Ho-Chunk history, as they now decided unanimously among the representatives of the various branches of the Ho-Chunk nation that some of the acts spoke for themselves and it was because of this true revelation of the character that was so precious to the Winnebagos, upon which they depended so much, that they decided among the members of the council that an exception was to be made and heroism in women was to be recognized and that the greatest honor could happen to any Ho-Chunk woman. They will be named the Mother of the Ho-Chunk.

"For Kisti was a true mother indeed. She had mothered

and suckled a Winnebago infant of the chief's house, which was evidence enough. She had mothered a daughter of the Foxes and brought her back to life through her care. She had nursed in sickness Ho-Chunk women and their children. There was ample evidence under many circumstances that her heart was truly for the Native people and the Ho-Chunk people. She had been heard to defend the Indian people to many white people. She had threatened to leave rather than to be a party to broken treaties. All of these virtues sum up to the ideal of the Ho-Chunk character and they wished to make her the official Mother of the Ho-Chunks.

"We see by the wampum around your neck that you have been given the honor of the Sauks, the Pottawatomies, and the Fox Indians. At this point, I wish to add the further insignia of the Ho-Chunk tribe, which has been made by the women of this nation in honor of this occasion. Wahopekau and Red Moon will confer this honor. From now on you are our Mama Manitou, meaning Spirit Mother."

Wahopekau and Red Moon came to Kisti and placed a beaded stole around her shoulders containing all the sacred symbols of the Ho-Chunk nation, including the Thunderbird, the Sunburst, and several others of the Winnebago, Pottawatomi, Sauk, and Fox insignias. As they did so, they kissed Kisti's forehead and knelt before her. Each of them took one of her hands and placed it upon their heads.

The drum began booming loudly once again. As its volume grew louder, the assemblage of people rose to their feet, and the women clapped their hands, and the men responded with, "How, How." The excitement increased until it became a tumultuous welcome. Hendrick and Kisti were standing in the middle of the circle with their arms around Ole. Hendrick looked very grave and dignified in his Winnebago headdress. Ole stood with his eyes on the ground, overwhelmed by the honor. Kisti looked about her with a big smile and tears streaming down her cheeks. They all came and shook hands very graciously with the family as the drummers began to sing with the drum a song of honor.

Everyone was happy and filled with good will. Soon the ceremony was closed with a prayer of gratitude by Yellow Thunder, and food was brought out and a great feast began.

Frank DuBey came over and said to Kisti, Hendrick and Ole, "I am very, very proud to have witnessed such a wonderful ceremony."

There was much talking, and games were played. There was a game known among the children as Moccasin in which four moccasins were placed together with a shiny little object inside one of them; the children had to guess which moccasin had the object.

The feast proceeded, the dancing began, and there was much good will, talking and happiness until late into the evening. As Yellow Thunder grew weary and entered his wigwam, the rest of the people began to disappear into their wigwams and dome-like houses.

When morning light began to appear in the east, they all wended their way homeward. Kisti, Hendrick, and Ole walked together in gratitude and silence through the October autumn woods as the great honor bestowed upon them that evening had touched them all very deeply.

Chapter Seventeen

Growing Slavery Discussion and the County Fair Debacle

Hendrick's and Kisti's children were growing rapidly. Ole was almost fifteen that winter. He had grown so tall that he was able to do everything his father could do with working the farm and hunting. Randine, entering her thirteenth year, was still working for the Bancroft family, and visited home when she could. Eivind was six years old, and beginning to show interest in reading and playing with his two-year old sister. Synneva was still very small, but she was developing normally. Her tiny little hands and feet were like miniatures. Baby Thomas was a smiling and active babe. He was a chubby little fellow.

Eivind would disappear for hours at a time to explore the woods and visit little Hans. Often Anna and little Hans brought him back home. Winona continued to be a daily visitor and had made herself indispensable to the household by helping Grandmother Synneva with the cooking and taking care of the children. After bearing two babies in two years, Kisti's health had greatly improved, and she felt as strong as a horse. Hendrick was home that winter, and Ole and Aspun worked in the woods cutting down trees and gathering firewood for his family. They gained much experience with their native friends in the forests, as well as spending time tracking animals.

Hendrick felt that it was no longer fair to burden Ole with the farm work. He wanted his son to have the right to work out his own destiny, which he could not do since his father was away from home most of the time. Ole had been freed to work in the logging camp with Aspun that winter. Ole and

Aspun would return home from the camp to visit their families over the holidays.

With the new baby, Hendrick wanted Kisti to be able to stay indoors with the children and not have to do any outdoor work. So even though she urged her husband to take advantage of employment, he remained at home to take care of the animals and the crop storage and look after his family.

This gave Hendrick more time for reading as well. He was a loyal subscriber to Mr. Medill's Tribune, and although the newspaper arrived several days late, he consumed every word of it. He was well informed on the affairs of the country. In fact, many asked his opinion on various issues, especially during the past election in 1856. Now that they were nearing another election in 1860, he was more sought after than ever for his knowledge and opinions. Slavery was becoming a huge issue in the South and this coming election concerned Hendrick and others a great deal.

The abolition of slavery in the South impacted the southern plantation owners. To them it was an economic disaster imposed by the people of the north. This, along with the increase in immigration and the rapid changes underway, worsened the economic issue. There was a panic in the economy created in part by the expansion of the railroads, and new lands opening up so fast. And, of course, the gold rush ten years before had brought many more people to the United States. Unemployment was rampant. People began selling their properties, some for less than half of the purchase price.

Families in the churches had divergent opinions about slavery, and neighbors turned against neighbors. Then the Supreme Court handed down the Dredd-Scott decision, which denied Dredd-Scott and his wife citizenship and the freedom to which they were entitled; after their legal owner died, slavery had extended into the new territories.

Kisti and Hendrick had enough money put aside and they had crops and some cows to sell. Their neighbor, Jenns, smelling trouble, made the most of the economic situation. He allied himself with the pro-slavery people and took advantage of people by buying items for little money, to resell them in larger towns to make more money. He cheated people out of their money when he could, especially if he knew their desperation. He made a general nuisance of himself everywhere he went.

The panic in the economy was on everyone's mind, with all the financial crashes and failures during that time. As the season turned into spring again, the forest was fast disappearing as people cut down trees to build new homes. Knute's house was now visible to the south of the Lysne's, and the Blaskys' was visible to the north. The woods were reduced by half that separated Mari's house from Kisti's. It seemed like their whole community was emerging out of the forest.

The Indian agents were making surveys to accede to the wishes of the Ho-Chunk, who refused their proposed removal to Iowa and Minnesota. Steps were being made to include them on several tracts of land deeded for permanent possession.

During the 1860 Portage County Fair, Hendrick and Kisti reunited with friends from far and wide that they had not seen for a long time. The fair was a huge success, as it was part of the harvest festival and an extension of the Fourth of July celebration. Those exhibiting their cattle gained credibility and status in the community with their livestock. Johan exhibited two of his cows and a calf, and the cows were so lovely and the calf so active and fit, he would easily sell the future offspring.

The biggest events of the fair were the parade and the horse races that followed. Horses were not too numerous, as oxen were used for farming. That year everyone secretly resolved to add a horse to their livestock before too long.

At the County Fair event, everyone was talking about two strange gentlemen who were making inspiring speeches about the wonderful growth of the country. The talked about the wealth from the lumber industry, and the farm produce, as well as the mines that produced minerals. Few people had heard about the mines, as they were not found in Wisconsin as much as in other states. The strangers spoke eloquently about the cities and how fast they were growing, which meant an increased demand for food. This inspired many of the farmers.

They pointed out that the chief bottleneck to progress was the lack of transportation and emphasized the need to extend the railroads. It was operating from Milwaukee to Horicon, and they were going to extend it from that point to St. Anthony Falls, through Amherst and Plover to the Mississippi at the DuBey Falls.

The fair goers were treated to visions of wealth when they saw how rail lines could distribute their produce much more efficiently. The speakers used a huge map to outline the route of the new Milwaukee and Horicon line. One of the men explained things, while the other man wrote down the names of those who were interested in investing in a railroad fortune. Many names were recorded on the stranger's list that day. The men said that the next week they would meet them at Plover, where the actual stock certificates would be delivered, and money exchanged. In the meantime, they would call on any other fortunate folks who had the vision and foresight to put their money in the country's assured future, according to their talk.

Mr. Bancroft heard about this investment scheme that the two men were selling. He sent Randine home on an emergency errand to tell her family and their friends not to be in a hurry to invest in this enterprise. As soon as the Milwaukee and Horicon Railroad people found out about these crooks taking advantage of its name, they sent their representatives into the territory to put them in jail. But when they arrived on the scene the men had fled for parts unknown, and many people were left empty handed with nothing but their dreams of wealth.

Hendrick, Anders, Johan, and Boes were safe, but the Blaskys and Jenns had taken the bait. No one knew how much, but Jenns was fit to be tied and took it out on Anna and poor little Hans.

The excitement of the Fair and the big swindle had diverted the attention of the community away from national affairs. Those who had lost money were really in a bad way. Although those who invested were pitied, many felt their circumstances were brought about by their own greed and stupidity.

The papers were diligent in reporting the financial panic. In his Tribune editorials Mr. Medill advised taking a cautionary course, citing some of the safeguards needed to prevent such a thing from happening again. As the drama of the swindle and the fun at the fair started to die down, the national stress began to be felt.

Chapter Eighteen

Uncle Tom's Cabin, John Brown and Citizenship

Kisti and Hedrick saw the play Uncle Tom's Cabin with Mari and Anders at a theater in Scandinavia, Wisconsin. Harriet Beecher Stowe's novel was showing throughout the country as a stage play. It became almost a patriotic duty to attend the play and weep for the misfortune of little Eva. The play had captured the American people's minds and hearts, and many clergymen felt called to preach from the pulpit about the issues of slavery.

Hendrick and Kisti opposed slavery just as they opposed the mistreatment of Native Americans. They could see little difference between the treatment of the slaves in the South and the way white people treated the Indians in the North.

One Sunday morning in church, the minister became vehement about slavery and the issues around the Dredd-Scott decision, and he brought up Uncle Tom's Cabin.

Hendrick rose from his seat and said, "While slavery is wrong, that doesn't mean our pastor is expounding right versus wrong. This is a time for sober reflection. Let's look at our own doorstep and how we treat the Indian people before we concern ourselves with the plight of the Negroes.

"At least the Negros in the South have shelter and crops they raise for plantation owners, and one could find them alive in the morning. But some of our abused native people have been found without shelter and frozen stiff in the morning.

"God knows no difference between the Negro, the Indian, and European Americans. Therefore, let the white people living among the Negroes straighten out their problems, and let those of us living among the Native people see to our responsibility here. Can we look at the speck of sawdust in our brother's eye but ignore the log in our own eye?"

Hendrick had never made such a speech, and some of the congregation broke with church decorum and applauded.

The pastor was about to respond to Hendrick, but Arund Brekke, at whose home the service was being held that day, got up and said, "We have an unwritten rule which states that there should be no show of pleasure or displeasure in the church, and I feel that a breach with secular affairs such as politics is just as harmful. We are in hard times, and I am sure that Hendrick spoke from his heart. I agree with him. But I can also see where we cannot afford to have this church split because we happen to differ in our opinions.

"I propose that we pray and each one of us ask ourselves for guidance and act upon it. If we want to discuss politics, let us meet outside the church and talk about these questions. But let us come to church to worship—not to condemn."

He received applause from most of the congregation and the minister thanked him and Hendrick, and then he continued to speak from the bible, not about the sins of slavery.

Many meetings and forums were held after Brekke made his statement that day. In community discussions about the declining economy, which was not as strong as the year before, some blamed the rich, some blamed the government, some blamed the slave owners, and other blamed the Indians. They came to see that the loss of trust among neighbors could be a problem for the whole community unless they came together as they had done since they settled in Amherst.

When the Fugitive Slave Act 1850 was brought up as an issue in Wisconsin, Hendrick and Arund Brekke were chosen by the towns of Amherst and Scandinavia as representatives to go to Madison and present a petition registering an unqualified 'no' to the legislation. Wisconsin was the first state to do so. Politics was the topic of the day and the forthcoming political convention in Chicago was watched with tremendous interest.

By autumn of 1860 the panic of the economy was nearing an end. Lumbering had resumed in the forests north of Amherst and the country was demonstrating a new vigor. Ole and Aspun were back in the woods working for the lumber mill. The gristmill at Amherst and Jerome Nelson's Mill were back in business and life was resuming its brisk tempo.

More people arrived in the area to take possession of new lands and new stores began to appear. There were still rumors that the railroad would come that way, but the subject was taboo in the presence of those who were stung by the Horicon fiasco.

Hendrick had taken his final oath of allegiance, along with the rest of his family, and they were now naturalized American citizens. Several other people in the community had received their citizenship at the same time—Mari and Anders, along with the Boes and Roes. Reverend Brandt held a special service for them in Scandinavia. It was such a notable event that there was a column about it in the Milwaukee newspaper.

At the next service, Rev. Brandt quoted from Ephesians 2:19: "Now therefore ye are no more strangers and foreigners, but fellow citizens with the saints, and of the household of God." The reverend said this text applied to the United States as 'One nation, under God'. When he had finished, they were a proud group, feeling even more dedicated to God and country. American citizenship felt like a brotherhood to them. Their neighbor's rights were of paramount importance, and they vowed to uphold those rights with all their worldly goods, as God gave them strength.

Hendrick and Johan and some of the others sat together after church and discussed the slavery question, which was the chief topic of most conversations. However, they felt that the issue would be resolved. The country had grown and was being settled from ocean to ocean. Texas was in the Union, and Hendrick was thrilled when he read what Sam Houston had to say about his new state regarding the Indian treaties; he would not withstand any violation of these treaties in Texas.

Stephen Douglas and Abraham Lincoln were debating the slavery issue and Lincoln made a statement that everyone would remember: "I hate slavery. It enables the enemies of our free institutions to taunt us as hypocrites and causes our real friends of freedom to doubt our sincerity; because it forces so many good men among ourselves into open war with the very principles of civil liberty." He added, "The holders of slaves are not to blame; they are just what we would be in their situation."

This statement was repeated over and over at every meeting Hendrick and Nils attended. As the election was nearing, John Brown, the anti-slavery man who attacked those supporting slavery, was again in the news. He had already committed some crimes in Kansas that upset people, but when he seized the arsenal at Harper's Ferry to free slaves, the government was angry with him and the whole slavery question could not be ignored. Most of the folks thought he was crazy. Yet he was admired greatly for his composure at his trial and subsequent hanging. John Brown left a sober impression on Hendrick and Nils and most of the men who met regularly to discuss the national issues.

The fanatics were at work on both sides of the slavery question. Secession became a threating word, especially when whiskey was around, and arguments over secession led to serious fights.

By the autumn of 1860, plans for secession were gaining support, and on October 25, 1860, at a meeting of South Carolina politicians, it was unanimously decided that in the case that Lincoln be elected president, their state would secede from the Union. The secessionist parties in the South were very vocal, which contributed to the rupture of relations between the North and the South. Hendrick and his friends were concerned that there would soon be a war if states began to secede from the Union.

Chapter Nineteen

Kisti confronts Jenns

Ole and Aspun had finally realized their dreams; they were riding on the lumber rafts running down the river towards Prairie du Chien. The river was swollen from the spring thaw and the current was very swift. They were cold and hungry, and their wet clothes froze stiff many times during the journey. But it was a great adventure for both of them.

Thousands of logs made up the rafts that floated along the current. The task of guiding them through the intricate currents of the river, avoiding the ever-present outcroppings of rocks, submerged sand bars, and other hazards, required skill that few could master. Ole and Aspun were a perfect team. Their movements coordinated so perfectly that it was as if they were directed by one mind. Often, one of them would break into the other's train of thought and start conversing on that subject. They would laugh and marvel, "How did you know what I was thinking about?"

The young men heard fabulous stories coming out of California about the gold rush, and new settlements, and the promise of the wonderful golden west. Many tales came to them from itinerants they met on the river, and of course the stories were fascinating to growing boys. As they took off down the river, they dreamed of traveling, because to them a future in Wisconsin seemed dull.

That year, after they returned home and then went back up north into the woods together, they were talking about leaving for California. Winona heard about it. Then, when Ole was home visiting, she made an announcement that she would be going to the white man's school when the snows came. Ole was stunned; suddenly, he felt as though he did not want to leave and did not want her to leave either.

Anna occasionally came over to Kisti's and Hendrick's and brought Hans with her. She timed her visits for when Jenns was away. He would be gone for several days at a time and Anna never knew where he went. Someone said they saw him in Stephen's Point in a linen duster, wearing a tall hat and high boots with big heels to give him more height. All of it added to his peculiar appearance. He was a man of mystery to many, but he wasn't much of a mystery to Kisti. She despised him, and she thought Anna was a saint to tolerate him. Kisti suspected that he was abusing Hans. While Jenns never attempted to visit, when Kisti went to visit Anna and whenever Eivind was with Kisti, Jenns showed his resentment toward her.

Hendrick was silent on the subject of Jenn's abuse, and he spoke to Jenns courteously and tolerated him. But one day Jenns approached him about the forty acres that he still claimed was his. He said that he was prepared to buy it if he couldn't get it any other way. He was being very obnoxious to a group of men in Amherst where Hendrick had stopped in to buy some whiskey. Hendrick rarely drank, but he liked to offer his visitors a steaming hot toddy. Jenns saw Hendrick and approached him with an officious air and said, "I still have my eyes on that forty acres you took away from me!"

Hendrick controlled his temper and said quietly, "Jenns, you know that is not true. I was here long before you came and I have a legal deed for it based on the surveyor's map, and it is properly recorded with the county."

"Well," said Jenns, "It was a mistake in the papers. I am getting a lawyer in Plover!" He saw Hendrick's anger rising and said he would pay Hendrick a reasonable price for it, but he would get it by legal means regardless.

A few days later a letter came from a new attorney in Plover, saying that he was investigating the title on the land in the interest of his client, Jenns. He stated that there was a discrepancy in the surveyor's maps, and he was going to contest the title.

Hendrick went to Judge Cate, and they went over the deed. The Judge pronounced the papers in order and said that Hendrick had nothing to fear. The controversy was contrary to Hendrick's nature. In talking it over with Kisti one day, they decided that maybe they would let Jenns have the forty acres for Anna's sake. This went on until the following summer, and no deal had been made. When it came to asking a price there was no disposition on Jenns' part to pay Hendrick anything.

That summer, Kisti and Eivind were on their way to see Anna when they heard screams and the sounds of whipping. They ran ahead and came upon Jenns whipping his son Hans. He had on his linen duster and beaver hat and was on his way to town. Eivind grabbed Hans and pulled him away. He gave Jenns a push, and as he did, Jenns switched Eivind's legs. Jenn's hat fell off and Eivind grabbed it and ran into the bushes with Hans where they could still hear Jenns yelling and swearing at him.

The two little boys ran and ran, with Jenns screaming and cursing at them as he ran after them. When he came upon Kisti in the narrow path thick with hazel bushes, he stopped short.

"You seem to be in a hurry today, Herr Jenns," she said.

"Your ill-mannered little..." Jenns replied.

Kisti held her finger up. "Ah-ah-ah; careful what you say. You have been warned before. I came to talk to you about the land you covet, but there are some stipulations if you wish to have it. First, we will give you the land for the thirty pieces of silver you offered, but you will have to promise that you won't lay your hands upon Anna or Hans or mistreat either of them. If I hear of any mistreatment, I will go to Judge Cate and place you under restraint, and I will tell everyone about the trouble you were in in Denmark. I will say that you bought Anna to use as a slave and bring her here to America. And you will never get your citizenship because I will stand as a witness against you. People despise you now, but when they hear the truth, you will wish yourself a thousand miles away. So you are in a spot, my friend; you had best be good to save your own hide."

"Anna told you!" he ranted.

"Anna has never opened her mouth about it. I know that fine person well enough by now to know that she would never tell a soul about the arrangement because of Hans. She suffers your cruelty for his sake. But your past will probably catch up with you soon."

He became so panicky, Kisti felt sorry for him.

He trembled and cried, "Who are they, when did you see them? Where are they now?"

She had no idea that her chance remark would come so near the truth. She suddenly realized that she had hit upon the fear that was the dominating force in his life. Here was an advantage she could press for the good of Anna and Hans.

"Why don't you leave them provided for and go out west to find better land?"

He began to talk more calmly. "You are saying that just so you won't have to sell me the forty!"

"I will sell it to you now. You can leave them better provided for with the forty acres. Leave them the land and some money; this one man I know you wouldn't want to meet."

Jenns quivered, "Was there something wrong with his ear?"

"Yes, I believe there was a scar."

Jenns whimpered, "Where did he go? Please tell me, you must tell me!"

"Well, he had another man with him. He asked about you and I told him I didn't know you, but that there was someone down on the other side of Iola by that name."

He took Kisti's hand. "Oh, thank you, thank you. They went east, so I will go west. All I have here is seven dollars. I will leave Anna enough to get through the winter and I will be back for them next year. I will go look for new land; anywhere but here." With that he ran home.

Eivind and Hans were hiding behind a hazel bush watching the conversation between Jenns and Kisti, though they could not hear the words. Eivind thought, 'Oh no, he is blaming her for the hat!'

Silently he crawled ahead and motioned for Hans to follow. They stealthily crept between the bushes, keeping their heads low, until they came upon the cow path leading to the Lysne barn. They ran as fast as they could, Eivind with a death grip on the hat. Just as they were about to run to the barn, there stood Grandma in the door on her daily mission gathering eggs. Eivind quickly swung out of sight onto the little path to the outhouse. The door was open, so in he sprang, with Hans close behind him.

Meanwhile, a short time later, Jenns came back to Kisti with a carpetbag and was soon on his way out of town, without the hat. In its place, he wore a low crown russet derby with a rolled brim, the linen duster floating in the breeze behind him.

Grandma's curiosity was aroused by the strange behavior of the two boys, and she started walking down the path. In his panic, Eivind thrust the long narrow crown of the hat into the hole. It fit nicely, except for the brim. He quickly pulled down his pants and sat upon the brim. When Grandma opened the door and found Eivind sitting there, she gently closed the door and proceeded towards the house with her egg basket on her arm.

Kisti entered the yard. "Mother, have you seen the boys?"

"Yes. They are in the outhouse, and such goings on, I never did see. They came here running like the demons were after them, and when they saw me they ran into the outhouse. It looked as if they had Jenns' hat with them."

"Oh, Hans," Eivind cried, "We are in trouble! Here take down your pants and sit on your father's hat. I'll go and talk to Mama, then when she goes into the house, we will hide the hat in the bushes."

Eivind came out of the outhouse trying to appear nonchalant, humming a little tune. He was such a poor actor that Kisti caught him and hugged him.

"What is my little man trying to hide from his mommy?" she said. "And where is Hans?"

"He is on the throne."

"Where is Jenns' hat?"

"What hat?"

"Now, you wouldn't try to fool your momma, would you? Where is the hat? I will help you. We will bring it home and Hans won't get spanked for it. Where is it?"

"Hans is sitting on it."

"In the outhouse?" She tried to be stern with him, but she broke out laughing, and the hearty sound brought both Synnevas out to see what was so funny.

"Sweetheart, I knew you hated him, but a prank like this I never expected to see."

"Hans is only fooling, Mama. He is just sitting on it to hide it. I tried to chuck it down the hole, but it wouldn't go all the way. It got stuck, and I sat on it so Grandma wouldn't see it. When I heard you coming, I made Hans sit on it."

Kist laughed, "I only hope Hans is hiding the hat as you say, but I am mighty suspicious."

Opening the door, she saw Hans partially submerged in the huge crown of the hat. He wasn't sitting on it. He was in it. Hans had done what came naturally, as he was in the outhouse after all.

Eivind clenched his little fists and stamped his foot. "Hans, you shouldn't have pooped in it, you should have just sat on it!"

"I had to go!" Hans explained.

Kisti cleaned him up at the outhouse and took him home to Anna. She placed the hat in the compost pile behind the barn with some ashes in it from the fireplace.

That night when everyone was in bed, Kisti went to her Königs Garten in the clearing where she loved to go at night. As she sat upon her favorite tree stump, she reviewed the events of the day, and chided herself for her impulsiveness. Still, she had felt a force that she was incapable of restraining when she saw Jenns torturing little Hans; the emotion took control of her, and it was as if she was given the instructions to follow from within.

While she had not seen a man looking for Jenns, his reaction to her chance suggestion brought such a response that she was impelled to press it until he ran away. By doing this she may have brought peace to Anna, and surely to Hans, but was it right? She struggled with her conscience and decided to pray for guidance.

In her quiet reflection, Kisti realized she could not condemn herself for trying to protect Anna and Hans. She would do it again if she had to. She hoped that Jenns would never return. She resolved to approach Anna on the subject and have a clear understanding with her... or was that wise? Well, there is always guidance. "I will place this in God's hands, and let him handle it," she mused, as she watched the fleecy clouds uncover the moon.

Chapter Twenty

River Runners and Baby Thomas

As winter drew near, Ole and Aspun returned home from their first log drive seeming almost like two strangers. They had matured and were very self-reliant, and now they were looking for more fun and excitement. They were determined to go to California, but after further consideration, and several heart-to-heart talks with his mother in her favorite Königs Garten, Ole decided to spend another winter in the woods and proceed on the log drive to St. Louis in the spring.

It was the first anniversary of their induction into the Ho-Chunk tribe when Ole and Aspun paid a friendly call upon Oshida's people. Winona, who was like a daughter to Kisti, had matured into a charming young woman. Ole was the light of her life, and she loved Synneva and little Thomas with a deep devotion. When the time came for her to leave, it was like losing a member of the family. Ole saw much of her before she went away, and when she left, he was very silent. He went out alone to sit in his mother's Königs Garten. Kisti went out and saw him weeping. She felt it was what he needed to do, and so she left him alone.

Ole and Aspun liked going to dances in Iola, Scandinavia, or Amherst in the evening to pass the time. While Ole never appeared to have been drinking when he returned, Kisti noticed that sometimes his knuckles were red and swollen from fistfights. This concerned her, but she felt he had been defending something important to him. So she did not confront him. Instead she asked Hendrick to talk with him.

Shortly after Winona left for the white school, Kisti and Mari called upon Anna Marie one day, and in her outspoken manner, Mari said, "I have been waiting for you to tell us when you are expecting the big event. We want to help you, you know."

Anna Marie thanked them and said that it might be any day now. Sure enough, Johan soon came over to the Lysne's house and announced the arrival of their first-born son. He said they were going to call him Nels. The women of the community went to their house to welcome the newborn, and soon there was a baptism at church.

The new church in Scandinavia was the center of activity for the farming community and already it was proving to be too small. There was some discussion about enlarging it, but there was also talk of establishing and building a new church in the New Hope Township, not far from Amherst. Eight to ten miles away from the church was quite a distance, with oxen carts and some on horses. In the dead of winter, it became almost impossible for many to attend church as it was, and many felt that the young people's religious schooling was being neglected. The baptism of Nels became another reason why they wanted to build another new church built closer to their farms, so their children could be integrated into Lutheranism.

The news that was coming through the papers was very disturbing. It was the election year, and everyone felt that the country had reached a crossroads. Abraham Lincoln was nominated by the new Republican Party to be president.

As the summer approached, it was very hot and dry and some of the wells ran dry. Several of the farmers had to drive their cattle to the lake for water, and the water in the wells turned brackish and many people became ill.

In August, Kisti realized that she was pregnant again and would be due around the middle of February. She nevertheless carried water to the garden and tried to help the crops survive the intense summer heat and drought.

Little Thomas did not seem well when Kisti returned from the garden one day. Earlier that morning, she had brought him a small green pumpkin that had fallen off the vine to play with. When Synneva called to her mother in alarm, she discovered that he had eaten much of the raw green pulp. Synneva said she had made him vomit it up by putting her finger down his throat. But little Thomas was still very weak and doubled over.

That evening, Winona's mother Odina brought over some herbs to brew a tea for Thomas, and he threw up the tea. Oshida came to see the child, and when he looked at Thomas, he shook his head and went away. Other Indian people came and went through the night. Towards morning, Thomas died in Kisti's arms. Only a few days before, his face was round and so cherub-like, now it was pale and still.

Lars brought over a tiny casket he had made from a poplar tree. Kisti thought it beautiful. She rubbed her hand over the wood and thanked him. Mari and Anna Marie brought them food. Anna came with Hans and brought a beautiful little burial dress and material to line the coffin. The entire neighborhood came the following day, and the little coffin was loaded upon the wagon and the family began the weary trek walking behind the wagon down the dusty road to the Scandinavia Church Cemetery. There they lay to rest one of their own in the soil of the new country.

Kisti grieved silently, dry-eyed. She could not cry as she was so shocked by his death. Hendrick, also in shock, seemed frozen and said nothing. That night, Kisti went to her Königs Garten after the household was asleep and reflected on what had befallen her and her family in the last two days. She recalled that when she first became pregnant with Thomas, she didn't feel the usual thrill of excitement. She had carried him without any difficulty, and he was born without any pain to speak of, and he never had been any trouble at any time. He was always a sweet loving baby.

Now, here she was, a shell without emotion, unable to shed a single tear. She asked out loud, "Lord, why do I feel nothing? Why doesn't my mother-love for my little boy bring tears?"

Hendrick heard her prayer and went over and wrapped

his arms around her and began to sob. Finally, she broke down and found relief in crying together with her husband.

After the burial of her little brother, Randine went to Chicago with the Bancrofts. The stories she had brought home about the trains, the stores, the theatre, and other wonders were most interesting to her family. Mr. Bancroft had attended the political convention in Chicago where Lincoln was nominated for President. Bancroft had much to say when Hendrick called on him while at Plover.

After Thomas's burial, Aspun and Ole took their lumber rafts down the Mississippi all the way to St. Louis. They lost two men in the treacherous river, and later told some hair-raising stories of their adventures with log jams and collisions. They were thoroughly sold on working another season on the river. They went by train from St. Louis to Chicago and took the train to Madison. So, when they came back home for Christmas, there was a wonderful reunion. All the family came together, except for little Thomas.

The drought had taken its toll. There was food in storage, but it was not plentiful. The lumber industry was getting back into full swing and there was much business activity.

Lincoln was to be the new President of the United States; South Carolina had seceded from the Union and there would be other states to follow. Lincoln would not take office until March, and President Buchannan was undecided in everything he undertook. Many felt sorry for him, and others condemned him for not taking a stand either for or against the southern state withdrawals. He was playing a waiting game until Lincoln took over.

While everyone feared for the future, the folks in the neighborhood were bent on having a great Christmas season. There were almost daily gatherings at the homes that went on well past Three Kings Day, on January 6th, until January 20th. The celebrations were much like they had been in Norway through the winter. They talked, sang, ate, and danced. There was poker playing in the barn, too, but nobody said much about it.

There was always venison, Juleale, lefse, fattigmans, bakel, kringle, and other Norwegian delicacies that were part of the Julefest, and the graver problems were forgotten in the spirit of the holiday.

In February of 1861, several of the other states began to secede in rapid succession. Tension rose with each issue of the Chicago Tribune.

In the midst of the uncertain future, on February 14th, Kisti felt the pangs of labor and in the early morning hours, little Anna was born. Hans's mother Anna was present, and so was Mrs. Boe.

Part Three
The Civil War

Chapter Twenty-One

Enlistment

Ole and Aspun were back at work in the woods that spring, having postponed their trip to California until after the next log drive. They were well on their way down the Mississippi with a huge cargo of logs when the American Civil War began with Fort Sumter's destruction on April 12, 1861. The excitement had reached a feverish pitch when they arrived in St. Louis to unload their cargo. They took the train back to Chicago, where the city was buzzing with excitement, and they were tempted to answer Lincoln's call for 75,000 volunteers to suppress the rebellion of the Confederacy against the Union. However, they decided to go home first; if they were to fight in the war, they wanted to join with the Wisconsin boys.

On their way back home to Wisconsin, they took a train through Camp Randall in Madison where they saw many recruits from Wisconsin organizing cavalry, artillery, and sections of infantry. There was already a Corps of Engineers building the housing for soldiers. Ole and Aspun recognized some of the boys in uniform that they had worked with in the woods the year before.

The day following President Lincoln's call for volunteers, Governor Randall issued a proclamation to the people of Wisconsin telling them that the state had responded to Lincoln's call and invited its loyal citizens to offer their services to fight the war. They were asked to serve for three months.

Ole and Aspun were in favor of going, but Ole said, "We must talk to our folks first. I don't want anything they or I will regret later. In war somebody dies. If it is to be me, I want to let my mother and father have something to say about it. I am sure

I know what their answer will be, but I am their son, so I want their opinion. I want to say goodbye to them too."

On his return home, as usual, Hendrick and Ole didn't have much to say to each other. However, Ole and his mother went out to her Königs Garten and talked for a long time. He told her about the drive down the river and how they had lost some of the men off the raft. Then he told her about the women, both Indian and white, that had cooked for the men on rafts in the river harbors. The women had built fires on shore where the curve of the river stopped the flow of logs, and pitched tents near the huge mass of logs.

He told Kisti about a fight between two men over one of these women; one of the men got thrown overboard and was never seen again. He told her about the gambling and the prostitution in St. Louis and Chicago. He also told her about the soldiers amassing at Camp Randall. Then he broke the news to her that he and Aspun had decided to join up.

Kisti stroked his blond hair as he sat next to her and said,

"Ole, my son, you are the most precious child I have, as my first born and the product of a wonderful love. But I cannot hold you back, even though my heart cries out to never let you go. Our little Thomas lies out there buried in this land we have learned to love. Now, part of us is buried there with his little body, and we cannot be separated. My precious son, if you feel you must go, then I agree that you must go, for it is destiny that speaks to you. I would be interfering with providence if I let selfishness sway my judgment. Go my son. I will hold my head high because of you and I will see you in every waving flag. From now on, until I die, you and the flag are one and the same."

Ole buried his face in her lap and wept softly. "Mother, I haven't cried since I came to this country, and I am ashamed. I will do my crying now mother."

"Hush Ole, you talk like a child. Don't be ashamed of tears. Jesus wept too, you know, but neither one of us will weep when you go away. We will not even say goodbye, will we? You will be going off to do your task and I will be here doing mine.

You have a proud heritage my son. You have a strong military tradition to uphold."

"Did you ever wonder about your name, son? What it means?"

Ole scooted closer to her. "No, mother I did not. Is there more?"

"Well, it means light, or dawning. It means the same as Wahopekau, "The Glory of the Morning," though we are unromantic Vikings. Anyway, as you know, the Sognfjord enters Norway on its western coast on its way through the mountains. For centuries it provided a safe place for ships that were pursued, because if they could enter Sognfjord, they were usually safe. Not only because they beached their vessels and got lost in the mountains but because there were numerous lesser waterways where they could fight off their pursuers. Therefore, the chief defense of the whole Norwegian peninsula centered upon the Sognfjord. It was the key to all Norway."

"What does that history have to do with my name?" Ole asked.

"Well, your forebears were placed on the most important promontory lookout over the western sea. They were the sentinels who served to protect the approach to the Sognfjord, for this was the duty of the family living there. The first rays of the sun would reach there first, and in the valley and along the fjord the bright golden morning light would be seen there while the rest of the valley was still dark. This is where your name came from son. So now you know."

"Dawn of Light. That is a good name to have." Ole sat up more straightly and smiled.

"Yes, it is. During one of many wars, and our forebears were always fighting, Knut of Salve, as he was called, came with the thousands of Danes in 1027. He had amassed and trained an army and entered the Sognfjord. His reputation had spread all over Europe until he was the most dreaded sea chief of all time.

"Our people were the ones to watch out for enemy ships and spotted him. The Lysne family at that time consisted of

Gudmund, his wife Bryta, and their two boys, ten and twelve. Bryta alerted her sister-in-law, Randi, with a blast of her trumpet and signals of fire. This was related to the other signal stations and Gudmund rode to the north to summon the aid of "Knut-i-aaska" in Årdal, who had their ships at Ulvik. Then the messages were relayed to Alf of Brekke and Aug of Lasse, who were at Vik and Hermanskiv. There, men battled Knut of Salve, and eventually vanquished him and broke his power; but it was a long and fearful fight.

"While Bryta waved her signal flags, the men of Salve ran her through with their spears. They were taking her body when Gudmund appeared and fought a score of men to prevent the defiling of her body. His war ax was taken from him, but his huge sword, "Storeesverdet," accounted for twenty of the deaths of Slave's warriors. The heroism of Bryta and Gudmund is the subject of pride as far as you and I are concerned. They sacrificed their lives to save our ancestors.

"The two boys were saved, because they remained hidden. The burial place was 'Steinhaugen,' which became a shrine for Leardal, and for our people in particular. 'Storesverdet' has been handed down and as far as I know, it is still in its accustomed place above the mantle in Storestua.

"Stein Haugen was erected in their memory and built around their bodies in the upright position, an honor accorded only to the most deserving. Their names were inscribed in blood on goatskins that they were wrapped in by the male members of your family who has taken the vow to defend our families. The Storesverdet was thrust into the ground before the altar at Stein Haugen. The vows were mainly taken to remain loyal to the traditions of Bryta and Gudmund, and serve truth and right, with their courage as an example.

"It is a beautiful and impressive ceremony performed at midnight on Midsummers Day following confirmations. The vows have been changed from loyalty to Odin and Thor to loyalty to the ever-living God and Jesus, since Norway was Christianized over a thousand years ago, but the signatures are still written in the candidate's own blood upon the parchment.

I witnessed your Uncle John's induction, and it was beautiful. I dreamed of yours, too. Your father says it seems too hedonistic and pagan, but I don't think so."

Hendrick joined them just as Kisti was sharing the last part of the story. He added, "Well, it is not exactly hedonistic, it is just not Christian, but it is an honor to be inducted. I was inducted. Ole, you have been inducted in the Ho-Chunks. This is very similar!"

"I wish I could take the vow, Mother and Dad. I would feel as though my ancestors were with me. I wish that I could be one of them, instead of the Winnebagos."

"That you mustn't say, dear one. You have inherited your ancestry nonetheless. I am so proud that a different race of people thought enough of you to make you a blood brother and honored your father and me the way they did. Can't you see, my son, that we must be the example for others? We must carry the ideal from our heritage. We have that commission from God, otherwise we wouldn't have been given these honors in this new land.

"You were born into courage, and you have shown us this spirit in you. When you leave here you will be going to your destiny, whatever that may be, and you will do it with your chin up and your head high. And so will I, my beloved son."

"How lucky I am to have you for my mother. What do you think father? I have not told you yet, but I am wanting to go to war."

Hendrick looked at him without surprise. He did not speak but looked at Kisti. She said, "Your father, is himself a soldier and an officer. You know what he will say. He wants to go too, and it is difficult for him not to. But he feels his duty is here now. After all, he is past forty, with a family to take care of, and he must be prepared to grow more crops and raise more livestock on the farm to give to the soldiers. I feel for him, yet if it comes to him needing to fight, he will go, and we will all do whatever God asks of us. You can remember this from your mother, if you wish, that we may be badly beaten, but we are never licked, even if we die!"

Kisti and Ole laughed with Hendrick.

"If you feel you are being called, Ole, you should go and do your best," Hendrick said.

"Let us make our farewell here, my son. Write to me often...and be of good cheer. Remember that I have consigned you to God's loving hands. At this time some other mother is giving her boy a similar message, and perhaps he will be your enemy. All I can say is, God bless her. We cannot be enemies, for we have the common bond of motherhood. Be your best, do your best, remember what you have been taught . . . God bless you, dear Ole."

"That is what I came back home to receive, mother and father, your blessing and God's." He bent over his mother's small frame and kissed her on the top of her head. Hendrick patted Ole on the back and got up and went into the house.

Hendrick came out when Ole and Aspun were ready to go. He saluted the two young men, and hugged his son goodbye and shook Aspun's hand. Then he sat down next to Kisti in the Königs Garten on the bench he had made for them beside the log she used to sit on. They watched Ole and Aspun reach the edge of the woods. The dark trees arched over them as they turned and waved to Hendrick and Kisti, and then disappeared into the forest.

Chapter Twenty-Two

Eivind Steps Up

With Ole gone, Eivind assumed many of the necessary responsibilities around the home: fetching water, providing firewood, and even milking the cows, whenever he couldn't avoid it. He hated milking cows and tried to bargain with Hendrick for other chores if he could. Hendrick would have to milk them if he resisted.

Anna's son Hans took to his duties very well, and already at eight years old, he milked their three cows, every morning and evening, with the regularity of a seasoned farmer, and he also fed and watered them.

Eivind wouldn't go near the horses. However, under the tutelage of their neighbor Jon Loberg, he had learned how to put the yoke on the oxen and drive them with considerable skill. Hendrick was amazed when he arrived home one day from a trip to Plover and saw Eivind with the oxen, pulling the poplar logs into a neat pile where the addition to the barn was to be.

Jon loved Eivind, and while he had no children of his own, he instructed Eivind in a playful spirit. The "gee and haw" to guiding the oxen was demonstrated with such humor that Eivind's hours with Jon were fun. He learned how to bind the bundles of grain one afternoon as they sat in the shade during "kaffe-tid, coffee time, which Jon observed with great regularity.

Every afternoon at four, the women came to the fields with coffee and freshly baked bread and pastry. Each woman tried to outdo her rivals in the neighborhood with some new venture into baking. The results of the contest were not known

until later, either at church or another gathering, when someone would say, "What did you give my husband the other day while he was at your place? He tried to tell me how good it was, but the way he explained it I am at a loss to know whether he drank it or ate it, or whether it was sweet or sour."
Kisti always chucked when this was discussed among the ladies.

During one 'kaffe-tid', Jon was helping Hendrick in the harvest field when he remarked to Eivind, "How about if I have you bind for me. I bet you and I could get these oats in shocks by tomorrow noon. Without your help I don't think I can get it done this week."

"But, Jon, I can't make a band like you can."

"A band? I don't make a band at all. I make an old witch dress. You know, when you make a witch's dress, she has to get into it, and if each bundle has a witch bound into it, then they will be tied to the bundle, and they can't do any damage. But I am talking too loud; the witches will hear me and think of something else for us to do. Come close while I show you how to make a witch dress."

He walked over to a pile of oat straw. "See" he said, "we take a handful of straw with all the heads of the straw together, then we take half of them and cross the two at the neck below the heads, like so. Now you hold your thumb on the cross while with the other hand you bring the straw behind up around and over, and there is your witch dress, with her head, her neck, and her dress. Now you pull her dress apart and hold her by the head in your left hand and wrap her dress around the bundle. With her head inside you twist her legs together and she is stuck for sure. And when she is stuck you can't pull the bundle apart; the harder she tries the tighter her bundle."

Within a few tries, Eivind learned to tie the bundle, and in this playful way, Jon had taught him how to drive the oxen and do many other tasks that were considered too much for a little boy.

Young Synneva had an unquenchable thirst for knowledge. She learned her letters, and quickly learned how to read. It was her nature to want to teach everything she was learning to others. And so, at Synneva's bidding, and with Kisti's blessing, Eivind, Hans, Ingeborg, Carl, and Albert cut down pine boughs and erected a little hut out in the woods where Synneva could gather the Indian children to teach them to read and tell them stories.

The family had begun to call the two Synnevas different names: both Grandma Synneva and young Synneva were now called Susan, or Susies. Their namesake was St. Synneva of Norway, who had been canonized in the early 15th century. Hendrick sometimes called his daughter Nonna, because she looked like the painting of St. Synneva in her nun's regalia at the church in Norway, as he remembered it. Once Ole left for the army, Grandma Synneva often called her granddaughter "Nonna," or "the Nun."

Aspun and Ole wrote letters to their families and Randine sometimes received letters from Aspun. In her letters to her mother from the Bancrofts in Chicago, there was news that Ole and Aspun had been in a severe engagement in battle, but they were well and unhurt.

Lincoln issued a call for more volunteers and the original three-month enlistment service had been changed to one to three years. Almost without exception, the three-month men were re-enlisting, including Ole and Aspun.

News continued to be unfavorable regarding the Union Army. It seemed they were being beaten at almost every turn. There appeared to be plenty of manpower; the problem lay in the hands of the leadership and the confusion in Washington. It wasn't Lincoln who was to blame, but the Congressmen, many who had insisted upon appointing their cronies as generals, even though they had no military qualifications.

Lincoln had few enemies in Congress, but many senators were quite outspoken in the face of overwhelming opposition to the appointed generals and their military strategy. But every fresh defeat gave weight to arguments against Lincoln and his generals.

Hendrick said after church one day, "This county had only sixteen thousand men in the whole army when this began. All of the good generals are in the South. They are the sons of planters and the Virginians around Washington. We have only a few good generals. Sherman, Sheridan, and Grant, who just took Fort Henry. We need more experienced generals and fewer politicians whose friends have assigned them as generals."

Jon asked Hendrick about General McClellan, and he said, "McClellan hasn't done a thing except drill soldiers. Now the weather is bad, but he had all summer to do things and he hasn't done a thing, except give out information to the papers that he is a great general."

The men at meetings and rallies always discussed the latest reports in The Chicago Tribune. Most of the men were pleased that Lincoln was eliminating generals that had been made generals by congressional friends. Camp Douglas outside Chicago, where many of the Wisconsin Boys had gone to train, was now converted into a prison for Confederate prisoners of war. Much concern was aroused by the appalling condition of the soldiers when people saw them marched through the streets of Chicago. Some wise and benevolent citizens erected a free hospital, which they called St. Luke's, to serve both Union and Confederate soldiers. This got the best of the Board of Trade, who wanted to treat them like prisoners rather than patients.

A community discussion was initiated at a luncheon after a church service.

"Suppose it was one of our dear boys there in that camp, how would we feel?" Kisti said.

Mari chimed in: "I wonder how many of our boys they bayonetted before we stopped them? I don't know how I feel about them. Anyway, I would feel safer if they were all behind a fence."

Over time, as more Confederates were captured, several thousand prisoners would be imprisoned at Camp Douglas. It remained a discussion in the Tribune and spurred much debate among the neighbors.

Chapter Twenty-Three

Letters from Ole and Aspun

Neighbors gathered whenever they received a letter from one of their sons to put together the picture of the battles their boys were fighting in. Hendrick and Kisti shared the letters they received from Ole. Ashbjorn, with his wife Randi Roe, also shared Aspun's letters with them.

Ole and Aspun had both fought in the Battle of Antietam, near Williamsport, Maryland, and they had been in one battle after another before Antietam, which ended in September of 1862. After that, both men were pulled out of the line of action to help take care of the wounded soldiers in the hospital. In their letters home during that time, there was much criticism of the command and their attitude towards the hospital. Ole wrote: "The Sanitary Commission has saved more lives than bullets have destroyed. And Mother, you can tell Mari that I have heard many a prayer of thanks because of what the hospital does for the wounded."

Mari had volunteered to raise money for the war effort to help the wounded and she had become a good fundraiser, working as far away as Waupaca and Stevens Point, as well as Portage County.

Shortly after these letters arrived, Hendrick's father Ole wrote to him from Minnesota, telling him that Hendrick's brother, Ole Olesson Lysne, had been killed in the Dakota Wars trying to save farmers and families in New Ulm, Minnesota. He was shot on the way back to a secured area in New Ulm, along with several other young men. It was "friendly fire" that killed him.

Hendrick was greatly saddened at losing his brother, and he and Kisti looked at each other when he had finished reading the letter aloud. They faced the real possibility of their own Ole being killed; the news had brought this reality too close to home. They were very relieved that he and Aspun were working in the hospital for now.

Hendrick went back to DuBey Falls and every man in the neighborhood went to work in the woods felling trees and cutting timber. Hans and Eivind were remarkably efficient around their farms and seemed to be able to cope with any situation that arose.

As soon as the crops were in, Kisti took over a space in the barn loft, as did her mother, to have a place of their own to read, sew, or rest. The warm animals living underneath in the barn provided natural heat for their spaces.

Eivind and Synneva went to school down the road from their farm in the schoolhouse built on their family property by the community. Eivind was slower in learning compared to Synneva (Susan), but she coached him along and he was near the head of his class because of her tutoring. She irritated him with her insistence, but he adored her and was her special charge.

Mari's Susan was like one of the Lysne family. They all vied with each other to do favors for Elsa, after her mother Ingeborg had recently died. Ingeborg was the matron of the group, and they all respected her. Her death came as a shock to many of the people in the original community. Now her children were surrounded by their community with love and support if they needed anything.

The winter was so severe that Chief Oshida's people suffered much neglect, as they did not receive the supplies and funds they were to be given by the government. Kisti and Mari saw that they were provided for by taking them meat and bread. They forwarded an appeal to their representative in Madison to secure the government help that had been promised on their behalf. Help came in the middle of December with food, supplies, and money for them to buy what they needed.

There was an occasional visitor to the Amherst area from the Kilbourne area, a noble stalwart Native man named DeKorra. He was a Christian with a good education and was a relative of Wahopekau. His original name was De Carrie, his first French ancestor having come to this country with the French army. He was trying to obtain an attorney for the Ho-Chunks and had succeeded in securing an Englishman by the name of Lee, who would be with them at the close of the war.

Kisti was pleased to make DeKorra's acquaintance, and glad to hear that Oshida had told him about her daughter's effort to teach the Indian children, and that it was appreciated by him. DeKorra was to be in Madison that winter to make an appeal to the assembly for recognition of the Indians who had served in the armed services.

Wahopekau was working at the army hospital, and she also served on the Christian Commission. No task was beyond her ability to serve others. Otwana and Winona were at a boarding school for Indians in the east, near Washington. Winona wrote to Kisti a few times, and she was articulate and affectionate in her letters, somewhat like the letters Randine wrote to her mother.

Spotted Deer and White Fang were in the army. Spotted Deer had been transferred from foot soldier to serve in the cavalry and had his name changed to Sam Smith. Otwana said in her letter that she was now known as Mrs. Sam Smith, and that she had even embroidered S. S. on the cuff of the gloves she had made for him. He and his horse were a great team, and there was some talk of his going to the Dakotas with a cavalry unit.

Ole's letters were cheerful, but the buoyancy of his early letters was gone. He never failed to praise Dr. Castleman, whose system of sanitation was now in general use in the entire army and was standard procedure at the hospital. Ole was sad that the doctor was not appreciated by the generals, which contributed to Ole's weariness and disgust at the management of the Civil War.

As Christmas approached, the sad news came that many of the Fifteenth Wisconsin regiment boys had been lost. There were services held at all the local churches for those who had passed on. Many others had been wounded or taken prisoner, which seemed worse than death to many.

Kisti learned by letter from Ole that he and Aspun had re-enlisted for the duration, and were at Brandy Station, the winter quarters on furlough. Kisti assumed that Ole had spent time with Winona on his furlough, though he didn't mention it. She was thankful when they received a Christmas letter from Winona and Ole and a package from Ole with presents for the whole family purchased in Washington when he was on leave.

Kisti wondered whether her son and others who were fighting in this war would ever be the same. Would the South ever be friendly with the North again? What would the soldiers do when the war was over?

Chapter Twenty-Four

War Comes Closer

Over the next two years, the North began winning more battles. Most of the politicians who were assigned to lead the North were replaced with real generals who knew better strategies, including General Grant. There was another presidential election year, and Lincoln won, after much political challenge. However, he was taking action, such as replacing generals, to make sure the war would soon come to an end.

Ole and Aspun had been helping the wounded in the hospital for over a year. But now they were reassigned to serve in a regiment and were sent to the front. They reported some of the details of their battles in their letters home. Ole wrote that he respected the new generals that had replaced the politicians, as they seemed to know what they were doing far better than the men who had been leading them before.

The folks in Amherst Junction were coming up with new ideas to help the community. One was to get a new thrasher that the farm community could share; the other idea was to build a New Hope Church of their own. Both had to do with the needs of their emerging community; there were fewer men around to help with harvest, and the Scandinavian Church was ten miles away. It took them all day to travel there by oxen cart, three to four hours each way. Only some of the people had horse carriages that went faster, but it was a still a long way. Church attendance had dwindled as a result. The community had wanted to have a church closer to Amherst for the past several years, but especially now during this war, as many casualties were coming in. Services for the departed needed to be closer than at the church in Scandinavia. After much discussion, the Scandinavia congregation offered to help build the new church because of their experience building theirs. So, the decision was made to found a New Hope Church in the area and start construction in the spring of 1863.

The women of the community actively participated; especially Mari, who had proven to be an amazing fundraiser for the War effort, and now she volunteered to raise money for the church.

The women of both communities joined the project and held meetings to organize events to raise money for the new church building. With Mari's ingenuity for raising funds, and the way people rallied around her charm, they were certain to raise the money they needed.

At one meeting, Mari quipped, "We could build this new church without any obstacles. Moses built one in the desert with less materials than we have!"

Her enthusiastic spirit and optimism inspired the whole community. Progress was rapid because more people than expected came and offered their help.

Rumors about the war were rampant, and it was important for people to focus on what they could do to improve their lives. Between the prospect of the new threshing machine for their next harvest and the church plans, everyone in the community looked forward to the fall when the harvest would be in and the New Hope church built.

The church was nearing completion as winter set in, but they had to stop working on it until the spring, as the weather would soon become severe. The demand for lumber was insatiable, and so was the demand for help in logging and at the mills.

The people around Amherst in Portage County had decided at meetings that a new church at New Hope was to be finished. Johan and Brandt had kept the idea alive for a long time, and they were excited to get the committees going to make the new church a reality.

Brandt saw that another minister would be needed at the new church, so he arranged for Amund Mikkelson to become permanently attached to the Scandinavia congregation. He called upon Hendrick to recommend him, since Hendrick had known him in Norway. Hendrick realized that Reverend Mikkelson was the son of the minister that had married Hendrick and Kisti. This inspired Hendrick to talk to him about serving both congregations in the future when New Hope was finished being built.

Meanwhile, Mari was busy raising money and materials for war relief and for the New Hope church. Dances, balls, and parties were frequently held and were very popular with the officers on leave in uniform. Strangers coming to the community were often looked upon as possible spies and were subject to much scrutiny. Between the dead soldiers sent home and the officers on leave, the people were beginning to see the war as something more real and deadly than the distant conflicts heard about secondhand.

The neighborhood came together even more closely around harvest time when the new threshing machine would be given a trial. The new thresher was a true marvel to the farmers. They were fascinated by the horsepower innovation with the turning rod spinning rapidly, in contrast to the slow turning when the teams pulled the main gear. It was dangerous, too. Halvor, who had a habit of wearing his trouser legs outside his boots, stepped over the spinning rod and had his pant leg completely torn off. If the material had been thicker, the machine could have taken his leg off or worse. However, the men realized the danger, and they laughed as Halvor just kept working with one leg bare and the other one covered with the pant leg.

Randine had gone with Mrs. Bancroft to Chicago. Mrs. Bancroft was an officer in the Sanitary Commission, and it was important for her to be there. Randine took over the responsibilities of the household and was invaluable to Mrs. Bancroft in her soldiers' relief work. Mrs. Bancroft came home from Chicago with a couple of great ideas that brought the state of Wisconsin to the top of the soldiers' support. One of the ideas was to sell the original copy of the Emancipation Proclamation. The auction raised $3,000 for the document. Another idea was to sell the Old Abe, the famous eagle mascot of the Eight Wisconsin. The army granted special leave on both the eagle and his keeper for the Illinois State Fair. About one-hundred-and-fifty-thousand pictures of the bird were sold to raise money. Old Abe's feathers had been shot from him during battles, even though he had survived, and the feathers collected in battle were sold at the event and brought a good price.

Homes were planned for disabled soldiers and orphaned children. Some people opened their homes to support orphans. Many kindnesses were offered to the bereaved families of those who were killed. These services extended even into the battlefield when someone was injured, and the soldiers were exceedingly grateful.

During her time in Chicago, Randine had met a young gentleman named Jonathan Evers. He had been attending college and would return for the fall term if he didn't go into the army. He was having difficulty with his mother, who did not want him to go into the war. She was ready to use her influence in Washington to keep him out of it.

Randine took her mother into her confidence about the young man. Kisti was sure that if the war didn't harm him there would be someone new added to the family. "You must decide this for yourself. Be sure it is the man you love and not the idea. What about Aspun?"

"Oh, Mom, he is like a brother to me. It's not the same with him."

"Well, you know best. Your heart is singing my dear. I have not met him, but you are the one who loves him and will be living with him. Time and circumstances will determine it for you. I am here for you, my dear Randine."

It turned out that Jonathan wanted to enlist. He was at the age where he felt he was letting his friends down if he didn't join the army. Nothing satisfied him but to become a soldier and serve his country.

A few weeks after his departure, Randine received a letter from Jonathan telling all about his life in the cavalry under the command of General Sheridan. Randine loved this young man very much.

Almost daily now, the papers reported some new phase of the war developing. Armies were on the move in both theatres. After the battles of Lookout Mountain, Chickamauga, and Missionary Ridge, where most of the Amherst, Iola, and Scandinavia boys were outfitted, everyone felt that the war would be over soon.

Chapter Twenty-Five

Hendrick Enlists

The country was growing despite the war. More Norwegian emigrants came to America and were welcomed by the northern Wisconsin community. Others joined the army before they settled and some of them died before they even had the chance to find where they wanted to settle.

Mari was pregnant again, as were Anna Marie, Tharand, and Anna. On April 7th, Mari gave birth to another son. They called him Martin. Anna Marie also had a son. They called him Carl. Anna's son was named Hans; Tharand's was called Julius.

Kisti's children were growing up so fast that she was surprised at what they could do. Eivind was managing the barn and the farm with his father, very well. He and Hans had become such good friends and talked about farming with each other.

Unlike Eivind, Anna's Hans felt stiff and uncomfortable in clean clothes in school and church and formal settings. He did not like to read, nor did he care about book learning. The two Susans tried to interest him in learning to read, but he would just sit at his desk staring into space, longing to be outside.

He was, however, an excellent caregiver to his animals. He almost lived in the barn. His livestock were cared for better than any of the animals in his Amherst township. Several farmers bought calves from him, and afterwards, Hans often checked to see how the calves were faring under the new owners' care.

The church was completed by Pentecost in the spring, and Rev. Amun Mikkelson dedicated it. The community felt proud of the new church; the builders and everyone who worked together to make it happen had done a fine job. There would be a confirmation class starting very soon. Rev. Mikkelson announced that services would be held every other Sunday, one in Scandinavia and the next in New Hope Church.

The congregation was so pleased to have their New Hope Church near Amherst. All the mothers with their new baby's father at home and not fighting in the war brought their babies for christening at the church after it was dedicated.

One day after church, the women were discussing the Reverend's sermon about the righteousness of the Union cause in the war. He said that God was with the Union troops. The Reverend had read letters from some of the young men that were in the war.

Later, when the women were preparing lunch, Kisti said, "God is also with the Southern troops."

The other women were aghast by her remark. Mari said, "Why Kisti, with Ole on the front lines, how can you say that?"

"Because I believe it. Don't you suppose there are thousands of mothers in the South praying for their boys just as we are here? Don't you think they believe in God's ability to care for their sons as well? God does not exact the justice upon us that we deserve, or we would be in a fix. Look at the way we have treated the Indians. God could have stopped this war if he had wished. There is some other purpose behind it, and I am not inclined to blame it on God. I think he just lets the stupid humans destroy each other so they may learn for themselves."

"You have an interesting argument there. You must do a lot of reading," Reverend Mikkelson said.

"No, Pastor, I don't have time to read as much as I would like. But I think a lot. One doesn't commit her son to God's care daily and bury three in a strange land. I fear to be alone while my husband may also go to war. It is only up to God and His mercy to have Hendrick return in God's own time and in whatever condition."

"I see."

"My conscience hurts, not for the slaves, not for the war, but for our own shortsightedness in our relationship with the

Indians. Let's forget about missionary ambitions for the Chinese or the Japanese or the poor Africans, and get to work right HERE. See what we can do for Oshida and his people. We don't even have to abandon our religion. They will be willing to learn what we know about God, if we are willing to be open to them. Some are already Christians. They also know God in their own ways."

"We will have to take that up at the Lutheran conference in Bergen, Norway. I will be glad to submit your idea to them, although I know there are plans for foreign missions as soon as we are able."

"Mari, it looks like we will have to go to Norway and appeal to their foreign mission to get help for our American Indians living right here beside us. Of all the stupid things I have ever heard, this takes the cake."

"Kisti, Norway isn't close enough! We just have something impossible and far away that gives it a romantic idea of service. The crisis with the Indian people is too close; therefore, it is ugly and unromantic," Mari said. "People like to fool themselves, and the church is the same."

"Mari, China and Indonesia are far, far away. Heaven is said to be far away too, when the kingdom of God is right here! Mari, my sweet friend, you have hit on something important!" Kisti replied.

"Well, I don't understand what you mean, but I am all for it."

There was no question now as to whether older men and heads of families could go to war. Hendrick wanted to serve but he was reluctant to talk with Kisti about it.

One day he mentioned Coronal Cobb, and Kisti said, "Why don't you come out with it? I know you will have to go, but I think you should exercise your prerogative and apply to the Governor for a commission and be allowed to organize your own group. I know these men here would be proud to serve under you."

"Kisti, I could not exercise military discipline upon these

men. I have worked alongside them, prayed, and drank with them, we've been in their homes, and I would have to be impartial with them as their officer."

Kisti gave him a kiss and said, "As you wish, my love."

Lincoln was reelected by an overwhelming majority. The people believed in him, trusted him, and they were war weary. He had already asked Congress for half a billion dollars to help the South get back on its feet. He had never seen the South as being out of the Union but considered it part of this country. Many feared the end of the war for the South if Lincoln was there, but his election was a great relief, and it proved how much the people in the country respected him.

When the 42nd Wisconsin Infantry was organized to serve one year, it meant the end of the hundred-day enlistments, which was neither practical nor sensible, since the war would end when it ended, and a hundred days may not be enough. Hendrick announced to his group of men at his Christmas gathering that year that he had been given an offer to serve in the 46th Wisconsin organized in Madison. He had been offered a captaincy, but he turned it down to enlist on an equal basis with his friends from Amherst.

Johan, Adam, Aspun, and David wished to enlist, but David was turned down because of the dependency of his children. Lasse, Lars Gordon, Lars Loberg, and Anders were in the group. When it came time for enlistment, Anders was laid up with a broken leg. He was so cross about it that Mari said, "I don't dare come near his bed. I think I will have to feed him off the end of a spade!"

Kisti walked through the snow to the Königs Garten and stood there as the cold January midday sun made bright jewels upon the snow. Hendrick walked out of the house with his arms around Susan and Eivind. Eivind broke away and made his way to the barn. He stooped to his daughter and hugged her and came slowly to where Kisti stood.

"Well, Soldier Boy, I have been anticipating this moment for four years, and here it is. I wondered what it would be like. I knew when we married that I had married a soldier and now it has all come to pass. I am proud and sad and happy. I didn't think my heart was going to break, but now I am not so sure."

She spoke very fast, as if her words would hold back her tears, but when he put his arm around her, she threw her arms around his neck and sobbed.

"I am so ashamed of myself for letting go like this. I hadn't wanted to cry."

Hendrick held her close. "I will be back, sweetheart, I will be back, I promise."

Regaining her composure, she backed away and looked at him. "That you will. I know for sure. I am sorry I cried, but don't you worry, things will be taken care of here. God will be with you and we will meet in our prayers. You will find us waiting when your return and maybe you will find someone new by the time you get back."

"You don't mean to tell me you are pregnant again?"

Kisti nodded. "But it doesn't need to interfere with your mission. After all, I am not exactly a novice at this, you know." She smiled at him and said, "So on about your business, soldier, and God bless you. Pray for our boy out there, the fighting is desperate where he is."

With that he bent over and kissed her tenderly, then he hoisted a duffle on his back, turned and began to walk across the field to the southwest. Kisti watched him leave, as she had watched Ole. Just as Ole had done, he turned toward her at the end of the field, paused to take a long last look, then waved and disappeared into the woods.

As she watched that place in the woods, she wondered whether she would see ever him again. It seemed so long ago that Ole had disappeared under those arching branches. But it was different that time. It was June then, with the trees in full foliage taking Ole in, and nature was in its youth, as he went off to war. Now it was the dead of winter, and Hendrick was in his maturity as he went off to fight and finish the war, and the trees were bare and black against the white snow.

"Oh Lord, there must be another way! Bless us and protect us in our ignorance," Kisti prayed.

Susan, Anna, and Grandma were silent as they cleared away the remains of the noonday meal. Kisti silently removed Hendrick's plate and coffee cup from the table and held them.

"Well, if we will all stay happy and cheerful and know that this is all for the best, it won't be so hard for us. I am going over to see Anna Marie this afternoon, and you and Anna can go down and see if you can be of help to Ingeborg's children."

Anna Mari had also accepted her husband's departure with great fortitude. She put the coffeepot on and served some Aebleskiver treats as soon as Kisti arrived, and they gossiped about trivial things, and the new baby to come.

Jon appeared the next day to see if there was anything he could do to help. The horses were sold by Hendrick, except Victoria, who was going to stay at Ander's place. He was entrusted to use and care for her when she had a foal in the spring and keep her until Hendrick returned.

Spring broke early that year and the winter wheat showed signs of early green growth. Eivind was disturbed to see the deer grazing on his winter wheat. Everything had taken on a brand-new meaning for him, for everything on the place was now his responsibility. At the ripe age of eleven years old, he had become quite the man of affairs and assumed the demeanor to go with it.

Jon was Kisti's advisor, but Eivind didn't know it, and Jon and Kisti diplomatically engineered the situation so that Eivind progressed very well. Several others came to Kisti's farm to help with the harvest. The chores were taken care of by the women of the household, and everyone cooperated with the spring sewing and planting of corn and potatoes. Eivind and his oxen prepared the ground.

The war news centered on the Richmond area and the papers proclaimed that the war would soon be over. General Lee and his troops were finally bottled up, and General Sherman was pressing north, and Sheridan was to the east; the anvil to receive the blows was set around St. Petersburg as part of their military strategy.

Hendrick arrived at Louisville in March with his regiment, and their General said his troops would be going to someplace in Alabama, and that Hendrick was to serve as a musician of all things!

"This is the army the world over! They make me a musician and I cannot sing a note! It must have been because of my association with the finest singer of them all that they thought some of it lingered about me. But how fortunate for the soldiers that they didn't make me a cook."

Kisti laughed as she read Hendrick's words to the other women who congregated as soon as they heard from their men in the army. That way their men didn't seem so far away.

On April 5, 1865, a letter came from Ole. It was a long, tender letter. He was very homesick, and his tone was different from any letters he had previously written. He told Kisti what a wonderful mother she had been to him, and talked about Eivind and little Susan and how he would love to see little Anna, and he mentioned what a fine woman Winona had become, and how she was ready to devote her life to service to her people.

Toward the end of his letter he said,

"Mother, this is the last battle of the war. We were told that this evening, a man from the Christian Commission was here and offered communion to the Fifth. Tomorrow, we will lead an attack, which we hope will be the beginning of the last battle. Yesterday I was on leave and went to City Point. I saw President Lincoln and General Grant and some of our other generals.

"Mother you seem so close to me tonight that I can almost touch you. By the time this letter is on the way we will be preparing to move up. You entrusted me into God's care, and I am there now. Whatever happens, I am not afraid. I have seen boys die by the thousands and neither Aspun nor I are afraid this evening. The moon is beautiful, and I am thinking of the Königs Garten. I hope to sit beside you again as on the night I went away. God bless you, my dear Mother."

Kisti wept as she read and reread his letter. She knew in her heart that her son had given his all.

On the way to the war rally for the soldiers, Mari stopped by the house to pick up Kisti, along with Anna Marie and the two Susans. There were several wounded soldiers on the street, an empty sleeve here, and a leg gone there. No, Kisti thought, Ole will not be like these poor soldiers.

As Kisti mounted the platform at the war rally to sing for the event, the postmaster came and gave her two letters. She glanced hastily at the letter and saw the inscription, War Department. The other was from Medill. She knew in her heart that dreadful news was here. Nevertheless, she thrust the letters into her pocket and sang as one inspired, "The Battle Hymn of the Republic." The crowd joined the chorus, "Glory! Glory, Hallelujah! . . ."

The stanza she sang:

"In the beauty of the lilies Christ was born across the sea, with a glory in his bosom that transfigures you and me; as he died to make men holy, My Boy died to make men free; his soul is marching on."

Mari greeted her off the stage and looked at her with concern. "Kisti, I heard what you sang. Do you feel Ole is gone?"

Kisti said, "I think so, Mari, here are the letters. I haven't opened them, but I have known for days."

"Maybe it isn't true, open the letters, maybe you are wrong."

"No, Mari, I am not wrong, my boy is gone. He knew I would know it."

They pulled away from the crowd to go sit under a tree, where Kisti gently opened the envelope. "The War Department regrets--- with the courageous...laid down his life for his country..."

A detailed letter from Medill reported:

"At about 2:00 a.m. on April 2nd, the charge upon the enemy works at Petersburg began. The Fifth Wisconsin and the 37th Massachusetts, led by Col. Thomas Allen, were in the extreme front supported by two lines in the rear. At 4:00 a.m. the signal was given to advance. As they appeared over the rise, they were met by an enemy shell that struck a pine tree that exploded, killing 29 of the advancing forces.

"Among them were your son and another from Company F, whose name was Albert Beggs. Ole would have been proud to know that the Fifth planted their flag upon the woods they had set out to take. Great must be your pride, however deep your sorrow. I think you should know that both my brothers went the same glorious road as your son. America is yours and mine and all of the mothers in this great struggle. The price has been terrible, but we own it now and it is ours to keep forever. May God give you strength."

Aspun's mother came toward them and put her arms around Kisti and wept. "My boy is all right. He was with Ole. He said Ole never moved a finger, he was perfectly calm."

Kisti looked at Mari, "Mari, darling, I want to walk home. Don't wait for me. Stop on your way back if you wish. Nonna, you and Susan have a good time if you can, if not come home with me. When I get there, I must be alone."

Kisti turned along the trail that, more than ten years ago, she had traversed for the first time with Ole with his carbine; Bless his precious heart, she thought, remembering how he looked so big and important.

"Well, dear Lord, how do you explain it? Why should my boys all die? What is Eivind to think now, that he should live and the rest die?"

As she walked along the path near the river, she pondered these things, and she soon came upon Oshida's camp. She was made very welcome and told them about Ole's sacrifice.

"Winona come home now, soon," said her mother Odina.

Kisti gave Odina a hug, and thanked her for her daughter's love and service to her family. "You have given a wonderful woman to our family, Odina, and I am grateful to share the love of Winona with you."

Kisti emerged from the arched opening in the woods at the bottom of the hill that rose to their farm. From there, she could see her favorite spot, her Königs Garten. The flowers around it were colorful strokes of white and yellow daisies. So this is the place where Ole and Aspun and Hendrick disappeared, she thought. She stopped to consider what it was that made it look like a cave entrance from where she sat.

There were two large white oak trees that made the entrance, with three pines behind them that darkened the passage, leaving the oaks to frame the entrance. She had never realized how pretty it was. Any figure standing there was framed by these trees and the dark background made them stand out. She pondered, "I will never see Ole come back through this opening!"

As she looked toward the Königs Garten she saw the faint outline of the bench Hendrick had made beside the stump where she used to sit with the large burr oak for a backrest. "Her throne," Hendrick had once said, "And there upon it sits my queen." She could see it plainer now and could imagine what they saw as they left. It must have been hard to leave the place. It appeared so peaceful and comfortable as she looked at the house and the barn nestled among the oaks.

Undoubtedly, Ole felt lonely out there many, many times. Well, maybe he is home now. Yet I feel he is right here, with his arm around my waist, telling me not to worry. "No, Ole, my precious boy, I will not worry," she said aloud. "If a sanctification is needed, you have done it for me. I will never see your face again, but my heart sees you and it will never lose you."

When she came to her farm and sat on the log in her Königs Garten, her heart felt lighter, stronger, and at peace. The dread of the war was over. God had had his way. The effect on the family was severe, but Kisti bolstered each one of her children in turn.

It was overwhelming when Randine came home a few days later, her face swollen from weeping, and announced that her sweetheart, fighting with Sheridan, had been lost too. This, coupled with Ole's death, was just about all she could stand. But youth and the fast-moving events lightened the burden with the news that the war was truly over.

The church bells at New Hope rang for an hour the following day, and everyone was beside themselves with joy. Kisti went on foot to the church and found others there on their knees in thanksgiving.

"I was pretty sure I would find you here," said Mari "There are some war widows here, too. They are fixing supper. I have sent Albert to get Susan and Eivind. We must be together on this day."

The evening gathering at the church was most satisfying. Victoria, their horse, had just given birth to a new colt, and Kisti immediately named her Elisabeth.

Mari, who had come with her horses and a wagon, took Kisti back to her house when she was ready. That night, coming through the woods, Kisti, Susan, and Dina, sang the old Thanksgiving Hymn, "Ros, takk, evig herlighet" ("Praise, Thanks, Eternal Glory.") Kisti recalled they had sung that same hymn when returning home from Amund Brekke's after having established the first congregation at Scandinavia, and that Ole and Aspun had invited the Indians over to see them.

She laughed at the memory of it. Bless Ole's heart. He certainly let his momma in for something amazing after the Indians ate the cupboard bare for the coming winter. As she looked up at the moon, she felt a surge of love and peace enter her heart. "Dear Lord, Thou blessed us indeed. Make me worthy of my son's sacrifice. Your son was taken too. You do indeed understand."

Soon after the war was over, a tremendous pall settled upon the entire country with the news of Lincoln's assassination. It re-awakened the old division of the North and South that had started the war. Services were held in the churches and in public places, and in a myriad of ways, the shocked public sought to show their grief and prove their loyalty to the Union. The war was over, soldiers mustered out almost every day; yet many husbands were still away in the army. Reports of Southern soldiers leaving the ranks before the end of the war were among the rumors spread. How they had fled to Montana, Arizona, and territories that were barely settled.

"We will have to try and understand all of this, I suppose," said Anna Marie. "They will come home when the time comes. We know now that there are no more battles to fight, and that their service is a peaceful one. That is something we can thank God for."

Lincoln's funeral was a huge event in Chicago. The Bancrofts, Judge Cate, and several from the community went there to attend. Randine could have gone with the Bancrofts had she wished to, but she was grieving her losses so deeply that she declined.

The summer wore on, and Hendrick's letters to Kisti were cheerful. He wondered what was happening at home, and he mentioned Ole, but was guarded in his statements.

July brought a heat wave in 1865, and on the 17th, Kisti gave birth to another baby boy that lived about two hours. She called him Hendrick. He was buried on a Saturday afternoon at the New Hope Church Cemetery. They were amazed that Kisti should be up and about, but she waved them away. She said nothing about it to Hendrick and asked the others not to tell their husbands. They had enough to worry them, just getting back home.

Eivind and Hans got the planting done. Jon, David, and Anders helped from time to time, but both boys felt they had arrived at manhood for sure, when they watched the crops they had planted grow and flourish.

The year's bountiful harvest was completed and stored away by the end of September. The corn was attaining great heights when the announcement came that the 46th was to be mustered out and was expected in Madison around the first of October.

Winona came home, and when she saw Kisti, she broke down and cried in her arms. She had seen much of Ole, she said. He had spent his leaves with her, and she loved him very much. She would never marry again, now, she told her. She was going to try to make Christians of her people. She had heard about Susan's attempt with the Indians and would help her with it.

She was a lovely young woman. Her clothes were well chosen, and her language was flawless.

Kisti took her out to the Königs Garten to sit with her.

"Winona, you are like a daughter to me. Did you and Ole marry when you were out east?"

Winona paused, and said, "Not in a Christian church, or in a Christian way, but we exchanged our commitment to each other, as he had done in the ceremony with our people. There was no time to find a minister, and no money to plan anything formally. But we loved each other, and we spent much time together, and we made a commitment to love each other to the end." Winona paused. "Ole knew at the end that he was going to die."

The two women cried together, and Kisti assured her that she would always be her second mother. Winona became a frequent visitor, but the merry little laugh that Kisti remembered was gone, as was the sparkle in her eyes.

Randine and Winona were as good of friends as ever, but they had both been scorched by the cruelty of war. What they told each other was not of Kisti's knowledge, but she wondered what they shared with each other.

Randine Lysne

Lallie Lysne, Susan Lysne, Randine Lysne Jaasted, Grandfather Hendrick, John Swenholt sitting, Henry Lysne on the ground, behind him, Sjur O. Jaasted, Martha and Evivind Lysne, Carl and Walther.

Part Four

New Life – Starting Over

Chapter Twenty-Six

Beginning Again

On a bright beautiful day in October, Kisti was sitting in her beloved Königs Garten reading a letter from Randine. She glanced up and saw a figure emerge from the opening in the woods across the field from her. It was a soldier. She knew instantly, from his bearing and familiar walk, that Hendrick was home. He waved when he saw her, and Kisti ran over to meet him. Neither of them spoke, they simply hugged each other. Hendrick held Kisti close and buried his face in her hair. When she could speak, she said with a slight smile, "Welcome home, soldier."

Great indeed was the joy of Hendrick's homecoming, but home would never be the same with Ole gone. It was almost impossible to realize that they would never see him again. Hendrick tried to remember Ole's face the last time he had seen him and grieved for his loss. But to Kisti, Ole was a constant presence. She felt him often, and knew he was in God's arms. The immigrant settlers who had died were now a part of this land, integrating into American soil, and the ties with Europe were completely broken.

Hendrick told Kisti and his mother-in-law about the many things he had seen during his time in Alabama and Tennessee. Coming home by way of Chattanooga and Nashville, he saw the battlefields there, and at Shiloh and Corinth. Seeing the damage to the houses, battlefields, and grave after grave, he realized what the soldiers and their families had gone through.

Hendrick felt deep sympathy for the people in the South and he understood their plight. But he could not understand why they felt such hatred for him and the soldiers from the

North. He said that one Sunday when he attended a church there in Nashville with some of the men from the Wisconsin 46th, the preacher stopped in the middle of the sermon and walked out. So did some of the church members. One of their men, a man from Oshkosh, went up into the pulpit and finished the sermon the minister had begun, and it was a fine one. He announced that if the regular minister was not present the following Sunday, he would officiate the service again himself. Hendrick said that those who remained for the service seemed amused by the antics. A man and his wife shook hands with the temporary preacher and thanked him for a real message of comfort.

The next Sunday Hendrick and the men went to the church again, and the regular minister was present and gave a short impersonal address. The men of the 46th contributed generously to the collection that day, and they would attend the services for several weeks. They had all vowed beforehand not to mention the war or do anything that would fan the flames of hatred. A social evening at the church was announced for the following week, and there was some discussion among Hendrick and the men about whether they should attend. When they shook hands with the minister after the service, none of them received an invitation.

The following Sunday, several folks came over to Hendrick and Johan after the service and invited them to visit their homes. They accepted and from then on, the soldiers had friends among two or three families there in Nashville. One of the southerners was bitter about losing a son at Chickamauga, and were trying, as Christian people, to break the resentment and find forgiveness. Hendrick told them about Ole, and said he was trying to overcome the grief of his own son's death by not holding any animosity toward anyone. This seemed to open the way to more empathy and their attitude toward Hendrick and the others became a bit less tense; but generally speaking, there was very little forgiveness. Their losses still felt very raw.

The resentment was so deep-seated that Hendrick said he feared the outcome. "We have freed the slaves," he said, "but we certainly have not solved the problem. And now we hear that there are short-sighted people who want to wreak vengeance upon already impoverished former slaves."

Kisti said to him, "Hendrick, I want you to stop worrying about this. You have done your part. We have done our part. Now it is up to God. Let us leave it there. This thing is not over yet. It will never be over for me with our boy gone. But I am content to wait and let destiny take its course. I cannot lose any more children at this point. We must think about our growing children. Eivind will soon be going to college. Synneva, Susan, as you know, wants to be a teacher. She is already teaching the Indian people. Randine will probably want to have a wedding one of these days."

Hendrick raised his eyebrows. "Yes, though her first love was killed in battle with Sheridan, I am sure there will be others."

My dear husband, you should see Victoria and her new colt, Elizabeth. She is just wonderful. There is always so much to do in a farming life, but we can relax a little with our family and enjoy this dearly bought freedom."

Hendrick hugged Kisti and decided it best to set aside any discussion of the post-war situation.

Aspun was a mature man when he returned home. After a joyful reunion with his parents, he walked over from the Roe house to visit the Lysne family. He said that he missed Ole very much and tried to make his loss as easy as he could for Kisti and Hendrick. He finally broke down and told them all he knew. He said he was convinced that Ole knew his time was near when he wrote the letter to Kisti the night before he died.

Aspun said, "I kind of knew it, too. I was tempted to give him something to knock him out, so he couldn't answer the call in the morning. Now I wish that I had."

"I am glad you didn't, Aspun. I know that sounds strange coming from his father, but Ole would never have forgiven you, and he would never have been satisfied. It is better this way. What is done is done, and I suppose there was no other way."

Aspun cried as he told them how much Ole had done to

help others when they worked together in the hospitals, and when he was fighting with his fellow soldiers. After several hours of deep discussion about the war, Aspun got up to return to his parents' home.

Kisti walked with Aspun across the field in the bright October moonlight. "Aspun, tell me about Winona and Ole."

Aspun looked at Kisti for a few moments. "I don't know what to say about it."

"Were they together a lot?"

"Yes, they were quite a beautiful couple. He was very fond of her. In Washington, she did not look Indian. She dressed in ordinary women's clothes. I doubt if anyone ever thought of her that way. She and Ole seemed very devoted to each other."

"Yes, that is what Winona said, too."

"I want to tell you about the time when I was with Ole in Washington and we met Winona. We were on our way to the theatre when Winona stopped us and stood in front of us."

"Have you written to your mother?" she asked. "Write first, then we will go to the theatre."

"Ole had written you. So, we went ahead to the theater."

"Bless her precious heart," Kisti said. "She is back home, but she doesn't look the same. She has grown so serious."

"Well, there is no joy in her life anymore," Aspun said. "And I don't blame her. Ole was her 'meant to be' love."

"Thank you, Aspun. Please come over like you used to. We are glad to see you anytime."

"Yes, ma'am, but I will be going to California soon, as Ole and I had planned to do before the war. I will go alone, but I will follow the plans we made for the journey. I'll write to you from there."

That winter Eivind was attending school without having to do as many chores as he had to when his father was gone. Hendrick had decided to stay home rather than being gone into the woods, and he had renewed his interest in the farm and was adding a room to their home. Anders had brought Victoria back with the new colt, and Hendrick was looking for a teammate for Victoria.

Susan helped Eivind to keep up with his studies, but he had taken on a new maturity, and resented his little sister's efforts to prod him. Susan tried to challenge him with some of the problems in math and history and he would ponder them silently and suddenly come up with the answer when she least expected it.

School was becoming fun for Eivind, and Susan continued to learn as much as she could. Albert, Carl, and Ingeborg were present, and even little Nels had entered school, along with Synneva, Susan, Dina, and Dena and her brother Ole, and the other children in the neighborhood. Winter slipped by rapidly for the busy youngsters.

Now that the men of the 46th were settling back into their community, they had begun to resume their interest in the affairs of the county. The women decided that, come what may, there was to be no more bickering and worry over what was happening in Washington as there had been in the years prior to and during the war. The soldiers were sick of Washington politics too, but no one could ignore how affairs were shaping up in the country.

Amherst was developing into quite a town, with new settlers arriving by the thousands, and vacant land was being taken up newcomers every day. The railroad was coming through the area; this time the government funded it, so the plans for developing Amherst and other small towns were realized.

The Ho-Chunck, Sauk, and Fox were being squeezed to leave their land again. One day Winona and Oshida came to see Kisti and Hendrick and told them about the land agent asking them to move; he said that someone had bought the land they were living on. DeKorra had also come with Oshida that day, and with him was Julia Marond, who was a relative of Wahopekau. They shared with the Lysnes that the tribes had secured the services of an English lawyer by the name of Lee, and they were taking their fight into the federal court. It looked as though the Indian camp would be broken up.

The Ho-chunks eventually decided to move into Marathon, or Shawnees County, and take up some land for themselves; they planned to break up the camp life and adopt the white man's ways, and each live on a patch of land as their own. Winona was active in this by encouraging her people to conform to Christian ways. Many of the tribes had already moved to Iowa, and some to the Nebraska territory; others moved north as soon as they had assurance they would be allowed to remain on their lands.

This was a step forward. Old Oshida decided there was no other way for them except to live on a reservation in the west and be dependent upon an Indian agent. This he had no stomach for, and he had lived through the Sioux massacre in the west. Yellow Thunder lived on his own land, and advised the others to do the same as soon as they could. Now was the time.

By the next spring, Oshida's camp had dwindled to nothing but the skeletons of wigwams, which came as a relief to some people, but grieved many.

Winona and Otwana came to bid Kisti and Hendrick and their family farewell. Otwana said, "Many in the Cavalry do not know that my husband is an Indian. I have been asked if I am. I am going to be careful of my ways and dress and I will make life easier for Sam." She was Mrs. Sam Smith now, the wife of Sergeant Sam Smith, who was stationed in the Dakota territory with the U.S. Cavalry. He liked the life, they lived well, and that is where they planned to stay.

Kisti was sad at her leaving, for she counted Oshida and his tribe among her very close friends.

"I will teach them, and you can come and help me," Winona said.

Kisti promised she would come often to see them.

Through the school district, Winona was able to open a school and get some books for the Indian children. Kisti tried her best to get some church help through Rev. Mikkelson. Mari managed to get enough support to help Winona, and promised that by the next autumn when her needs were fully known, she should come back and there would be help for her school.

There were several pleas for help from Winona during the summer, and when Winona appeared again in Amherst, supplies were available that would assist her work substantially. Kisti was sure that it would take consistent pressure for the church to become interested in Indian affairs. 'Someday,' she thought, 'we will capture the imagination and hearts of the American people and we will give these Native Americans some of the blessings that this country provides the foreigners from other countries.'

Over time, DeKorra and others pushed the State of Wisconsin to grant some of the land in Marathon and Shawano Counties for the Indians' use. In Shawano County, an especially a large tract was given over to the Menominee tribe, and they were protected from exploitation by white lumber and mining interests.

Susan Lysne

Chapter Twenty-Seven

Eivind finds Music

The Amherst children were delighted to have their fathers, big brothers, cousins, and neighbors home again. There were homecomings held at the Scandinavia and New Hope Churches, as well as parties for the soldiers in many homes in Amherst, which were a bit rowdy. At the town hall the soldiers were honored for their service. There was an occasional fight when some of the participants had too much to drink. There were also card games at many of these parties. Mostly, there was a spirit of good will and fun at these events.

Hendrick could hardly believe the wonderful progress his children had made, both at school and in their religious instruction. Susan was a natural teacher, and she was never happier than when she could share what she knew with her students. Mari's Susan was also gifted and bright. She enjoyed making light conversation, and there was never a situation where she didn't find humor in it. The folks in the community called them "the two Susans," and whenever there was a public program they performed together as best friends.

Eivind was good at arithmetic, woodcarving, and building, and of course he loved the animals. And then he discovered another gift. While over at Jon's one day after supper, Jon reached for his violin and played a few tunes. Jon allowed Eivind to hold it and he showed him how to produce the various sounds with the bow. The boy was so fascinated with the instrument that he went home and tried to make one for himself.

One day while Jon was over, he came upon Eivind's

masterpiece and resolved that anyone so interested in the instrument really deserved to have a good fiddle of his own. On Eivind's 13th birthday, Jon gave him his violin, and then he taught him how to play a few songs.

It was wonderful to hear him playing the fiddle, once he knew how to play the tunes. Grandma and Susan enjoyed it immensely, and when the two Susans, Dina, and Little Anna were together, they would all dance to his music.

That spring Hendrick was searching for a teammate for Victoria. One day he came riding into the yard on what looked like a perfect match, a beautiful bay. It was supposed to be a workhorse, but it looked, for all the world, like a racehorse.

Kisti was surprised that the horse he brought home looked like a racehorse, but she pretended not to be. "Such beautiful horses. I see you have an extra one now."

Well, a third horse is always useful, Hendrick said. "Sometimes we need a third one on the breaker plow, the reaper should have three horses, and there are many occasions when a third horse is really needed."

"Of course," Kisti said. "And he can run, right?"

Hendrick knew he was caught. He grinned and said, "Yes, he can run. I have always wanted a good road horse and I fell in love with this one."

"I'm glad you did. It is time we had some fun around here."

The new arrival caused much speculation, and the roadster was receiving a lot of attention. Hendrick found a place beyond the Königs Garten that was well hidden from the public road where he could clear away stumps and brush; soon a paddock was taking shape with Jon's help.

Eivind's violin playing aroused great displeasure in Hendrick. He acted as though the instrument was an agent of the devil. At first, Kisti forbid Eivind to play before his father, and she instructed the others not to mention the violin in Hendrick's presence. But one day, after Hendrick had left for town, Eivind sat on the steps playing a merry tune. The Susans were dancing, and little Anna was trying to do a pirouette on her bare toes. Suddenly Hendrick appeared, as he had forgotten to bring a sack of wheat with him, and the children scattered in every direction—all except Eivind.

Hendrick reached for the violin. "Give me that!"

"NO!" shouted Eivind.

"Why do you defy your father? Give me that fiddle."

"No. It's not a fiddle; it's a violin and you will break it!"

Hendrick reached for it, but Eivind jumped out of the way, and with tears streaming down his cheeks, he broke into a dead run. Hendrick was about to follow when Kisti appeared.

"Well, what is happening here? Why is Eivind running away?"

"I demanded that he give me that fiddle and he refused. Imagine! He said no to his father! I'll break that violin into a thousand pieces."

"Sure you would, and the boy knows it. He would just as soon have you break his body rather than his violin. You fool; can't you see that the boy loves it? Just like you love that racehorse, Hendrick. If the violin goes, that horse goes! If you are going to deny your child, who is like a man at thirteen years old, this outlet for the beauty in his soul, then you shouldn't have the horse to nurse your gambling instinct, either. Now make up your mind to like the violin and its music, and I will make up my mind to like the horse. We can have a lot of fun here, but we have to learn to live with other's likes and dislikes."

"Where did he get the violin?"

"Jon gave it to him because he thinks Eivind is naturally gifted. What is your aversion to it? I never knew you hated violin music."

I don't hate music; it is just that my uncle was like that. He played all the time; we thought he was a bit odd. He sat on the steps like Eivind, fiddling away. He said the elves danced for him while he played."

"I bet he was a genius and perhaps could really see the elves and trolls. As for you, none of your family could imagine anything that good could come from you."

Maybe that is it, I don't know. There is nothing wrong with a violin unless one plays for dances."

"There is nothing wrong with it if one does play for dances either. Hendrick, I hate this narrow viewpoint of yours. For God's sake, let us get out of this prison we have built for ourselves. We are so busy with our 'don'ts' and our 'must nots' that I want to break out and fly away."

"Well, the devil is a powerful adversary."

"Fiddlesticks. He has no more power over me than I will give him. I can never get used to that idea. What about the violin, does he get to keep it, and play it?"

"Yes, he can keep it."

"He is not your uncle! He is your son!"

"Well, then, tell him he can keep it."

"You call him over and tell him, Hendrick. Put your arm around him and tell him how proud you are, what a fine boy he is, and what a good job he did while you were gone. Tell him you have heard of his excellent schoolwork, and how wonderful it is to have a boy that can do so many things, so well.

"Unwrap your own soul, Hendrick. Maybe you love him, but he doesn't know it. He feels about you, the way you feel about God. He is scared he might break a rule you have made and provoke your wrath. I don't think he knows whether he really loves you or not, you have been gone so much. Well, you had better try and find out and then I'll let you keep your horse."

She tipped his hat over his nose, and as she went into the house, she heard Hendrick call out, "Eivind! Come here, son."

After a time, she saw them standing by the barn, holding hands, with the violin tucked under Eivind's arm. They walked along in deep conversation. When she rang the bell for the evening meal, there was Eivind sitting on a stump, with his father sitting on the ground beside him. Eivind was playing his father's favorite hymn, "Der er Glaede hos Gud I Himmerig" ("There is joy with God in his Kingdom.") Hendrick was singing along, a bit off pitch, but singing the words as Eivind played. The world now looked bright once again for their family.

Chapter Twenty-Eight

Railroad Passage

Hendrick returned from Waupaca full of news. There was a new high school in town, and a group of people busy negotiating for the new railroad and buying up the right of way for the line that would come from Oshkosh and extend to Minneapolis and St. Paul. There was also a branch line going from Minneapolis to Duluth and Superior. The surveyors near Fremont, in Waupaca County, told him that the railroad also had branches into Neenah and Menasha and going towards Stevens Point and the one going northwest would be coming through Amherst. This would increase food distribution for farmers in Amherst to all over the country! Hendrick said the railroads would be all over and that in a few years one could travel from New York to California.

As he got into politics, Kisti said, "Hendrick I don't want to hear a thing about politics or world affairs. We are going to live here awhile and enjoy this patch of ground and our home! You can have fun with your horse, Eivind can play his violin, and Susan and Anna have their books. I am going to have a good time just being alive and chatting with my neighbors, and not worrying about what they do in Washington or any other place!"

"But Kisti, what they do in Washington affects everyone..."

"When the railroad comes to town, we will take a ride on it, and when our children get old enough, they can go to high school in Waupaca if there isn't one built here by that time. I think you and I should get our fishing poles and go fishing tomorrow. There hasn't been fresh fish in this house since Oshida brought us some last year. We will pack a lunch and go to the lake, just you and I." Kisti did not wait for an answer from Hendrick. She knew he would like the idea.

Early the next morning, after the milking was done, they set out in the late September sunshine for the lake. On the way, they passed the remains of Oshida's old camp and saw some wigwam skeletons still standing. They gazed with nostalgia upon the deserted site and realized that another era had passed. But from the latest reports, the Ho-Chunks were better off now, at least Kisti prayed for them to be. They had a sense of permanency now that they didn't have before. Winona was a great force in bringing this about, and now that the Indians had a lawyer to represent them, there was some assurance of having a place to live well into the future.

Hendrick and Kisti had been fishing for only a short time, getting a few nibbles, when there was a loud gunshot in the woods by the lake, and soon Johan emerged.

"Did I scare you folks? I just shot a bear. I have trailed it for two days. I saw he had been in the cornfield, and I trailed him through your place, David's, and Blasky's. He is a big one. I will give you enough for a roast, but I will need help to bring him home. If I go home to get a horse and my stone boat, will you help me load him, Hendrick?"

"Sure enough, Johan. I'll be waiting for you."

Within an hour, Johan returned with the horse and his stone boat. They rolled the huge animal onto it and dragged the boat behind the horse to Johan's house. Hendrick divided the fish he and Kisti had caught with Johan and Anna Marie. She served them coffee and the special cakes that she always had on hand.

"It's nice to be neighbors again, Johan, to eat our wives' cooking and to be back with our families in our own homes," Hendrick said.

"It sure is better than that awful army grub we had, and not knowing whether we should eat it or throw it away. I guess we fared pretty well, though, after listening to some of the boys in the Eighth. But we couldn't think of anything except to get home to our beautiful women awaiting us."

Johan tried to get his arm around Anna Marie, but she deftly avoided him.

"Drink your coffee. And you have a bear to skin, remember?" She smiled at him and kissed him on the cheek.

"I wonder how they are making out down there without us?" Johan said.

"Where?" Kisti asked, "down South?"

"Yes, I bet they are going to have the devil's own time."

"Now, no more talk of politics or war, no problems except Portage County, town of Amherst, home, school, church, and the price of hogs. Didn't you say so Anna Marie?"

"Yes, you are absolutely right. No more talking about subjects that do not have to do with our home and our children, and maybe some new clothes for us women. We were good ladies while you were gone. We didn't dress up, and now I want a new winter coat and a new dress for Christmas," Anna Marie said.

"I am with you, Anna Marie. And if we run out of ideas for what we need, we will call on Mari."

"Good Lord, Hendrick, let's go back to the army," said Johan.

Hendrick laughed and said, "You know that the railroad is coming!" He lifted his coffee cup and clicked it with Johan's.

The railroad was indeed coming. The number of men working on the right-of-way, the amount of food, clothes and supplies they needed was fantastic. The local merchants scurried to meet the demands.

Many of the railroad workers boarded at local homes. They were a motley crew, and on payday they were loud and boisterous, spending their money and drinking freely wherever they wanted to.

Anders increased his acreage and decided to take in boarders to help around the place. One was a handsome young immigrant by the name of Alfred. This young man had herculean strength. His muscular prowess was greatly admired by the men, and the women fancied his curly blond hair.

During gatherings, feats of strength were often the subject of entertainment. At such times Alfred was provided with a horseshoe, and he would pull the ends of it apart with his powerful hands. He had been a sailor and had traveled everywhere. He had gone "around the Horn" and had fought pirates, and he had the cutlass scars to show for it.

During the war he had been at sea, but upon arriving in Boston, he made his way to this settlement in Amherst to find himself a "good woman" and build a home.

He became acquainted with another young man named Nils. Nils could pull a horseshoe apart by his strength as well. But he was younger and not as experienced as Alfred. Nils had worked in pine logging and had served on the log drive down the river.

Alfred and Nils loved playing poker, and this is what brought them to Stack's Bar on Saturday nights. They both had plenty to drink and became reckless at betting, and they lost more money than they thought fair. Nils wanted to clean out Stack's and break the bar into pieces, but Alfred chose to bide his time.

"Nils, when you go after these fellers you have to go all the way. You can't leave a single bottle or a single skull in one piece. If you tickle them with a few scratches, they will look you up and kill you, or hire a drunken jailbird to knife you. But if you ruin them completely, they will have respect for you. But only if you lick them good."

Nils knew that Stack was a real crook and probably had been a pirate at one time. "He looks yust like 'em," he said to Anders in his Norwegian accent.

"Ah, Nils, we will have a good time one day!" Alfred said to him.

A few weeks later, that "good time" arrived. It was Amherst County Fair time in the early fall. The Fair attracted many Indians; some came out of curiosity for a sojourn in the white man's world to enjoy the new sights; others came to sell ponies, trade dogs and furs, and buy whiskey. Winona came to town for supplies for her school. The churchwomen and some folks from the school at Amherst had donated money for her to purchase what she needed.

The Fair was a wonderful annual event for the farmers and their families. Farmers from the county exhibited cattle, mares with colts, single horses, teams, sheep, and the men participated in team pulling contests. The women had weaving and fancy work on exhibit, and there were contests for baking and other homemaking skills.

Thursday during the fair week was payday for the railroad gang. They were told they could have Friday off, but they had to work on Saturday and Sunday afternoons in place of it.

As was their custom, Mari and Kisti found a table where they could sit and enjoy supper together at the fair. Andes had gone home to do the chores and Alfred had been promised the day at the Fair. He passed them and waved, as he headed to the cattle barn to see the animals.

"Hello Alfred," said Mari. She turned to Kisti and said, "It is better if Alfred takes the week because he won't be worth anything for a couple of days anyway."

Alfred and Nils came back to the table and joined Mari and Kisti and the two Susans. The men kept the two Susans and their mothers in hysterics with their witty talk and imitations of Stack, and others who frequented the bar.

Eivind was over near the band and Albert, Mari's oldest son, was with his horse in the horse barn. "We won't wait for them. They are too excited and will eat when they are hungry," said Mari.

While they were eating dinner, Winona came stumbling over to the table with her dress torn from her shoulder and a scratch on her face. She dropped on her knees and buried her head in Kisti's lap and sobbed. She had gone in search of one of the young women from the Indian neighborhood only to find her and a friend at Stack's. They were both drunk, sitting in the back room of the place. Stack was giving the girls all the whiskey they could drink, and he was charging the men one dollar each to lay with them. Winona went into the back room to get the girls out of there, and the men set upon her and almost tore her clothes off. She pulled herself away and ran out.

While Winona was crying and explaining what had happened to her, Alfred rubbed his hands and smiled. "You hear that Nils? You hear that?" He stood up. "Don't cry, little ma'am, we will get your girls out of trouble, won't we Nils?"

"By golly, this I want to see!" Mari said. "We will take on the team. You two Susans stay here. Come Kisti, we'll drive over in my wagon," Mari said.

"Mari, we may get ourselves killed, but I'm in. Let's go."

So Kisti, Winona, and Mari set out in Mari's light wagon. They made their way through the crowd and the traffic to Stack's establishment. The noise coming from the place was filled with snatches of songs, lewd ditties, crashing glass, yells, clacking dice and poker chips, and loud laughter.

Mari caught up with Alfred and Nils, who had stopped on the way to Stack's to pick up some railroad tools for the important work ahead of them.

"Now ma'am," said Alfred, very businesslike, "you drive around the back. Don't get too close, you won't be able to tell who or what comes out that back door, but that is where your friends are—in the back room."

"Ve get 'em out all right, you can hang your hat on that, you bet ya," said Nils. "But be ready to go. Be careful now. Vi vil få disse drittsekkene." (We will get these assholes!)

Kisti looked at Mari with wide-open eyes and nodded toward the back door. "Let's line up the wagon over there," she said.

The two men set off towards Stack's front door and the women drove around to the back where Mari turned the horses around to be ready to drive away with the girls if she had to.

There were conflicting stories of what happened that day, and all of them were very descriptive. The most accurate ones were did not mention promiscuity, but the later court version came up with this story:

Upon entering Stack's, Alfred and Nils proceeded to the bar and asked for a drink. Nils refused to give up the bottle until he had poured another for Alfred. Stack was sitting at the poker table facing the bar.

"Alfred approached him and said in a loud voice, "You got women in the back? We want to go in."

"Pay your dollar and wait your turn. They are busy now."

"They've been in there too long. We're going in now, we'll throw the guys out."

Stack nodded to the bartender, who led them through the crowd to the back door of the bar into the back room. They knocked on it. Someone yelled for them not to come in, but one kick from Alfred's boot and the door flew open. Alfred picked up the man on top of one of the Indian girls and with a kick to the outside back door he threw him out. Mari later said, "All I saw was the back door give way and two men came out head first. Neither of them touched a one foot on the ground. One of them looked as if he had been thrown out by his feet. Then came the two girls, too drunk to stand. The men pushed them out."

"Well, it is up to us, I guess, to take it from here," said Mari.

So Kisti and Winona got the women and helped them into the light wagon while Mari tried to manage the horses, frightened by the commotion. Hearing the noise and seeing the door to his backroom broken, Stack ran out with a pistol in his hand. Someone got in his way and a small oak herring keg hit him in the midriff; his arm went wild, and he fired a shot into the air.

A barrel of beer went sailing and landed on the bar with a tremendous crash. Stack was picked up bodily and flung sprawling amid the broken glass. Another herring keg completed the damage to the bar, then some of the customers caught the general idea and added to the destruction.

Winona would nurse the two misguided girls back to a degree of health. They were brought home to the Lysne's, and although Kisti had no room in her house, she provided beds in the new granary. With the faithful Winona in attendance, the girls were ready to resume their journey home a few days later, terrified by the horrible memory of the Fair at Amherst.

Alfred didn't come home for several days, and it was rumored he had been put in jail. The story was never substantiated, and he was home in time to shuck the corn. The following winter he went logging in the woods. In the spring he went on the log drive. Alfred eventually migrated to Minnesota and would become a legend among the folks at New Hope and Amherst.

Nils found a wife and bought a farm. He was always a champion. Some of his feats of strength were challenged by men in many social contests and folks gossiped about his ability to lift the heaviest logs and break horseshoes in two.

Despite the fighting at Stack's during the Fair, which took up most of the news about the fair, there were many new things on display at the Fair.

Several new inventions had been shown, including sewing machines. Anna Marie bought one, as did Mari. At one of the ladies' meetings, Mari and Anna Marie demonstrated how to use the sewing machine, and that winter almost every household owned one of these marvels of the age, a godsend for the women.

Then there were the new oil lamps for the homes; coal oil was becoming readily available to everyone. The new lamp was a great improvement over the candles, so often causing fires, and the lamps made the parlors beautiful and bright. Folks were also buying the new chairs and furniture being made in Rockford, Illinois, called the Forest City. Some of the chairs and couches were done in red plush with carved frames. It was a real treat to go into the better stores and see the abundant luxury that was becoming a part of this wonderful country.

Hendrick and Johan and other farmers from their community went to New Hope to talk with the railroad committee to have them bring a branch line to Amherst so the farmers could get their grains and supplies to market. After much debate, they succeeded in getting a rail line to come through Amherst. It was the topic of much conversation and excitement. Immigrants were coming in even greater numbers, and land prices were increasing due to the population growth. The Union Pacific had been completed, and one could go from the east coast to the west coast, and the telegraph grew right along with railroad tracks. Newspapers came daily instead of weekly.

The school at Amherst was well established, and a new school building was being built; there were nearly forty pupils altogether. Life was changing rapidly for the growing community. Kisti and Mari and their husbands often talked about the changes they had seen since first settling there.

Kisti became pregnant once again. She felt that perhaps this would be the last one. But she was able to enjoy the time, with Hendrick at home working the farm, and the Civil War behind them. They were enjoying this new life with their children and Kisti's aging mother.

Chapter Twenty-Nine
Eivind's Decision, Randine's Dream

Eivind was in high school now, and he was thinking about going to college. He discussed possible career options with his parents. He did not want to be a lawyer or a doctor, "I don't want to shoulder people's troubles. Nor watch people suffer."

"Why not relieve people of their suffering, Eivind?" Kisti said.

Eivind replied, "I want to protect people but not get caught up in their daily problems. I want to go to West Point."

Hendrick responded, "No, no more war, or anything connected with war."

So Eivind did not mention the subject again.

In the meantime, Eivind's Grandfather Ole Thomas Lysne had written to them about his other sons, who now owned stores and tool shops in Northfield, Minnesota. Hendrick thought maybe they would have a place for Eivind. He wrote to his father and asked about the possibility.

The next time Eivind talked about school and work, Hendrick mentioned his half-brothers and their business. "You could go to Luther College or Carlton over near Northfield, and you could study for the ministry at Luther, and I will be glad to help you either way."

"I want to go to Northfield," Eivind stated clearly.

It was Eivind's first experience leaving home. He would get to know his uncles and his grandfather Ole and his wife Anna. It was hard to leave his little sisters. But Susan would continue high school and would carry on without him this year.

She hoped he would marry her best friend, Mari's Susan someday.

Randine came home to visit her family before Eivind left for Northfield, with stars in her eyes. Sjur Jaasted came to see her the following Sunday and asked for her hand. He was teaching school in Scandinavia, Wisconsin, and was a deacon in the church. With a new railroad coming through, he would make connections with many more people, and he assured Hendrick he would be able to support his daughter in the manner to which she was accustomed.

"Well, Sjur, that is better than I can do. She has been with the Bancrofts for so many years and they live a pretty fine life. If you can support her in a manner that pleases her, I will be satisfied, and my blessing will be forthcoming."

Sjur acted as a visiting deacon at the church that Sunday. He showed his ability to serve the church community. Randine and Sjur announced that all were invited to their wedding in July. The wedding date was set for July 26, 1869 at the New Hope Church.

Mrs. Bancroft insisted that Randine go with her on one more trip to Chicago. She wanted to assist Randine in selecting her wedding trousseau.

There were dresses to make, the house to be cleaned, and so many things to do. Randine came home on the weekends, and she was home the week prior to the wedding. Randine wanted Pastor Mikkelson to marry them, but he resigned in July to accept a call at Luther College. Young Pastor Berge would officiate.

Sjur made impressive decisions around the wedding and reception. He told Hendrick he did not want to have drinking at his wedding.

Hendrick responded, "Well, there will be wine at your wedding. I have already ordered some from Chicago. It will be served properly, as it should be, and your happiness will be toasted with wine, not milk."

Sjur bought a corner lot between Iola and Scandinavia, halfway on the Torgerson corner on the way to Amherst, and he had already begun to build a house for his bride. Kisti was overjoyed that Randine and Sjur would be living nearby.

On the wedding day, dawn was bright and beautiful, and Randine and Kisti were up early to finish some tasks before the wedding. Susan and a young student at Luther College served as bridesmaids and the best man named Carl was a friend of Sjur. Lollie Ingeborg and John Scindholt's youngest daughter, Lollie, served as the flower girl. Her pretty little white dress and laced pantalets highlighted shiny new shoes as she scattered flower petals from a tiny basket while skipping down the aisle, enjoying her first public appearance. Whenever a petal landed off the path she would stoop down and put it on the path, revealing her round lacey panties.

Coming down the aisle with beaming Randine upon his arm, Hendrick could scarcely refrain from laughing at the sight of little Lollie. But he composed himself, realizing the significance of this moment, walking with his daughter down the aisle.

Randine was so lovely in her white wedding dress. With the lace around her neck and chest and her dark hair tied up with flowers behind her head, she looked so beautiful as she walked slowly down the aisle with Hendrick to meet Sjur. Hendrick suddenly felt moved by giving his first daughter away to her soon to be husband. He stopped and kissed her cheek, and squeezed her hand before he sat down next to Kisti.

Wahopekau and Winona were present; Oshida, who was too feeble to come, sent his blessings and greetings through Winona. After the ceremony, Sjur was not certain whether he could accept Winona, but when he saw Randine's affection for her, and the devotion in Winona's eyes, he bowed from the waist in greeting. Both Winona and Wahopekau congratulated Randine and Sjur and nodded to return his respectful bow.

After the dinner held at Kisti's and Hendrick's, all the neighbors were present at the reception in the town Hall, where there was a dance as well as a dinner for the guests. That evening, after Sjur and Randine danced with their friends, Sjur's best man, Carl, took Sjur and Randine to the train for

Chicago. The crowd of merry makers remained at the town hall to dance and celebrate until the wee hours.

Susan was much taken with her escort, Jonathan. He was to return to college for the fall term, and she promised to write to him. Mari's Susan had an escort, too, with whom she was very well pleased, and she no doubt would see much of him, because he lived only a few miles away.

Kisti went out into the summer moonlight to the Königs Garten to contemplate the events of the day. Susan came over to join her after bidding her escort goodnight, thrilled to have met such a fine young man. She sat on the ground beside her mother, who put her strong arm around her daughter's tiny shoulder and gazed into the soft night with a wistful smile.

"You like your young man, don't you sweetheart?"

"Oh, yes, ever so much, Mother."

"I can see it in your eyes. I know the feeling; he is very handsome."

"Oh, I am so glad you think so, Mother. I want you to like him."

"Of course, I will like him. If my girl likes him, there is every reason why I should. Some day you, too, will ride away like Randine did today. Time will bring it about."

"Oh, Mother, I hope that is so, but when I think about it, I want to cry, it seems so sad."

A chill gripped Kisti's heart, like a cold hand squeezing it.

"Oh no, darling. Don't let these thoughts of the future make you sad. This is your first wedding; it always does that to us. There is a mix of love and sadness, as change closes one door and opens another. You are just tired. Run along now, to bed, darling."

Susan kissed her mother good night.

Hendrick came out and stretched out his long arms toward the moon. "Well, it has been quite a day. They're still having a party up at the hall. I hope they are having fun."

"Hendrick you surprise me. Who would think you would ever condone such a thing as a dance? You objected to your son's violin playing and you only acquiesced so that he might play hymns on it, and here you are now, hoping they are dancing their heads off at Randine's wedding. You are a strange one."

"It isn't every day that one has a daughter married. People are young only once, and it is natural for them to express their youth. I wish I felt like that."

"I am so glad to see that you have come out of your shell. Still, you and I didn't meet at a funeral, did we? I think that was about the luckiest wedding party I have ever attended."

"Yes, and when I think that I attempted to get a leave to go back to Leardal that night, I shudder to think of it. You know, they could have granted it, and then all this might never have happened."

"Yes, but I am sure it would have happened some other way." Kirsti took his hand as he sat next to her. Hendrick kissed her. "We are meant to be here together my darling, Hendrick. Just think, we have a married daughter, and I think our little Susan has met her husband, too."

"He seems like a nice chap. Rather weak looking though, don't you think?"

"Well, he is a rather disciplined type."

"I think he is sick."

"Oh, I hope not. She is anything but robust, but she has never been sick a day in her life. She is just tiny all around. The shoemaker told her at Oshkosh that she would have to have her shoes custom made as long as she lived."

"Yes, she is small, but she is strong. However, her friend is sick. I saw too many of those people in the army. They died before the year was up. I hope she doesn't fall too hard in love with him because I just can't be too hopeful for his prospects. He should quit school and go into the woods or go out west in the mountains and recover his health."

"Oh, Hendrick, I hope you are wrong for our daughter's sake. I got a strong sense that he would not be at their wedding, yet I just couldn't stand to see her hurt."

"What made you want to marry me?" Hendrick said, slipping his arm around into his wife.

"When you gathered up the breakfast porridge in the mess hall and poured it into the lieutenants dress boots."

"He was really insufferable."

"I have never laughed so much over such a silly prank. But I loved you for it, and I was glad to have such a witty companion. I just knew that from then on, we were going to be very happy. This wedding today is the first time I have seen a revival of that old spirit with your interactions with Sjur. I hope you will recapture it!"

"Well, I did have a lot of fun then, and it has been a hard row to hoe with much responsibility."

"That I know, but I do believe we take things too seriously. There is a lot of happiness to be had, Hendrick, if we just accept it. The trouble is we feel that in our religion we must put on a long face and expect damnation or something, but from a loving God, who is all love, that is just not true. I just can't think that he is sitting up there ready to pounce upon me, watching every little move I make to call me into account. No Hendrick, THAT is OUR thorny problem. We have learned to fear and not to love God. Let's take another look at it and see if love does not bring more joy than fear."

Kisti looked at Hendrick with eyes full of love, and Hendrick tightened his arm around his wife, and kissed her. They snuggled together. "You are right, my dear. Love is stronger than fear."

Two days later Kisti gave birth to her fourth daughter, Olena. Her nickname was Lallie; she was born on July 28, 1869. This one was strong and healthy, and she had a great smile when her mother held her. Kisti knew this would be her last child to be born. She became very attached to her youngest baby daughter, Lallie.

Chapter Thirty

Changes for Susan, Kisti Returns Oshkosh

In September of 1875, Kisti and Susan took the train to Oshkosh to make the necessary arrangements for Susan to go to the New State Normal School in Oshkosh. The school had degrees in liberal arts, and Susan was excited about studying to become a teacher.

It was over twenty years ago when Kisti came through this town for the first time in 1855. She was stunned by how many of the old buildings had been torn down with new modern ones in their place. The stores were amazing, a source of wonder. Once her daughter was safely established in the school as a new student, Kisti went on an Oshkosh inspection and shopping tour. She wondered whether the sudden decision to leave Oshkosh twenty years before, and go settle in Amherst, had been a wise choice.

On her way home on the train, she decided the answer was yes, yes, indeed. Home was like no other place. She doubted whether she could have had the same feeling for a home in Oshkosh, had she stayed, that she had for her modest home with her Königs Garten, and the lovely trees, and the meadow, and her wonderful neighbors. She was supremely happy with her home and felt so content that she had no desire to go anywhere else.

Home was the place where her children were born and raised, where several babies had died, where every stone in the chimney, every shingle of the roof, and every nail in the walls were the result of Hendrick's and their neighbors' handiwork.

Now Eivind was in college, Randine, married and settled into her new home, and Susan starting at Normal School. Anna would soon be ready for high school, and little Lallie was such a dear, ready for second grade. How the time has flown by.

At the train stop in Waupaca, which was now a town, Kisti recalled the time when their wagon train had camped on the outskirts. She remembered the night when she, Randine, and Mari, guided by Wahopekau, had all gone swimming in the lake. It was a wonderful memory. As the train sped down the tracks to Amherst, she knew that their home was where she wanted to be and nowhere else.

Anna met her at the station in Amherst and helped her with packages. "Mother did you buy up the town? I have never seen so many packages."

"Well, I shopped for Christmas. I know it is only September, but I just couldn't resist buying a doll for Lallie. And I bought something special for the family for Christmas, too, but I don't dare to tell you about it before I speak to your father."

"Mother, you mean I will have to wait three whole months before I know what I am getting for Christmas? I will be ravaged by curiosity by that time."

"Oh, there is Albert! He wants to see if he can beat me home. He has a new horse."

Kisti drove the wagon while Anna climbed on Prince, who was in tow, just in case she had the opportunity to race a bit. So out of town they went, and as soon as the road was clear, the two horses set out with a burst of speed in a cloud of dust.

Anna held the reins of her horse tightly while Albert and his colt, a beautiful black horse with white spots, rode behind. When she saw him gaining on her, she said, "Come on Prince, let's pick up those feet, you can beat him!"

As the street narrowed into the single lane, Prince edged out Albert's roan and made it to the road first.

When Anna came back to the wagon, Kisti said to her quietly, "You know dear Anna, he let you win because he is a gentleman. You know his horse is larger and could be faster."

"Mother, that is the meanest thing you could say to me. I

beat him fair and square. Now I am going to challenge him to a race with judges and everything. I am going to get a cart, and he will have to get one too, I won't quit until I do it!"

"Sweetheart, I am only joking with you. You scared me to death. Do you drive like that often?"

"Well, we have raced before, and I have beat him every time. Prince can out run any horse in this county, and I aim to prove it."

"Heavens, you inherited your father's sporting blood. Now I see it clearly in you. How much of this racing have you done?"

"Only a few times. Nils, Dina, Albert, and I tried it with Jon a couple of times. Jon has a good horse too, named Oscar. Nils rode Oscar and I rode Prince. I bet if Dina rode Prince, and I rode Jon's horse, I would beat them anyway! Dina can ride better than Nils."

"Sure, she is a woman."

"Mom, are you making fun of me?"

"No, I am not. Really, I am so surprised and amused. I want to laugh. I just can't get used to my kitten being a race-horse rider!"

"Does your father know about this?"

"No, but he doesn't need to know. You won't tell him, will you?"

Albert came alongside.

"That is a good horse, you have Albert," Kisti said. "I told Anna that on a regular racecourse, I bet you two would come pretty close."

"Yes, Ma'am, he is a good horse, and he sure can go, but your Prince has a better rider, and a pretty one too. Even I couldn't win a race with my horse with a rider like that."

"That is enough for you today. See you later Albert," Kisti said.

Anna waved at Albert as she rode alongside her mother in the wagon. Anna's cheeks were pink, and she was smiling.

This was the first time Kisti had been away from home by herself. As she drove home with Anna riding on Prince, it dawned on her how the soldiers must have yearned for home when away, in danger, and confronted by the enemy. It must have been unbearable at times she thought. "No, I will never leave here again!" she said to herself.

She had much to tell Hendrick about the trip to Oshkosh with Susan. She was happy and tired and so glad to be home.

That night she said to Hendrick, "I don't know how you soldiers could have stood being away."

"Well, we knew you were here, waiting. That helped, and we also knew that someday it would be over."

"I am so glad we are home together. Now do you want to know what I spent our money on in Oshkosh? I bought a lot of Christmas presents!"

"No, I don't need to know until we open them. I know you had a good time shopping."

"Well, there was something I bargained for, though I hesitated to buy it."

"What was it?"

"I don't know what you will think of it."

"Okay, tell me."

"I am sure the children will love it. I think it will give them a sense of pride."

"Kisti, what are you talking about?"

"I bought an organ."

"You bought what?" He stared at her.

"An organ."

Hendrick broke into laughter.

"I bought one, too."

Kisti sat down and laughed with him.

"Oh, how funny my dear one, we had the same idea!"

"Well, I bought it tentatively," Hendrick said. "I paid no money down and I can cancel the order without any embarrassment."

The two of them smiled at each other and held each other close.

"What a wonderful gift we will be giving to our children," Kisti said.

The organ was delivered as scheduled in time for Christmas that year to Kisti's and Hendrick's house. Their place became the scene of many a party.

The women were busy that season preparing packages for the unemployed, as the stock market had fallen and there was an economic squeeze. Mari was a welcome organizer for this community project.

Pastor Berge was impressed with the two Susans for their efforts on behalf of the Indian people, especially after having met with Winona. He observed the women's interest in the Indian affairs. He saw to it that the Indians were the recipients of a fair share of the relief efforts.

Mari made sure that the local people who needed help received what they needed. The Indian project worked well, and there was less need in Winona's group than the winter before.

The holidays feasts were as delicious as ever, with rib roasts, venison, lutefisk, lefse, kringle, fattigmans, bakels, and Uleale or Christmas beer, made from old Norwegian formulas.

The young people had their own gatherings. The two Susans and Anna, along with Ingeborg, had their own groups with young people over, too. And singing and drama clubs from the school gathered for performances; the young people stayed and enjoyed their friends long after the older ones had gone home.

Randine and Sjur were home for the holidays and were present at some of the festivities. Randine reported that she was very happy in her new home and loved being a hostess, and Sjur was indeed the head of the household.

Hendrick and Sjur met on common ground at the gatherings around the needs of the church. They reviewed the Calvinistic viewpoint, which had more restrictions. Kisti and Randine would have none of it. After the holiday party was over, Sjur told Hendrick that maybe the animals in the barn would better appreciate their discussions. Kisti encouraged them to discuss their philosophy with the horses and cows.

In the spring, Randine confided to her mother that she

was pregnant with her first child. Kisti made preparations for her birth by buying clothes and hosting a baby shower. She was there when Randine gave birth to help her, along with a midwife Randine had hired, and on October 11th, there was a new baby boy in the family who they named Otto Dietrich Justad.

Ander's and Mari's Susan became engaged the following spring, and they began to plan her wedding scheduled for the 21st of June 1878. Mari and Anders had rebuilt their house with larger rooms and Susan wanted to be married at home. There were three bridesmaids, and her friend Susan was the hostess at the reception. It was the most wonderful gala event of the year. Susan and Anders spared nothing and made it a memorable event. Flowers were everywhere, and food was abundant. They had even imported wine from France, and had other refreshments for everyone.

The day after the event, Kisti stopped by to help Mari clean up after the wedding. Mari poured her a cup of coffee and they sat behind the house under the apple tree.

"Well, sister Kisti, we have in-laws. You have a grandson, and it won't be too long before I have one too. Tell me, where has the time gone?"

"Isn't it nice Mari that we don't have to go it alone! That our friends go right along with us. We have both gained new sons, and soon we will sit back and watch our young brood spread all over the place, just like a couple of old clucking hens!"

Nonna, Kisti's Susan, was teaching again in Nelsonville for another year. Dina was also teaching, but closer to home.

The following spring, Nonna learned of the fatal illness of her intended love, who was in his senior year at Luther College. She resigned from school and went to his home, where she was with him until the end. She was silent in her grief, and upon her return, she was such a changed person that Kisti was thoroughly alarmed.

Susan returned from her visit to the Indian country and there was not much joy in her soul. She took her mother by the hand and went out to the Königs Garten and sat upon the ground with her head in her mother's lap. Kisti sang the little lullaby that had calmed her nervous daughter many times when she was a baby; the song she had taught Otwana and Winona.

"Have you been able to cry, darling?"

Susan shook her head, no.

"You and I are denied the luxury of tears, my dear. Why that is, I don't know. I envy those who can open the floodgates and let the sorrow drain out. They have a much easier time of it than we do. But we mustn't become bitter. I have sat here when my world dropped out from under me, several times, and each time it seems harder. Sometimes I feel there is no real reason for me to sit here any longer, but there always is. You have had a great loss, but it would have been greater if you had married him."

"There will never be any marriage for me, now," Nonna said.

"I wouldn't say that. God determines these things, and you have no right to say what you are going to do. Your motives may be ever so pure, and your desire to sacrifice your own will and emotions to what you think the greatest service, but it might be the opposite of what God wants. So let us not be hasty in our vows."

"Oh, mother, why should I be denied what every woman wants; a home, someone to love her, children of her own?"

"But you haven't been denied them, dear Nonna. You have focused all these things upon one man and God said, "No, not this one."

"Of course, you loved him. He was sweet and pure, and all the things girls dream of. But Susan, you were with him such a little while. God has other plans for you."

Tears began to flow and Kisti held her daughter tight while the floodgates burst open. Kisti rubbed Nonna's back as she wept on her mother's lap.

Susan decided to return to the Indian school in Nelsonville, as Winona and DeKorra were striving to get the Indians interested in their own problems, but so many years of broken promises had broken their spirits and they remained impassive. Susan realized that many were grieving the loss of their land and culture.

DeKorra and Mr. Lee went to Madison, and at long last, there was a representative from Washington to look into the problems of the Ho-Chunk people. The result of the meetings was that they could obtain land if they wished, and a reservation would be established in which they could retire. It took some time for them to decide. Those who wished to go to the reservation would have to migrate to Nebraska. Other could remain in Northern Wisconsin. For those who remained, Susan and Winona were promised government help, and if the church wanted to establish a mission, help would be readily forthcoming. This was the message given to the new Rev. Homme, who married Jonas's sister. He was interested in the North Country, and especially in the plight of the Native American people with so many orphans and elders. Finally, Susan saw in Rev. Homme the answer to her prayers to get the church interested in the Indian people.

The following winter, Chief Oshida passed away. He left a message for Kisti which was delivered by Winona.

"He thanks you for all you have done and wants you to know that he loved all of you very much. He hopes you will live to see the Winnebagos, Ho-Chunk people, be the first-class citizens he always wanted them to be."

He was buried in a place called Ingersoll, which was a little log cabin chapel near the school. Winona used the log chapel for her school in Ingersoll.

The New Hope Church had continued to grow and there was now a large congregation and talk of building three new churches. Amherst had already organized its congregation. There was a rumor that one would be in Nelsonville and another in Alban. Disturbing doctrinal points were being discussed with theological differences involving the lay people in all of the congregations. These discussions marked the beginning of various Lutheran synods with strong disagreements in philosophy from the lay people, even though they were all Lutheran Christian churches.

"I don't understand it," said Mari one day at the ladies meeting. "Why should we bother our heads when we have gotten along with each other all these years, and supported each other. Isn't that what a church is for? If the ministers don't have enough to do without inventing arguments, send them over to our place, and I'll find something for them to do, sure enough."

The other women laughed with her. Yet the spirit of controversy prevailed. In every publication that came out, the first thing people looked for was which side the arguments favored. People began to take sides.

Even Hendrick was disgusted with the discussions. "These questions have appeared from time to time since the reformation and have only resulted in creating more factions within the protestant church. Nothing has been solved, except it has given willful men a great opportunity to become important people in smaller groups."

Kisti was sitting in the October night, enjoying her Königs Garten, and feeling closer to God than she felt in any church. She remembered a text in Exodus 23:20: "Behold I send an angel before thee, to keep thee in the way, and to bring thee into the place which I have prepared." This was the place where she belonged, her and Hendrick's home, the place for her mother, her children, and her friends such as Winona and Mari and her beloved Hendrick. She felt such joy sitting in her special place overlooking the fields.

Hendrick came home from a meeting and found her in the Königs Garten. He walked over and sat down beside her.

"Aren't you cold my dear, it seems the frost will come soon."

He put his arm around her as they sat together.

"No, it's lovely, the air is so fresh and clear. I can hear the trains passing at the Spur and at Amherst. I wouldn't be surprised if there is a heavy freeze coming soon. Oshida used to tell me that a sure sign of frost was when there was a ring around the moon; he said the snow would come before the next full moon."

"Yes, well, here we are in October, which is often when the heavy freeze comes in Wisconsin, we all know that. December is just down the road."

Kisti asked him about the meeting, and he said he was frustrated by the arguments, which delayed any new church policies for another year. They discussed the challenges caused by those who divided the people with their philosophical arguments rather than uniting everyone with prayers.

"Hendrick it will heal, just listen to what God says to you in your heart and follow that. Let them alone and keep your peace. We have been guided here, and in this community. That we cannot deny. Now you are being asked to lead the people in a new church and they are looking to you. But just turn it over to God and you will be guided, my dear."

Hendrick drew her closer. "I am so grateful for your clarity, wisdom and support, my darling Kisti."

Hendrick and Kisti Lysne

Chapter Thirty-One

Death at the Door with New Days Emerging

The month after Oshida's death, Kisti's mother Synneva died in her sleep. Kisti was aware that her mother's health was declining rapidly over the past year, and she had taken on more of the work to ease the strain on her mother. When she died, their neighbor Johan brought over a casket he had made for her, and they held a sweet funeral at the New Hope Church with Pastor Berge officiating. She was laid to rest in the graveyard next to Kisti's and Hendrick's three sons, Ole, Thomas, and the infant Henry, who died two days after birth.

Synneva had been a wonderful mother to Kisti; she was by her side with every baby born and every child that was lost. As a grandmother to Kisti and Hendrick's children, she was always loving and happy to care for her family. She managed the house when Kisti was away at gatherings or meetings. She cooked their favorite Norwegian recipes; she darned the socks and mended the shirts and other clothing for the family. She did everything that Kisti could not find time to do herself. And she did all of it quietly, without complaint or asking for anything for herself.

Now that her mother was gone, Kisti was managing the house full of the younger children's activities. Henry, who was age twelve, and Lallie who was now six years old, often came home from school with friends to play, as the schoolhouse was just down the road. Both of them loved the animals and their friends loved to visit their farm animals too. Henry liked building things with his friends. Lallie loved the horses and was already learning to ride.

Henry was interested in woodworking and made picture frames and furniture. He made a chair for his little sister to sit on and built furniture for her dollhouse.

Henry was a bright and carefree boy who loved to work on projects he invented. But he was teased and bullied at school because of the cowlicks in his hair that made it uncontrollable, especially in the front where it stood straight up.

One day after school, Henry stood in front of the mirror, after plastering his wet blond hair to his head. He gazed at the flattened hair with satisfaction, but the cowlick in front soon stood up again. He stamped his foot angrily.

"Darn it, I can't make it stay!" He began to cry.

Kisti was watching him and then said. "Now wait a minute, Sir Knight. What might be the trouble here?"

"Mom, the kids at school make my life miserable because of this cowlick in my hair. They call me a rooster! Today when the rooster crowed outside, Olavus said, 'Henry, Hank, there is your brother calling you,' and they all laughed.

"Mom, I hid myself in the back room at school and cried. Someday I am going to fix Olavus so that he will cry every time he hears my name." He clenched his fists and his mother could see his muscles tighten as she drew him towards her.

"Little Hendrick, your father has a cowlick too, and so does your nephew Otto. Wouldn't you rather be a rooster than a pig? You have been reading about the Norwegian Knights. Well, let me tell you a story.

"You have heard the story of Gunmund and Bryta. It was the rooster that awakened Bryta to the danger of the invasion, and the bright sunrise illumined the home of your ancestors before any other homes in the community. That is where the Lysne name comes from, the "Land of Light." The rooster and sunrise were the insignia for all the shields of the brave knights. It was on the dress sword your father had in college and in the army in Norway. Don't be ashamed of the cowlicks in your hair, it is a mark of knighthood. And don't mind the rooster either. It plays a bigger part than you know. Don't tell the others! Just keep it to yourself. So now that you know, I hope you will feel better."

He smiled through his tears, and now he did not feel quite as bothered by his unruly blonde hair.

Over the next year, Henry grew taller and was becoming a teenager. He loved reading poetry books and drama. He especially loved the stories of knights and ladies and their kings. He asked Hendrick about the old shield in Norway that belonged to his people. He made a wooden sword with the rooster carved on it and started making a shield with the image on his father's military shield.

During the afternoon recess at school one day, Henry was brought home by two of his schoolmates. He was doubled over with pain and crying. "Oh, Mommy, my stomach, it hurts so! Beads of perspiration stood out on his forehead, and he was very pale.

"Olavus jumped on his stomach," said one of the boys.

"He didn't mean to, Mother."

"He did too, he wanted to hurt him. He has always wanted to lick him," said the other boy.

"Well boys, thank you for bringing him home. Please tell his father out in the barn to come in right away, will you?"

Hendrick ran into the house after the boys told him about Henry. He hitched up the horse and wagon and drove at breakneck speed toward Amherst. He met the doctor as he was coming out the door, and he got in the wagon with Hendrick, and they drove home. Hendrick couldn't give much account of the accident except that one of the boys had jumped on his son's stomach.

When they drove into the yard, they jumped out the wagon and their neighbor Isaac took the horse by the bridle and led the horse and wagon to the barn. Kisti opened the door and brought Dr. Guernsey inside and then she put her arms around Hendrick, "Oh, our little boy!"

Dr. Guernsey examined him and said, "His liver is probably ruptured, and maybe some of the abdominal vessels. The abdomen is full of blood."

Little Hendrick was very pale and still. The shield he had started was hanging on the wall over his bed. The doctor took Kisti's hand. "I am so sorry. There is nothing I can do for him."

Not long after, the poor child bled out and took his last breath at under thirteen years old.

Isaac who was a friend of Henry and brought him home, set upon the saddest task of his entire life: to make a casket for his friend, Henry. Isaac brought the casket over the following evening and Hendrick Olai Lysne was placed in it by his father. A new minister, a fiery young evangelist by the name of Eidahl, officiated. The theme of his sermon was on the beauty of youth, like the flowers of springtime. It was a touching, beautiful service that brought peace to Henry's parents.

The older children did not all come home, as Eivind was not notified right away, and Anna could not be located. The message reached Susan too late for her to come for the funeral.

Hendrick and Kisti spent time in the apple orchard he had cultivated, where the trees were loaded with spring blossoms. Amid this beauty, they were left to contemplate their loss. Everywhere Kisti looked around the farm, her eyes came upon some of her boy's handiwork. Birds were building nests in little cabins and churches he had built for them near her Königs Garten. The sword and unfinished shield were tucked away in the iron bound chest that contained many of their possessions from Norway.

Lallie was silent and stoic in her grief, as was Susan when she arrived a day after Henry's funeral. Lallie spoke very little, and sat at her schoolwork with profound concentration, even though she had little to do as a first grader. On the paper in front of her, she drew pictures of Henry and herself.

Two days after Henry's funeral, their wonderful neighbor Jon passed away. By that time all the family had arrived, and he was buried in the cemetery not far from Hendrick and his three brothers and grandmother. Rev. Eidahl, who also officiated Jon's funeral, noticed that the flowers on little Hendrick's grave had already wilted. At the gravesite service, Eidahl spoke of the frailties of human existence symbolized by the wilting flowers. Jon was the first of the original male pioneers to pass on after Ingeborg. And the significance of the event was not lost upon those who remained.

The saddened community began to recover from the loss with the coming of summer.

Two months after Henry's death, Hendrick received a letter from Jonas Swenholt in Scandinavia, Wisconsin.

Dear Sir,

I am sending you a letter asking for Anna's hand in marriage. Will you bless us and honor me with her beautiful presence? You will make me the happiest man ever.

Sincerely,
Jonas Swenholt

Hendrick and Kisti were both surprised, as they knew Anna was seeing Jonas Hommes Swenholt, but they did not realize the relationship had grown serious. Anna was busy at the Mission at Wittenberg with her sister Susan. Jonas' uncle, who had been involved with the Mission at Wittenberg, was living in Wittenberg, and so frequent visits between Jonas and Anna were inevitable.

Hendrick sent Jonas his consent to marry his daughter Anna. The wedding was set for later in the year. Kisti and Anna would need time to make the wedding plans. It also gave their family time to recover from the loss of little Hendrick. The couple wanted to be married in the New Hope church at Amherst.

Jonas was interested in lumber and iron lands near Ironwood, where he had worked the summer before so there was ample field opportunity and he had started great things in the development of the northern Wisconsin territory. Jonas and Eivind had become friends and explored much of the territory near Ironwood together. The new territory up north was mushrooming into the city of Wakefield with all the good and evil aspects that come with cities. Eivind had finished college and was running a store and a hotel there. Jonas was gathering up mining rights and contracting land in the region where expansion was bound to come.

When Anna came home to prepare for her wedding, she told her family about the rough life Jonah and Eivind were living in Wakefield. She had wanted to visit both of them before coming home, but Jonas wouldn't let her. He told her, "That is no place for a woman as pretty as you, it could cause a riot and men might be killed or hurt. I know you don't want to be party to that, do you?"

Then she said, with a twinkle in her eye, "It's nice of him to protect me like that isn't it, Mother?"

Her mother agreed; she could not afford to lose another child. Eivind was the only son that she had left. While questioning Jonas, when he came to see Anna, Kisti discovered that he was the Sheriff of Wakefield, and Eivind was a deputy. She recalled the Cole brothers and how they harmed people to get what they wanted. She mentioned the Coles to Jonas and said she was worried about her son Eivind.

"He is in no danger. Everyone likes him. There are a group of rowdies, but they don't mean any harm. Why, one night they even warned him there was going to be a rough time. The saloon next door, which Eivind and I own, was having trouble with some of the men and they began shooting. Meanwhile, Eivind laid on his stomach in the store next door as holes were being shot in canned goods on the shelves through the saloon wall. Leaking cans of beets, corn, peas, and oysters. Oh, it was a mess! Eivind invited the boys in, and they opened the cans. They had a party and paid for every can they had punctured. He gets along fine with them."

Kisti replied, "But some day, someone will come along who will not like him so well."

"They had better keep out of Wakefield. Eivind's friends would take care of them."

Kisti was not happy about it, but she felt slightly better.

Susan came home for the summer vacation and dedicated her time to working with the Indians. Her hopes were being fulfilled as she watched the students at the growing Indian school respond to their attempts to help them learn.

The wedding of Anna and Jonas in July was yet another gala event for the community, and while it lacked the merrymaking following Randine's wedding, it was a wonderful affair. Jonas's brother-in-law officiated in the ceremony and after the dinner, the newlyweds went to Chicago for their honeymoon.

Eivind came home for the wedding and Kisti and Hendrick were surprised at what a man of the world he had become. He had a well-groomed mustache, and he was dressed in a somewhat elegant fashion. He wore a collared shirt with a satin vest, and a suit with matching jacket and trousers that were tailored to match his boots.

"I guess we are getting old Hendrick. Look at our son. I can't imagine where the time has gone. Our two girls are married, and Eivind and Susan are old enough to be wed, and our youngest is growing so fast, she is already riding a horse!"

"Don't worry dear, there will soon be other little ones coming along to keep us company."

Eivind left the next day, and Susan went to Randine's to spend a few days. The household settled down to the old routine again, and Hendrick and Kisti seemed to enjoy the solitude.

Lallie was a great help, even though she was barely seven. Hendrick and Kisti were pleased to see how good she was at farming tasks and that she loved being in the barn with the horses.

The rest of the year went by fast. Jonas and Anna had a wonderful time in Chicago, where they saw the sights and went to many theatre events. They returned north, and decided to settle near the Indian school, as Anna wanted to work with Susan and Winona.

August was dry, and the dust was piled high, and some of the wells went dry. Many farmers drove their livestock to the lakes and streams for water. There was much sickness that summer among both cattle and people.

One day Lallie came in from riding in the field and threw herself on the wooden bench, exhausted. The horses were still standing in the yard, as she had made no effort to unharness them. She looked pale, and perspiration stood in great beads on her head, and she made little response to questions.

Hendrick once again went to fetch Dr. Guernsey and brought him back as quickly as the horses would carry them. When they returned, the doctor examined Lallie.

"It's cholera!" the doctor said.

Kisti was stunned and felt as though another death sentence had been given. Susan came back from Randine's and helped her mother tend to Lallie. She was a wonderful nurse to her sister, and she sat stoically by her bedside. She kept her cool with wet cloths and gave her as much water as she could drink.

The doctor came twice a day for several days, and then he announced that there was likely to be a crisis soon; he had never seen a case last so long, but he felt there was hope that she would recover.

Kisti went out to her Königs Garten after the doctor left in the evening and tried to meditate and calm herself after his challenging news. She couldn't cry, but her prayers for her daughter calmed her somewhat.

She heard Susan scream, "Mother! Come quick!" Kisti rushed inside and listened to Lallie's heartbeat. It was very faint, but Kisti could hear it.

A wild feeling of frenzy and defiance seized her. She sat on the bed, lifted Lallie's almost lifeless body to her heart, and screamed, "Death, get out of here! You don't get another one of my children, especially not this one! You have taken four others and I defy you in the name of God. Now, God, don't fail me again!"

She laid Lallie down on the bed and began to pace back and forth. She heard a weak voice, "Mother..." It was Lallie's voice, and Kisti ran to her side, "Yes, darling, you will be all right. We will get you some soup."

Susan ran to the kitchen to get the soup and water for her and hurried back.

Lallie swallowed a few spoonfuls and drifted into a sound, natural sleep. Kisti sat there beside her and wept for the first time in many years.

"I can't seem to weep from sorrow, but I sure can make it come in thanksgiving," she said to Susan.

When the doctor came the next day, Lollie was sitting up in bed and eating breakfast.

He announced happily, "She's weathered the crisis!"

While Lallie was recovering in bed, the family gave prayers of thanksgiving at the dining table during every meal. Susan stayed for several days to be sure her sister was getting better.

At dinnertime one evening, Susan said that she had heard Dr. Guernsey in town discussing the recovery of another townsman. He asked Susan how Lallie was, and he said, "Why, that girl had absolutely no chance of recovery. All her vitality was gone, and I had expected her to expire within the next few hours. I can't explain it."

Kisti looked at her, and said, "All I know is that I was at war against death at that moment. I didn't fear it; I challenged it, as her mother. I was death's master, calling in Jesus and God for that moment, and I told it to leave. I did not plan for her recovery. I knew she would recover when I laid her back down."

"Mother you scare me. Still, it is wonderful how strong in faith you are."

"If she had died, I would have lost my faith. I could not bear to lose two children in one summer, so I could not compromise with death."

Susan grabbed her hand and kissed it.

Over the next few years, Lallie went back to school, and grew fast. Susan, Winona, and Anna worked at the Indian school, shaping the curriculum to include stories of the Native people along with the Christian teaching. They were working hard with fifty children in their school. One year they invited Kisti to come and talk to the children about Oshida and the other elders who were part of the tribe when she came to Wisconsin.

Kisti came in wearing clothes made for her by her Native American friends, and the strands of beads that the Ho-

Chunks had given her. She shared stories of their early travels with the children: stories about Ole and his carbine, Wahopekau's baby, Frank DuBey, and all the events that united them with the Ho-Chunk people. She was so proud of her daughters and happy to come to the school and share her stories of how she and her family had become part of the Native Ho-Chunk/Winnebago tribe. Her stories were written down by Susan and would be included as part of the new teachings that the children would learn about their people.

It was a great day at the school, and on the way to Susan's there was much laughter. Kisti understood why Susan loved teaching so much. She returned home refreshed and grateful.

Eivind finished school and started work with his uncles in Northfield, Minnesota. He had met a woman at school that he was interested in named Martha Havey, who was back in Northfield. Now that he had his own businesses with Jonas, and life had settled down a bit, he wanted to travel back to Northfield to visit his uncles and tell them of his success in Northern Wisconsin. He also wanted to talk with them about supply access.

Eivind contacted many friends from school and was invited to several parties. He saw Martha again at one of the parties, and several days later, after several more dates, he asked her to marry him. They got married at the courthouse in Northfield so he could bring her home with him on his return to Amherst to meet the family.

Randine's second baby was born, a healthy little boy, and he about to be baptized. Kisti asked her daughter what they planned to name him.

"Oh, we decided right away that he will be named Hendrick Olai."

"Oh, Randine, you wouldn't."

"Yes, that is what he will be named."

"Oh, but Randine, child, there have been four of them and none of them lived!"

"I am not superstitious, Mother. I am going to call him

Hendrick Olai."

"And defy fate?"

"Yes, we will defy fate!"

So Hendrick Olai it was. Kisti said no more, and he was baptized in the Scandinavian church. Sjur was very proud to officiate in his capacity as a deacon that day.

Hendrick was deeply involved in the challenges between the newly developed synods that were philosophically in different camps. The Scandinavian church was at the heart of the conflict, and Hendrick decided with others that they needed to create another New Hope Church under a synod that was less restrictive than those that forbid dancing and celebrations. He was done with those restrictions. And these synods focused on suffering and repentance, rather than on love and forgiveness.

The women were not comfortable with the situation, and felt the storm browing, so they came together and recalled all the things they had done together to help each other. Mari, Kisti Anna Marie, Tharand, and many other women couldn't understand the synod break-ups. Such a proposal seemed so unnecessary.

Mari said," Remember the first time we walked five miles down to Brekke's to establish the Scandinavian congregation? That was the night that Ole and Aspun first stopped at Oshida's camp. Ole invited them to come to the house and they ate up everything you had stored away for winter. Remember, Kisti?"

"I will never forget it! I thought the world had come to an end after they left. There wasn't even a cup of meal left. I sat down and cried. Mari, I will never forget how kind you all were. I never knew until later that all of you had contributed to help us with flour and potatoes. Oshida did, too. He brought us fresh meat all winter."

I haven't had the opportunity to thank all of you. That was thirty years ago, you know. And here we are, we are still growing with each other's kindness. I intend to keep appreciation for one another and love as the core value, even as this storm is raging over our heads."

Mari laughed, "Yes, we are like cows; when there's a storm, we all huddle together under a tree until it passes over!"

Anna Marie said, "I think we should thank you, Kisti. The little we contributed at that time was more than made up for when the Indians went out west on the great migration some years ago. When the government had them leave for new lands out west, there were thousands of them. But not a thing of ours was touched, while north and south of us they butchered cattle and hogs. There were no guards, but there wasn't a thing touched here because they were your friends, Kisti."

Mari added, "Once a calf got loose, and a young native woman caught him. One of the native men led him by the ear into our yard, and said, 'We don't touch anything of yours. You friend of Spirit Mother.' Some places distant from here lost everything."

"I never knew that," Kisti said.

"I don't know why I never told you. But you saved many of us because of your relationship with Oshida and his tribe," Anna Marie said.

"There needs to be a new church regardless of the synods, as New Hope is growing," Kisti replied.

"Let them build it, we will be as we have always been. No one can destroy us as friends," Mari said. "It will be hard for us, especially for you Kisti, as you have your mother and five of your children buried in the graveyard at our New Hope church."

"Yes, but Hendrick is seeing the future, he wants to build a big enough place for the young people. The land has already been donated in a beautiful location, and there is more room for the graveyard. But I will be buried at the current New Hope, as will Hendrick. So many of my family are there already," Kisti said.

Chapter Thirty-Two

Eivind, Martha and Kisti's Sanctuary

Eivind sent Kisti and Hendrick a letter in late November saying that he and his bride were coming home from Milwaukee after their honeymoon. They would be arriving by train a week before Christmas. The household buzzed with excitement as they prepared to welcome the new bride.

The day of their arrival, Kisti and Hendrick drove the carriage to the Amherst railroad station. When Martha stepped off the train with Eivind, Kisti liked her daughter-in-law Martha instantly. By the time they had reached home from the railway station, the two of them were chatting like old friends. The next day, Hendrick and Kisti hosted a reception for the newlyweds at their home. Anna came with Jonas, who had to leave the next day. Randine stayed at home with her family for a few days. Eivind and Martha described their plans during their time at home with their family. There was a possibility that Eivind would go into business in Amherst with a brother of Aspun.

The newlyweds went back home to Northfield a few days after Christmas. Martha wrote to Kisti regularly throughout the winter. After they were able to tie up their work in Wakefield, and Eivind sold his businesses in Northern Wisconsin, he and Martha moved back to Amherst, where Eivind became a teacher at the local high school.

As the dedication of the new church grew closer, Hendrick felt nervous, concerned that the new church would fracture the community. Kisti reassured him.

"Hendrick, my dear, you have listened to what your

guidance has told you. No matter what the conflicts are with this, I want you to know you have done the right thing. No matter people's opinion, we are entitled to peace and tranquility for the rest of our lives. You have done nothing wrong."

On the morning of the dedication, Kisti and Hendrick arrived early at the new church to go over everything. The outside was painted white with a bell tower that was two stories high. The new steps were sturdy, with fourteen-inch planks planed smooth by the Mill and painted a blue-gray. The gray paint on the steps to the choir loft contrasted nicely with the white walls. Ingeborg's painting above the pulpit reached almost to the ceiling. She had focused her theme on, "He is risen."

Everything was in order. Mari's and Johan's boys had built the picnic tables out in the grove. The new paddock fence looked clean and white, with a flat board placed along the top. The youngsters would be tempted to climb on it. But for now, there was a freshly painted frame around the church property, including the new cemetery.

To Kisti and Hendrick's surprise, all of their children and their spouses came to the event, along with many young local people and their families. More and more people kept coming. Hendrick and Kisti greeted everyone and shook hands with them as they came into the church.

"See, Hendrick, they are not letting you down! They are coming from all directions. This is a new church, and these are young people. They are our young people. They will carry this church on and it will grow!"

The organ began playing the Bach prelude Emma had chosen to play for the occasion as everyone took their seats. The service was profoundly focused on God as love and hope, especially in their new location. This helped everyone look towards the future with optimism.

After the service some folks came up to Hendrick and Kisti and thanked them for their contribution, and said they were excited to have a new church.

"Look Hendrick, this is a youthful place, we have built ours at New Hope and at Scandinavia. This church is for them.

Maybe that is why you had to build it. Come let's celebrate at Mari's. She is having a reception for all of us."

The reception was a joyful gathering that celebrated the new life emerging from the community. People were happy to be there. They were proud and grateful to everyone for all their hard work in building this new church for the next generation.

Later that night, after they had returned from Mari's reception, Hendrick decided to go to bed early, as he was exhausted from the tension surrounding the opening of the new church, not to mention all the celebrations that followed.

Kisti went out to her Königs Garten and sat down at her favorite spot under the bright June moon. She remembered the day the tree had been cut down, leaving this stump where she had so often sat. Most of it had long since disappeared, leaving only the part she used for a backrest, now worn smooth. Hendrick's beautiful wood bench was large enough to sit on with others who wished to join her there. The fields beyond were sprouting with wheat and corn, with new grass along the edges of the field, and the oak trees at the top of the hill were in leaf, forming a green archway at the opening of the woods.

How many of her old friends were gone? She did not know. She thought of William DeWitt, Frank DuBey, Otwana, and Wahopekau. She thought of her boys that she had held to her chest when they died; her two Hendricks, her Ole, and little Thomas. Her blessed mother came to her thoughts, and her dear neighbor Jon. All were gone. She was so proud of Susan and Winona and their dedication to helping the Indian children. Kisti wanted to return to the school to share many more stories of their wonderful relatives. She thought of Randine with her two children, and another one on the way, and her new daughter-in-law Martha and Eivind returning home to Amherst. Little Lallie was not so little anymore, now in college. At this moment, with so much love present in her life, she felt deeply grateful for all that she had lived through with Hendrick. She was so grateful for his wisdom and dedication to the community.

Now she knew there would be more grandchildren and she felt life would go on beyond her and Hendrick. This gave her a sense of peace. She was grateful for this farm, and this Königs Garten that was her place, her church. Nothing was greater than witnessing the awe of God in nature. She would always have her place here under the stars, and she had never been happier than she was at this moment, at one with Mother Earth and Father Sky, and the constellations glowing bright in the dark blue-black sky.

Eivind Lysne, 1888

Walther Herman Lysne's Acknowledgement

From his Original Draft

In writing this story, I have had to rely on my memory of tales told me as a boy, by my father and his sisters, Randine, Susan, and Lollie. Vivid in my mind are those wonderful days when there would be visitors, or we would be guests, and we "the small fry" would sit quietly out of sight and watch the history of the community unfold, as painted by the colorful words of the founders and their sons and daughters.

The cemeteries, of course, supply many of the dates of births and deaths. Family papers, and many letters and periodicals hold much of the data that I used in this book. Especially I want to mention Thor Helgeson's, "Indianernes Lande," and my brother Karl for obtaining this copy for me.

I also owe much to my dear friends, Stella Anderson Bidwell, Olga Jaastad Myhre, Edna Swenholt Williams, and my brother Henry. The Portage County Historical Society, under the able direction of Clifford Swanson, the Stevens Point Library, Malcolm Rosholt, for his very entertaining and informative books, Town 25 North, and Luther England of the Wittenberg Enterprise, and Miss Beulah Folkedahl, author of A Dream Come True, for their information concerning the life of Rev. E. J. Homme and the Indian Mission.

I am also indebted to Thor Hanson, of the Adjutant General's Office, State of Wisconsin, and Margaret Fleason, of the Wisconsin State Historical Society, for the informative material they gave me concerning Wisconsin's glorious part in the Civil War. The Aurora Public Library and the bookshop helped me with a great deal of information, as did Earl and Lillian Dwyer, in preparing my manuscript. I am grateful to Lillian Budd, author of April Snow and Land of Strangers, for her valuable advice and encouragement. And also to my wife, Jo, who from the beginning has been my most enthusiastic supporter.

Helpful material has also been found in "The History of Portage County," published in 1919 by the Lewis Publishing Company, Chicago and New York. Also helpful, Wisconsin in the War of the Rebellion by Wm. De Loss Love, published in 1866 by Church and Goodman. And Chicago and the Military History of Wisconsin Civil War by E. B. Quiner, Esq., published in 1866 by Clark & Co., Chicago.

To all mentioned above, I am grateful. And I stand in true humility before the memory of a heroic people, unheralded and unsung, who stand upon the sturdiness of their character and their uncompromising stand upon the side of right, "as God gave them to see the right," went about their tasks, ignorant of the fact that they were laying a foundation for the citizenry of the finest quality, to shape a building block, perfect and true in its dimensions, for the structure that is America. "That house not only made with hands, eternal in the Heavens."

Walther Herman Lysne

This following section is from Grandpa's first chapter, which was about the history of the New Hope Church that he visited with his wife, Grandma Jo Lysne, his oldest daughter Martha Lysne Heerens, and his first granddaughter, Kisti Heerens, who became Kisti Beckwith many years later.

KISTI
By
WALTHER HERMAN LYSNE

"Behold, I send an angel before thee, to keep thee in the way and to bring thee into the place which I have prepared." Exodus 23:20

*T*he South New Hope Church, built on Plank Hill, called "Plankebakken"; then, as it is now, is as fresh and clean as it was on the day of its dedication. The oaks have taken on a dignity as they become of age and environment. The white paddock fence, with the flat board along the top, has been replaced by the wrought iron ornamental one bought by the Ladies Aid.

Concrete steps with a sturdy iron rail, to assist the aged and infirm into the church, have replaced the fourteen-inch planks, planed smooth by the Wrolstad Mill.

The wide double doors are the same now as then. The leaded window above the door bears the original date, 1889. It is still white, and the tower bell is still a clear note in the key of F, selected to harmonize with the old New Hope Church in the key of A. "We will have harmony in spite of them, at least in the pitch of the bells," exclaimed the chorister, Kalstad, when the order for the bell was placed. "From the way some of them sing, few will ever know the difference."

The barn for the comfort of the preacher's horse has long since been removed, much to the relief of Susan, who always resented the fact that her parents were buried "behind the barn."

Time has brought electricity and a basement with a modern kitchen, but the devotion of the sons and daughters, the grandsons and granddaughters, and their sons and daughters, has kept it pretty much as it was.

The Sexton continues to dig the graves by hand, mounts the circular stairway in the tower to toll the bell, and still pauses to view the unforgettable panorama from the tower along the road to the north, the rich valley below the hill, and to the west an occasional glimpse of Rhinehart Lake, sparkling in the sunlight.

In earlier days, one could see the tower of the South New Hope Church had become a rebellious symbol from the previous New Hope Church, but still united in a common cause. To the west, the verdant pastures and down the south, the busy crossroads of Benson Corners.

Time and again, this pause has been interrupted by sounds from below, as Emma played the organ prelude. Great was the pride of her father, Johan, who sat in his pew, thrilled to his daughter's and granddaughter's talent, his attention probably diverted for a moment to the massive silver candlesticks guarding the silver service of the Holy Supper upon the crisp white tablecloth, catching the rays of the mid-morning sun filtered through the multicolored glass window.

Above the pulpit is Ingeborg's canvas in its gothic frame entitled, "He is risen," her contribution of love, rather than art. It became to them, and is to the succeeding generations, a thing of beauty. Woe unto the art critic, who even in this day would express his honest opinion, "What atrocious art!"

On the hallowed ground these ancient oaks stand as silent witnesses to the marble and granite gravestones bearing the names and life span of those they commemorate. Bearing witness, too, of a glorious past, for here lie the men of the Forty-Sixth Wisconsin Volunteers, of the Fifteenth, and Twelfth, the Eighth, but none of the Fifth. Here also are their sons of San Juan Hill, their sons of American Expeditionary Forces of Soissons Cantigny in France, and the Meuse-Argonne, one of the last battles of WWI, and their sons; not found wanting in the holy essence born in them, still as strong in the fourth generation as in the first, sacredly corroborated by Malmedy massacre, Anzio, Guadalcanal, Iwo Jima; proclaiming to the world that they are worthy of the trust invested in them by their forebears.

Kisti, of the fifth generation, blissfully ignorant of the heartbreak out of which all of this had evolved, skipped happily between the rows, reading the inscriptions: Johan and his wife, Anna Marie; David Anders and his wife, Mari. Much impressed by her recently acquired knowledge that history is prone to repeat itself, she pondered the inscription: Hendrick, Olai, and Kisti, his wife.

Jill Heerens, Granpa Lysne
and Kisti Heerens

Grandma Lysne, Robin Heerens Lysne
and Grandpa Lysne at
Robin's High School Graduation
1971

Jo and Walther Lysne

Walther Herman Lysne, D.C., was born in Amherst Juntion, Wisconsin October 11, 1897 on the farm where his grandparents settled in 1855. He lived there with his father, mother (she died when he was eight) and two brothers until he joined the Army reserve and met his wife, Gladys Egathaline Collins, known as Jo. They were married on January 31, 1920 and moved to Amherst Junction, Wisconsin, and lived with his father Eivind. Their first daughter, Martha Virginia Lysne, was born December 19, 1921 on the same farm as Walther.

They moved to Batavia, Illinois, and opened a practice in Aurora. As a Doctor of Chiropractic, he was nationally known in his profession for over fifty years. Jo worked as his office manager for many years. She also managed their finances and was an amazing cook. He and Jo had two daughters, Martha and Doris who gave them nine grandchildren, and nine great-grandchildren.

He belonged to the Sons of Norway, the Medina Temple (Chicago), The Aurora Commanders, AF and AM Chapter Jerusalem #90 and the Aurora, Illinois Chapter of Masonic Knights Templar. He was a stalwart in the Illinois and National Chiropractic Association in his efforts to continuously improve the quality of care in his profession.

When he and Jo retired to Flat Rock, North Carolina in 1971, he joined the Henderson Shrine Club and the Hendersonville Art League. The twelve years in this community were the happiest years of his life with Jo.

Besides being an active Chiropractor he was also a visual artist, loved to carve wood, and made many bowls, spoons, sculptures, and paintings. He also wrote the first manuscript called "Kisti" about his grandmother. His research included history of his ancestors, the Civil War, Egypt, and Middle Eastern biblical history. He also wrote and gave to all his grandchildren a book of his and Jo's genealogy along with copies of his manuscript "Kisti."

Two weeks after his sixty-third anniversary with Jo, he died at age 87 from an intestinal blockage, February 16th, 1983 in Hendersonville, North Carolina. He was surrounded in the hospital by his wife, daughters and granddaughters.

Row one: Kisti and Sidney Beckwith, Lysne Beckwith, baby Nick, Ralph Knudson and Nancy Heerens-Knudson, Dave and Jill Windahl, Andres Kratchowil (Argentina exchange student), Robin Lysne, Sara Heerens and Doug Zimmerman, with their son Keegan Zimmerman.
Row two: Laura Knudson, Robert Heerens, Jo Lysne, Walther Lysne, Martha Lysne Heerens.
Row Three: Toben Windahl, Nate Beckwith, and Ben Beckwith

Robin H. Lysne, M.A., M.F.A., Ph.D. is the author of ten books; two poetry, five non-fiction, two novels and this narrative non-fiction, *Kisti's Royal Garden*. She is also an artist and energy medicine practitioner, medium and psychic. Currently she is launching a "Legendary Women Ancestor Series," with three works of historical fiction/narrative non-fiction to bring to life the courage and wisdom of her Norwegian ancestors.

The Legend of Randine: Entering the Sisterhood is the first book in the series and was launched in November, 2021. The second novel: *The Legend of Randine: The Laerdal Letters* has been released in March, 2022. The third book is *Kisti's Royal Garden*. She is also working on a new poetry collection called *Luminaria*.

Her previous books are: *Ceremonies from the Heart, for Children, Adults and the Earth, Mosaic: New and Collected Poems, Poems for the Lost Deer, Heart Path, Heart Path Handbook*, which contains some of her drawings and paintings, as well as poems. (all published by BlueBoneBooks, Santa Cruz, CA) Earlier works are: *Sacred Living, Dancing Up the Moon,* (Conari Press). Her poems have been published in: *Fog and Light, North American Review, Catamaran, Porcupine Literary Arts Magazine, Monterey Bay Poetry Review, Rattle, Phren-z online Magazine, Porter Gulch Review, Samizdat, Awakening Consciousness Magazine*, and others.

She is a member of: Poetry San Jose, Poetry Santa Cruz, and the Emerald Street Poets in Santa Cruz, The Santa Cruz Art League and member of the Mountain Art Center in Ben Lomond.

Her websites are: www.thecenterforthesoul.com, www.RobinLysne.com and www.bluebonebooks.com. On her days not writing, she paints, dances, sees clients and enjoys her friends.

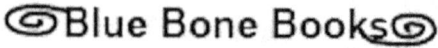Blue Bone Books
Santa Cruz, CA

Blue Bone Books Publications:

Narrative Non-Fiction
Kisti's Royal Garden

Novels
The Legend of Randine: Entering the Sisterhood
The Legend of Randine: The Laerdal Letters

Poetry
Mosaic: New and Collected Poems
Poems for the Lost Deer

Non-Fiction
Ceremonies from the Heart, for Children, Adults and the Earth,
Heart Path, Learning to Love Yourself and
Listening to Your Guides
Heart Path Handbook, for Therapists and Healers
all published by Blue Bone Books, Santa Cruz, CA

Sacred Living, 365 Meditations and Celebrations
Dancing Up the Moon, A Woman's Guide to Creating
Traditions that Bring Sacredness to Daily Life
(both published by Conari Press)

A memoir is ready for publication:

Two Worlds One Light, A Memoir of a Medium,
and *Luminaria* a new poetry book.

Some endorsements for previous books:

Legendary Women Ancestor Series: Book One and Two
The Legend of Randine, Entering the Sisterhood and
The Legend of Randine: The Laerdal Letters

Robin Lysne transports us to nineteenth century Norway in this beautifully written story of the spirited midwife Randine. I admired this atmospheric and carefully researched historical novel immensely.
Elizabeth McKenzie, author of *The Portable Veblen*, and *The Dog of the North*, Santa Cruz, CA Editor for Chicago Quarterly Review and Catamaran Literary Reader

My own Norwegian ancestry initially drew me to The Legend of Randine, and I was quickly engaged by the story of Randine. I highly recommend this beautifully written novel, not only for its compelling characters, but also for its previously untold drama of the development of midwifery in rural Norway.
Ruth Olsen Saxton, Professor Emerita of English, Mills College, Oakland, CA

Heart Path and Heart Path Handbook:
"Learning self-love is something everyone needs to learn. Heart Path offers readers a way to love themselves without limits."
John Gray, Ph.D. author of *Men are from Mars, Women are from Venus.*

Poems for the Lost Deer
"*Poems for the Lost Deer* is much more than poems. It is a tract that is, at once, lamentation and praise song, dirge and testament and manifestation. And an inquiry into values and hierarchy and a series of addresses to the faces of power. ... *Poems for the Lost Deer* invites readers to try to comprehend the scope and scale of the hillsides and of "what humans do."
C. S. Giscombe, author of Into & Out of Dislocation, Professor at U.C. Berkeley, CA

"*Poems for the Lost Deer* is passionate, compassionate, skillful, meticulous, graceful, vital, and heartbreaking..."
Heather Nagami, Editor of Overhere Press, Professor Northeastern University, Boston

www.ingramcontent.com/pod-product-compliance
Lightning Source LLC
Chambersburg PA
CBHW050314120526
44592CB00014B/1903